A Popular Survey
of the
OLD TESTAMENT

A POPULAR SURVEY OF THE OLD TESTAMENT

NORMAN L. GEISLER

BAKER BOOK HOUSE

Grand Rapids, Michigan

Copyright 1977 by
Baker Book House Company
ISBN: 0-8010-3684-4
Library of Congress Catalog
Card Number: 77-78578

First printing, October 1977
Second printing, November 1978
Third printing, August 1980
Fourth printing, April 1981
Fifth printing, December 1981
Sixth printing, July 1982
Seventh printing, March 1983
Eighth printing, January 1984
Ninth printing, August 1985

Scripture references are from the Revised Standard Version, © 1941, 1952 by Division of Christian Education of the National Council of the Churches of Christ in the United States of America.

PHOTOLITHOPRINTED BY CUSHING - MALLOY, INC.
ANN ARBOR, MICHIGAN, UNITED STATES OF AMERICA

Contents

PART ONE
Introduction

PART TWO
The Books of the Law:
The Foundation for Christ

PART THREE
The Books of History:
The Preparation for Christ

PART FOUR
The Books of Poetry:
The Aspiration for Christ

PART FIVE
The Books of Prophecy:
The Expectation of Christ

Illustrations

*The chronological charts were taken from *Moses and the Gods of Egypt* by John J. Davis and *Solomon to the Exile* by John C. Whitcomb. Used with permission.

PART ONE

Introduction

1

Christ: The Key to the Inspiration and Canonization of the Bible

What is the Bible all about? How can I understand its meaning? Why are there sixty-six books in the Bible? How do I know it is the Word of God? All of these questions can be answered in one word— Christ. Jesus Christ is the key to both the inspiration and the interpretation of the Bible. Further, it is Christ who confirmed the collection of books as both complete and authoritative.

In this introductory chapter we will examine just how it is that Christ confirmed both the authority and the extent of the Bible as the complete Word of God. The divine authority of the Bible results from its "inspiration" by God. How the Bible came to have only sixty-six books is the problem of "canonization."

I. Christ and the inspiration of the Bible.

A. THE NEW TESTAMENT IS A HISTORICALLY ACCURATE DOCUMENT.

It is a historical fact that Jesus Christ lived and taught what the New Testament says He taught. The Roman historian Tacitus (A.D. 112) said that Christ "...was put to death by Pontius Pilate, procurator of Judea in the reign of Tiberius" (*Annals* XV.44). Lucian, the second-century satirist, referred to Christ as "...the man who was crucified in Palestine," and who "persuaded [His followers] that they were all brothers," and that they should deny the Greek gods and worship Him (*On the Death of Peregrine*). The first-century Jewish historian Josephus wrote of Jesus "the so-called Christ" whose disciples "reported that He had appeared to them three days after His crucifixion and that He was alive" (*Antiquities* XVIII.33; XX.9.1). Suetonius (A.D. 120) alluded to the Jews who were expelled from Rome because they were

11

". . . making constant disturbances at the instigation of Chrestus [another spelling for Christ]" (*Life of Claudius* 25.4). Pliny the Younger (A.D. 112) recorded that early Christians met to sing ". . . a hymn to Christ as to a god, and bound themselves to a solemn oath, not to do any wicked deeds . . ." (*Epistles* X.96). Thallus, the Samaritan-born historian (A.D. 52), wrote in the third book of his histories, "It was at the season of the Paschal full moon that Christ died" (as recorded by Julius Africanus, A.D. 221). The Jewish Talmud says, "On the eve of Passover they hanged Yeshu (of Nazareth) . . . in that he hath practiced sorcery and beguiled and led astray Israel" (Babylonia, *Sanhedrin* 43a).

The best source of information about Jesus of Nazareth, however, is the historically verified documents of the New Testament. The English scholar F. F. Bruce (in *The New Testament Documents: Are They Reliable?*, 1960) agreed with the renowned scholar Sir Frederic Kenyon that "both the *authenticity* and the general *integrity* of the books of the New Testament may be regarded as finally established." Contrast with other writings from the ancient world underscores the fact that the New Testament is uniquely well-documented. The *Histories* of Tacitus are known only through two manuscript copies which date from about a thousand years after he wrote. There are only ten copies of Caesar's *Gallic Wars*, eight of Thucydides' *Peloponnesian War*, and twenty partial copies of Livy's *History of Rome*. The New Testament, in stark contrast, has over five thousand manuscript copies which began to be produced less than fifty years after the New Testament itself was written. Studies on the accuracy of the copying of ancient books reveal that the Hindu *Mahabharata* has been corrupted by copyist errors so that we are sure of only about 90 percent of the original text. Homer's *Iliad* has been copied with only 95 percent accuracy. Similar studies of the New Testament reveal that it has been copied with over 99 percent accuracy, the remaining portion of less than 1 percent affecting no significant teaching. Since these works were regarded as religious writings, the accuracy of their transmission was important. All of this means that the New Testament is not only the best-documented but also the most accurately copied book from the ancient world with the exception of the Old Testament, which was copied equally as well or better.

The result of this historical verification of the New Testament is that the modern reader can be sure as he reads the Gospels that what they record is indeed what Jesus of Nazareth taught and did. According to the famous archaeologist, William F. Albright, every book of the New Testament was written by A.D. 75. This means that the entire New Testament was written while most of the eyewitnesses were still alive. The New Testament is a first-century, firsthand report of what Jesus taught.

B. WHAT JESUS TAUGHT ABOUT THE INSPIRATION OF THE BIBLE.

In brief, Jesus confirmed that the Old Testament is the divinely authoritative Word of God and He promised that the Holy Spirit would lead His disciples in writing an inspired New Testament. Let's examine in particular what Christ said about the Bible as the Word of God.

1. *Some general claims about the Old Testament.* Jesus said many things about the Old Testament in general, all of which amount to an unmistakable acknowledgment that it is the authoritative and unbreakable Word of God. (1) He said, "Scripture *cannot be broken*" (John 10:35); (2) it *"must be fulfilled"* (Luke 24:44) ; (3) *ignorance of the Old Testament is the source of error* (Matt. 22:29); (4) Jesus said, "... till heaven and earth pass away, *not an iota, not a dot, will pass from the law until all is accomplished*" (Matt. 5:18); (5) following Jesus, the New Testament writers also considered the Old Testament to be Scripture which is *"inspired by God"* (II Tim. 3:16). These and numerous other passages leave no doubt that one of the central teachings of Jesus was that the Jewish Old Testament Scriptures are the divinely inspired Word of God with full and unimpeachable authority to teach God's truth.

2. *Some specific claims about the Old Testament.* In addition to the general claims Jesus made about the Old Testament inspiration there are numerous specific citations of Old Testament persons and events which reveal what Jesus taught about the authenticity and historical character of the Old Testament. For example, Jesus personally confirmed (1) that Adam and Eve were created by God (Matt. 19:4); (2) that Abel was killed by Cain (Matt. 23:35); 3) that a flood destroyed the world in Noah's time (Luke 17:27); (4) that God spoke to Moses through a burning bush (Luke 20:37); (5) that Elijah performed miracles (Luke 4:25); (6) that Jonah was in the whale three days (Matt. 12:40); and (7) that Daniel made true predictions (Matt. 24:15). What is significant about these teachings of Christ concerning the Old Testament is that they force us to choose between Christ and the critics of the Bible. Virtually everything major the critics deny about the Old Testament Jesus affirmed to be true. The dilemma is either to accept the authenticity and authority of the Old Testament or to impugn the integrity of Christ. In plain language, either the Old Testament is the Word of God or Christ is not the Son of God. Either it is true that the Old Testament is God's Word or we cannot believe Christ's word. Conversely, if Jesus taught the truth, then the

Old Testament is the historically accurate and divinely authoritative Word of God.

3. *Was Jesus an accommodator?* Some clever Bible critics have devised the "accommodation theory" to evade the above conclusion. They claim that Jesus did not verify these teachings about the Old Testament but merely accommodated Himself to the accepted (though false) beliefs of the Jewish people to whom He was speaking. The critics say He did this in order to get His own message to the Jews without entering into an unnecessary dispute with them over the nature of the Old Testament.

This ingenious accommodation theory does not stand the test of the historical facts which are known about Christ. Jesus was far from an accommodator; He was a forthright rebuker of error and tradition. (1) Six times in the Sermon on the Mount Jesus corrected false interpretations of the Old Testament by using such phrases as "you have heard that it was said . . . but I say to you" (Matt. 5:21-44); (2) Jesus rebuked the Jews who followed the "tradition rather than the commandment of God" (Matt. 15:1-3); (3) on other occasions, Jesus told them, "You are wrong, because you know neither the scriptures nor the power of God" (Matt. 22:29); (4) the Jewish rabbi Nicodemus was rebuffed by Jesus for not understanding the truth of the Old Testament (John 3:10); (5) Matthew 23 is one of the most severe denunciations of error to be found anywhere. Religious leaders are called "blind guides" and "blind fools" (Matt. 23:16, 17). Whatever else Jesus was, this much is clear, He was not an accommodator. The accommodation theory is ruined by a brutal gang of facts.

4. *What Jesus promised about the inspiration of the New Testament.* Not only did Jesus confirm the inspiration of the Old Testament but He promised the inspiration of the New Testament. Although Jesus never wrote any book, He did promise on several occasions that the Holy Spirit would direct His disciples in proclaiming God's truth. (1) When the Twelve were commissioned to preach He promised them it would be "the Spirit of your Father speaking through you" (Matt. 10:20); (2) in sending out the Seventy, Jesus gave them authority, saying, "He who hears you hears me . . ." (Luke 10:16); (3) in the Mount Olive discourse Jesus told His disciples, "It is not you who speak, but the Holy Spirit" (Mark 13:11); (4) in the Great Commission the disciples were given "all authority in heaven and on earth" for "teaching" men to observe His commandments (Matt. 28:18, 20; cf. John 20:23); (5) the promise to send the Spirit to direct His disciples into *"all the truth"* was clearly given by Christ after the Last Supper (John 16:13). Likewise, He told them that the Holy Spirit would "teach

you all things, and bring to your remembrance all that I have said to you" (John 14:26).

This promise of Spirit-directed teaching was claimed by the apostles in several ways. First, they claimed to be continuing what "Jesus began to do and teach" (Acts 1:1; cf. Luke 1:3, 4). Indeed, the early church continued in "the apostles' teaching" (Acts 2:42), and the New Testament church itself was "built upon the foundation of the apostles and prophets" (Eph. 2:20). Second, whereas the official oral pronouncements of the apostles were authoritative, it is also true that their writings were considered equally authoritative (cf. II Thess. 2:15). Peter even classed Paul's epistles with the inspired "scriptures" of the Old Testament (II Peter 3:16), and Paul quoted Luke's Gospel as "scripture" (I Tim. 5:18 from Luke 10:7). Paul reminded his readers that his own writings were equally as authoritative as other Scripture (I Tim. 4:11, 13) and that they were to be read in the churches (Col. 4:16). Since the twenty-seven books of the New Testament are the only authentic literature we have from the New Testament apostles, we may conclude that the promise of Christ to give us *all the truth* by the Spirit through the apostles has been fulfilled in the writings of the New Testament. As a matter of fact, this is precisely what both the apostles and early Christian church claimed for the New Testament Scriptures. Jesus' promise was fulfilled and the New Testament took its place alongside the inspired writings of Old Testament Scripture. The Bible was complete.

II. Christ and the canonization of the Old Testament.

Jesus is not only the key to the divine *nature* of the Old Testament, He is also the key to the *extent* of the Old Testament. The "extent" of the Old Testament refers to the question of which books belong in it. This issue is called the "canonization" of the Old Testament. The word *canon* means "rule" or "norm," and refers to the sacred writings which are the rule or norm for faith and practice among believers. More specifically the canon is concerned with the extent of the inspired or normative writings of the Old Testament.

Dispute arose over the claim by the Roman Catholic Church at the Council of Trent in 1546 that eleven books which Protestants excluded are to be included in the Bible. These books are called the Apocrypha. The books under dispute were Tobit, Judith, the Additions to Esther, Wisdom, Ecclesiasticus, Baruch, the Letter of Jeremiah, the Prayer of Azariah, Susanna, Bel and the Dragon, and I and II Maccabees. These books were written between 200 B.C. and the time of Christ. They reveal the religious history of the Jews between Malachi and Matthew. However, neither the Jews, Jesus, nor the early Christian church considered them to be part of the inspired Old Testament. Christians rejected them for several reasons. (1) The Jews, who are the custodians of the Old Testament (Rom. 3:2), never considered these books as inspired. (2) Jesus and the New Testament writers never quoted any of these books as Scripture. (3) No church council included them in the Bible until almost the fifth century. (4) When they began to be accepted by some Christians it was under the questionable authority of St. Augustine, who was refuted by St. Jerome. (5) St. Jerome, the most biblical scholar, emphatically rejected the books of the Apocrypha. (6) These books were not officially added to the Catholic Bible until 1546, and even then the basis for their acceptance was their support of such doctrines as Purgatory (II Macc. 12:45) and salvation by "works" (Tob. 12:9; Ecclus. 3:30). (7) Actually there are fourteen books in the Apocrypha. One of those which Catholics rejected has a strong verse against praying for the dead (in Purgatory) (II Esdras 7:105, called IV Esdras by Catholics). (8) In those which were accepted by the Council of Trent, there are historical contradictions (cf. Judith 1:1 and 14:11). (9) In addition, the Apocrypha never claims to be inspired. On the contrary, there are indications that there were no prophets of God at the time (I Macc. 4:46; 9:27). (10) There is no predictive prophecy in the Apocrypha as there is in the Old Testament prophets. (11) The Apocrypha adds nothing to our knowledge about Christ the Messiah, though the New Testament says that "the testimony of Jesus is the spirit of prophecy" (Rev. 19:10).

Of all these reasons, the most definitive for the Christian is the fact that the Apocrypha was never quoted or approved by Jesus. In fact, the Apocrypha was never part of the Jewish Old Testament which Jesus accepted. The Jewish Old Testament at the time of Christ consisted of the same thirty-nine books as the English Old Testament (though they were grouped differently so as to number twenty-two). The Old Testament is referred to as the "Law and the Prophets" (cf. Matt. 5:17; Luke 16:16). Jesus called these two sections "all the scriptures" (Luke 24:27) containing "everything written" about Himself (Luke 24:44). Elsewhere Jesus said the Law and Prophets contained God's Word up to the time of John the Baptist (Luke 16:16). Even books like Job, Psalms, Proverbs, and Daniel, which were later classified by the Jewish Talmud in a third section called "Writings," were included under the earlier and more basic division of "Law and Prophets" (cf. Matt. 24:15; Luke 4:8-11; John 10:34; I Cor. 3:19). From this it is evident that up to the time of Christ the whole inspired Old Testament included what is commonly called "Law and Prophets" (and later divided into "Law, Prophets and Writings"), which, on the testimony of both the Jews and Jesus, did not contain any books of the Apocrypha. Even the advocates of the Apocrypha admit that it was never included among the Law and the Prophets. They propose a third section of "Writings" in order to accommodate the Apocrypha. But the fact that the "Law and Prophets" are said to contain the whole of Old Testament inspired Scripture means that the Apocrypha was not considered by Jesus to be part of the Scriptures. Hence, Jesus is the key to the canonization of the Old Testament, and He clearly quoted from and affirmed to be inspired only the thirty-nine books of the Old Testament.

STUDY QUESTIONS

1. Distinguish between the meaning of *inspiration* and *canonization*.
2. For what reason does the critic raise the "accommodation theory"? Why is it fallacious?
3. Why ought one conclude that there are thirty-nine (no more and no less) books in the Old Testament canon?
4. "Either the Old Testament is the Word of God or Christ is not the Son of God." Explain.
5. Upon what grounds can one say that the New Testament, which was written after Christ, is also inspired?

2

Christ: The Key to the Interpretation of the Bible

What is the correct way to interpret the Bible? It is sometimes imagined that there are as many different interpretations of the Bible as there are readers. How should the Bible be understood? As the Ethiopian eunuch asked, with the Bible in hand, "How can I [understand] unless someone guides me?" The answer to this problem for the Christian is clear. Christ is our guide; He is the key to the interpretation of the Bible.

Jesus claimed five times that He is the theme of the entire canon of Old Testament Scripture. Speaking of the Law and Prophets He said, "I have come not to abolish them but to fulfill them" (Matt. 5:17). Jesus walked with two disciples on the road to Emmaus, and "beginning with Moses and all the prophets, he interpreted to them in all the scriptures the things concerning himself" (Luke 24:27). Later, to the ten disciples in the upper room Jesus said, "Everything written about me in the law of Moses and the prophets and the psalms must be fulfilled" (Luke 24:44) In dialogue with the Jews Jesus charged, "You search the scriptures . . . and it is they that bear witness to me" (John 5:39). The writer of Hebrews ascribes to Christ these words of Psalm 40: "It is written of me in the roll of the book" (Heb. 10:7). These five times our Lord affirmed that He is the theme of the whole Old Testament. We may conclude then, on the authority of Christ, that He is the theme of the entire Bible.

The Bible must be interpreted Christocentrically (i.e., Christ-centered). There is no other way for a Christian to understand it. There are at least three basic senses in which we may see Christ in the Bible as we survey its contents: (1) Christ is the theme of both testaments of the Bible, (2) Christ is the theme of each of the eight sections

of Scripture, and (3) Christocentric themes and truths may be found
in each of the sixty-six books of the Bible. Like a puzzle, once the
overall picture (theme) is understood, it is much easier to put all
the pieces together. The overall picture in the Bible is the person of
Christ. Once we see this, all the parts of testaments and books will
fit more easily in place. We can see Christ as the theme of the Bible
by examining the way Christ unites it in each of these senses.

I. Christ is the theme of both the Old and the New Testament.

The most basic division of the Bible is that of "testaments,"
"covenants," or "compacts" between God and His people. Both of
the testaments are centered in Christ. The Old Testament views Christ
by way of anticipation; the New Testament views Him by way of
realization. The Old Testament is incomplete without the New Testament. The salvation prepared for in the Old Testament was provided
by Christ in the New Testament. What is commenced in the Old
Testament is completed in the Christ of the New Testament. Christ
was enfolded in the truth of the Old Testament but is unfolded in
the truth of the New Testament.

The New is in the Old concealed, and the Old is in the New
revealed. What the Old Testament contains about Christ implicitly,
the New Testament explains explicitly, for the truth only latent in
the Old Testament is made patent in the New. The moral precepts
of the Old Testament are brought to perfection by Christ in the New
(cf. Matt. 5:17). What the Old Testament foreshadowed, the Christ
of the New fulfilled (Heb. 10:1). The ritual which prefigured Christ
is done away with in the reality of Christ (Col. 2:17). Old Testament
types become New Testament truths. Further, the many Old Testament prophecies which foretold of Christ are fulfilled in Christ in
the New Testament (cf. Isa. 7:14; Mic. 5:2). Christ often appeared in
temporary preincarnations in the Old Testament (Gen. 16; Exod. 3;
Josh. 5), but in the New Testament He is manifest in a permanent
incarnation (John 1:14). God manifested Himself through laws in the
Old Testament but in the life of His Son in the New Testament.
The Old Testament revelation was one of symbols, but in the New
Testament God spoke directly through His Son (Heb. 1:1, 2). In short,
the promises of salvation in the Old Testament are brought to fruition
in the presence of Christ in the New Testament (Matt. 1:21). The
thematic unity of both testaments is Jesus Christ. What the Old Testament says by way of anticipation of Christ, the New Testament says
by way of realization in Christ.

II. Christ is the theme of each of the eight sections of the Bible.

The Bible is divided into eight basic topical sections. There are four in the Old Testament and four in the New.

The Law (Gen.—Deut.)   Gospels (Matt.—John)
History (Josh.—Esther)   History (Acts)
Poetry (Job—Song of Sol.)   Epistles (Rom.—Jude)
Prophecy (Isa.—Mal.)   Prophecy (Rev.)

Each of these sections has a direction in its movement of thought which forms a perfect parallel between the Old and the New Testament. In the Law there is a *downward* movement as the Jewish nation is chosen to provide the foundation for the coming Christ. In History there is an *outward* movement as they make preparation for Christ. In Poetry there is an *upward* movement in their aspiration for Christ. In Prophecy there is a *forward* movement in the Jewish expectation of Christ. The exact New Testament parallel to this fourfold movement in the Old Testament is a *downward* movement in the manifestation of Christ in the Gospels, an *outward* movement in the propagation of Christ in Acts, an *upward* movement (to the ascended Christ) in the interpretation of Christ to the believers in the Epistles, and a *forward* movement to the consummation of all things in Christ in Revelation.

As a result, the whole Bible takes on a Christocentric structure. This structure may be seen in the following section-by-section overview:

A. LAW—THE FOUNDATION IS LAID FOR CHRIST.

The first five books of the Bible lay the foundation for the coming of Christ in that God here effects the *election* (Gen.), *redemption* (Exod.), *sanctification* (Lev.), *direction* (Num.) and the *instruction* (Deut.) of the Jewish people through whom He will bring into the world its two most treasured gifts, the Living Word (Christ) and the Written Word (Scripture). It is the foundation for this task which is laid by God in the first five books of the Old Testament.

B. HISTORY—PREPARATION FOR CHRIST.

In order for Christ the King to come through the chosen nation, the kingdom had to be formed. Under Joshua the Israelites took *possession* of the land for the kingdom (Josh.). Because of incomplete obedience, this was followed by the *oppression* of the nation (Judg.). But *devotion* within the nation (Ruth) brought a long-needed *stabilization* (I Sam.) under Saul's kingship. This was followed by the *expansion* of the nation under king David (II Sam.). After a brief period of Israel's *glorification* under Solomon (I Kings 1-10), we witness the *division* of the nation into two kingdoms (I Kings 11-22). Eventually this led to the *deterioration* of the northern kingdom of Israel (II Kings 1-17) and the *deportation* of the southern kingdom of Judah (II Kings 18-25). Chronicles reviews the prophetic history of Samuel and Kings from a priestly point of view, showing the *deprivation* (I Chron.) and ultimate *destruction* of the Temple (II Chron.). All is not lost, however, for God's providential hand is witnessed in the *protection* of His people in Babylon (Esther), the *restoration* of their Temple (Ezra), and the *reconstruction* of their nation (Neh.). Thus the checkered history of the Old Testament ends with the returned remnant awaiting the coming Redeemer.

C. POETRY—ASPIRATION FOR CHRIST IS EXPRESSED.

All of the poetic aspirations of the Israelites arise out of the previous historical setting. In suffering they aspired for *mediation* by someone "who might lay his hand upon us both [God and man]" (Job 9:33) and explain their plight. This was an implicit longing for Christ the Mediator (I Tim. 2:5). Throughout their history there was an aspiration for *communion* (Ps.) which blossomed forth in the messianic Psalms later fulfilled in Christ. Likewise, the aspiration for *wisdom* (Prov.) was finally fulfilled in Him who is the Wisdom of God (Col. 2:3). In philosophical aspiration for ultimate *satisfaction* the wise man found that it rests in God and the truths which come from "one Shepherd" (Eccles. 12:11, 13). The longing for *union* in love (Song of Sol.) was ultimately fulfilled in Christ, the lover of their souls. In short, the spiritual desires of Israel found in the Poetical books are fulfilled in Christ for whom Israel implicitly, and sometimes even unwittingly, aspired.

D. PROPHECY—THE EXPECTATION OF CHRIST.

Along with their moral exhortations, the writing prophets kept alive Israel's messianic expectation. The early prophets (Hosea, Joel and Amos) held out the hope of national *restoration* by Christ while Isaiah and Micah spoke of the even broader international *salvation* through Christ. Obadiah, Jonah, Nahum, Habakkuk and Zephaniah, on the other hand, found it necessary to call down the *retribution* of Christ on the sinful nations. Just before their exile (the seventy-year Babylonian captivity), Jeremiah reminded Israel of the future covenantal *reaffirmation* which would be made with Christ. During the exile the nation was reminded of its glorious *restoration* by Christ (Ezekiel) as well as its political *destination* in His kingdom (Daniel). After the exile both Haggai and Zechariah pointed to Israel's religious *restoration* through Christ, and Malachi pointed to the need for their moral *reconstruction* by Christ.

E. GOSPELS—THE MANIFESTATION OF CHRIST.

The anticipation of Christ in the Old Testament became the realization of Christ in the New Testament. In the Gospels this realization began in the historical manifestation of Christ in the world. The manifestation was fourfold. In Matthew Christ was manifest in His *sovereignty* (as King) to the Jews. In Mark he was manifest in His *ministry* (as servant) to the Romans. In Luke Christ was manifest in His perfect *humanity* (as man) to the Greeks. And in John He was manifest in His *deity* (as God) to the whole world. This messianic manifestation was the culmination of the anticipation of Christ in the Old Testament. The Old Testament hope became the New Testament reality, when deity entered into human history.

F. ACTS—THE PROPAGATION OF CHRIST.

The historical manifestation of Christ in the Gospels was limited to Palestine. In Acts the worldwide *propagation* of Christ began in Jerusalem (1-6), moved to surrounding Judea (7), Samaria (8) and finally to the whole world (9-28). That is, the historical manifestation of Christ in the Gospels was carried by the disciples into a worldwide proclamation of Christ in the Book of Acts.

G. EPISTLES—THE INTERPRETATION AND APPLICATION OF CHRIST.

In the Gospels there was a historical manifestation of Christ and in Acts a global propagation of Christ. In the New Testament Epistles there are a doctrinal interpretation and practical application of Christ for the believers. The key to discovering the specific theme of each of Paul's doctrinal epistles is the phrase "in Christ." The first use of this phrase in each epistle always occurs in connection with a word which is the interpretive theme of that epistle. For example, in Romans it is *redemption* in Christ which is the theme (3:24). In Corinthians it is *sanctification* in Christ (1:2) and in II Corinthians it is *jubilation* or triumph in Christ (2:14). Galatians reveals the believers' *emancipation* in Christ (2:4) and Ephesians their *exaltation* and resultant unification in Christ (1:3). Philippians declares the Christians' *exultation* (joy) in Christ (1:26) and Colossians speaks of *completion* in Christ (1:28). In I Thessalonians there is *expectation* in Christ (1:3) of His return and in II Thessalonians there is the future *glorification* in Christ at His coming (1:12). In I Timothy believers are urged to *faithfulness* in Christ (1:14); *soundness* in Christ is the theme in II Timothy (1:13). Titus is admonished to a life of *steadfastness in Christ* (1:9; cf. 2:1) and Philemon reveals an act of *benefaction* (benefit) in Christ (v. 6).

Paul's epistles are characteristically an *exposition* of what believers have in Christ, whereas the General Epistles stress *exhortations* to follow Christ. There is the exhortation to *perfection* (Heb. 6:1), to *wisdom* (James 1:5), to *submission* (I Peter 1:2) and to *purification* in Christ (II Peter 1:9). John exhorts the churches to *communion* with Christ (I John 1:7), to a *continuation* in Christ (II John 4) and to make *contributions* for the cause of Christ (III John 5-8). Jude exhorts believers to stand in *contention* for the faith of Christ once for all delivered to the saints (Jude 3).

H. THE REVELATION—THE CONSUMMATION OF ALL THINGS IN CHRIST.

The final section of the Bible shows how all things will find their consummation in Christ. Through Him all things were created and in Him all things are directed toward their final consummation. Christ is the beginning and the end, the Alpha and the Omega. In the Gospels He is *prophet* to His people. In Acts and the Epistles He is *priest* for His people and in Revelation He is *King* over His people. The foundation was laid for Christ in the first books of the Old Testament; the culmination of all things in Christ is found in the last book of the Bible. The plan of God for this planet ends in Christ's reign. The Book of Revelation reveals the final consummation of human history in Christ's person (Rev. 1), His possession (2-3), and His program for conquering this world (4-22).

III. Christ is found in each of the sixty-six books of the Bible.

As we have just seen, Christ is the theme of both testaments of the Bible as well as each of the eight sections of Scripture. In addition to this, Christocentric themes are found in each one of the sixty-six books of the Bible. As a sample, Christ is the Seed of the woman (Gen. 3:15); He is the Passover Lamb (Exod. 12:3f.), the Atoning Sacrifice (Lev. 17:11), the Smitten Rock (Num. 20:8, 11), and the Faithful Prophet (Deut. 18:18). Christ is the Captain of the Lord's Host (Josh. 5:15), the Divine Deliverer (Judg. 2:18), and the Kinsman Redeemer (Ruth 3:12). Christ is anticipated as the Anointed One (I Sam. 2:10) and as the Son of David (II Sam. 7:14). In I and II Kings Christ may be viewed as the coming King and in I and II Chronicles as the Builder of the Temple (I Chron. 28:20). Ezra represents Christ as the Restorer of the Temple (Ezra 6:14, 15), Nehemiah shows Him as the Restorer of the Nation (Neh. 6:15), and Esther portrays Him as the Preserver of the Nation (Esther 4:14). Christ is also seen as the Living Redeemer (Job 19:25), as the Praise of Israel (Ps. 150:6), the Wisdom of God (Prov. 8:22, 23), The Great Teacher (Eccles. 12:11), and the Fairest of Ten Thousand (Song of Sol. 5:10). Christ is the Suffering Servant (Isa. 53:11), the Maker of the New Covenant (Jer.

31:31), the Man of Sorrows (Lam. 3:28-30), the Glory of God (Ezek. 43:2), and the coming Messiah (Dan. 9:25). He is also depicted as the Lover of the Unfaithful (Hos. 3:1), the Hope of Israel (Joel 3:16), the Husbandman (Amos 9:13), the Savior (Obad. 21), the Resurrected One (Jon. 2:10), the Ruler in Israel (Mic. 5:2), the Avenger (Nah. 2:1), the Holy God (Hab. 1:13), the King of Israel (Zeph. 3:15), the Desire of Nations (Hag. 2:7), the Righteous Branch (Zech. 3:8), and the Sun of Righteousness (Mal. 4:2).

In the New Testament Christ is presented as the King of the Jews (Matt. 2:2), the Servant of the Lord (Mark 10:45), the Son of Man (Luke 19:10) and the Son of God (John 1:1). Christ is the Ascended Lord (Acts 1:10), the believer's Righteousness (Rom. 1:17), Sanctification (I Cor. 1:30), Sufficiency (II Cor. 12:9) and Liberty (Gal. 2:4). He is revealed as the Exalted Head of the church (Eph. 1:22), the Christian's Joy (Phil. 1:26) and the Fullness of Deity (Col. 2:9). In the Thessalonian epistles Christ is the believer's Comfort (I Thess. 4:16, 17) and Glory (II Thess. 1:12). He is seen as the Christian's Preserver (I Tim. 4:10), Rewarder (II Tim. 4:8), Blessed Hope (Titus 2:13), and Substitute (Philem. 17). He is also High Priest (Heb. 4:15), the Giver of Wisdom (James 1:5), the Rock (I Peter 2:6), and Precious Promise (II Peter 1:4). John represents Christ as the Life (I John), the Truth (II John), and the Way (III John); Jude portrays Christ as the Advocate and Revelation shows Him as King of Kings and Lord of Lords (Rev. 19:16). It is literally true that the Bible is all about Christ!

STUDY QUESTIONS

1. In what three senses can Christ be seen in the Bible?
2. Contrast the way in which the Old Testament and the New Testament view Christ.
3. List the four divisions of the Old Testament. How do they each relate to Christ?
4. From what four complementary perspectives do the Gospels present the person of Christ?
5. How do the General Epistles differ from the Pauline Epistles in their presentation of Christ?

PART TWO

The Books of the Law:

The Foundation for Christ

3

Introduction to the Books of the Law

I. The general structure of the Old Testament.

The books of the Bible have not always been numbered or grouped as they are today. There have been several stages in this development.

A. THE EARLY TWOFOLD DIVISION.

The earliest division of the Old Testament was a simple twofold division of Law and Prophets. The first five books were called the Law of Moses or the Books of Moses. All the other books were called the Prophets.

The Law	Genesis-Deuteronomy
The Prophets	Joshua-Malachi

Special place was given to the Books of Moses because he was the great deliverer and lawgiver of Israel. Beginning with Joshua a succession of prophets appeared who added their books to the sacred collection.

There are several reasons for believing that this twofold division was the original and most basic format of the Old Testament Scriptures. (1) It is the primary way the New Testament refers to the divisions of the Old Testament (cf. Matt. 5:17; 7:12; 22:40; Luke 16:16, 29, 31; 24:27; Acts 13:15; 26:22). (2) Even within the Old Testament itself there was a basic distinction made between the writings of "Moses" and "the Prophets" (cf. Dan. 9:6, 11, 13). Nehemiah spoke of the "Law" and the "Prophets" through which God warned Israel by His Spirit (Neh. 9:29, 30). Zechariah referred to "the law and ... the former prophets" (Zech. 7:12). (3) During the period between the Old and the New Testament the Second Book of Maccabees mentioned "the law and the prophets" (15:9). (4) The Qumran community of Dead

29

Sea Scroll fame consistently referred to the Old Testament as the Law and Prophets (*Manual of Discipline* I.3; VIII.15; IX.11).

That this twofold division of Law and Prophets included all thirty-nine books of the Old Testament (twenty-two or twenty-four as numbered by others) is confirmed from several sources. (1) Jesus and the New Testament writers cite eighteen of the twenty-two books of the Jewish Law and Prophets. These include all but Judges, Chronicles, Esther and the Song of Solomon. (2) Fragments of all but one (Esther) of the twenty-two books of the Old Testament were discovered in the Dead Sea Scrolls. (3) Josephus, the first-century Jewish historian, lists twenty-four books of the Old Testament (*Against Apion*, I.8). (4) Jesus declared that the Law and Prophets were *"all* the scriptures" of the Jews, and promised not a part would pass away "until *all* is accomplished" (Matt. 5:18; Luke 24:27). (5) The apostle Paul defended his orthodoxy by saying he believed *"everything* laid down by the law or written in the prophets" (Acts 24:14; cf. 26:22).

B. THE THREEFOLD DIVISION OF THE JEWISH OLD TESTAMENT.

There was an early tendency within Jewish circles to divide the Prophets into two sections called Prophets and Writings, thus making a threefold division of the Old Testament. Some feel that those books written by men who held the prophetic *office* (like Isaiah, Jeremiah, Ezekiel, the Twelve) were listed among the Prophets and those written by men who were not prophets by calling but who nevertheless had a prophetic *gift* (like David, Solomon, Daniel) were listed among the Writings.

1. *Before the time of Christ.* In the prologue to the apocryphal Book of Sirach (c. 132 B.C.), the writer refers to "the law and the prophets and the other books of our fathers." He mentions that these books had been read by his grandfather (c. 200 B.C.).

2. *At the time of Christ.* The Jewish philosopher Philo lived at Alexandria and made allusion to a possible threefold division of the Old Testament when he spoke of "the [1] laws and [2] oracles delivered through the mouth of prophets, and [3] psalms and anything else which fosters perfect knowledge and piety" (*De Vita Contemplativa* III.25). On one occasion Christ implied a threefold description of the Old Testament when He said, "Everything written about me in the law of Moses and the prophets and the psalms must be fulfilled" (Luke 24:44).

3. *After the time of Christ.* Josephus, the first-century Jewish historian, referred to the twenty-two books of the Hebrew Old Testament. He identified them as, "Five belonging to Moses, ... the prophets in

thirteen books. The remaining four books containing hymns to God and precepts for the conduct of human life" (*Against Apion* I.8).

By the fifth century A.D. at the latest, the Jewish Mishnah (*Baba Bathra*) listed eleven books in a third section of the Old Testament called "Writings" (*Kethubhim*). Since that time Jewish Bibles have continued to use the following arrangement:

I. Law of Moses (Torah)—5	II. Prophets (Nebhiim)—8	III. Writings (Kethubhim)—11
Genesis	A. Former Prophets	A. Poetical Books
Exodus	Joshua	Psalms
Leviticus	Judges	Proverbs
Numbers	Samuel	Job
Deuteronomy	Kings	B. Five Rolls
	B. Latter Prophets	(*Megiloth*)
	Isaiah	Song of Songs
	Jeremiah	Ruth
	Ezekiel	Lamentations
	The Twelve	Esther
		Ecclesiastes
		C. Historical Books
		Daniel
		Ezra-Nehemiah
		Chronicles

C. THE FOURFOLD DIVISION OF THE OLD TESTAMENT.

The Hebrew Old Testament was translated into Greek at Alexandria, Egypt, around 280 to 150 B.C. This translation was known as the Septuagint or LXX. At that time the books were rearranged according to subject matter. This arrangement later served as the basis for the modern fourfold division of the Old Testament into Law, History, Poetry, and Prophecy. Jerome's Latin Vulgate (c. A.D. 383-405) followed the Greek fourfold division, as do modern Christian editions of the Old Testament. This familiar arrangement is as follows:

I. Law (5)	II. History (12)	
Genesis	Joshua	I, II Samuel
Exodus	Judges	I, II Kings
Leviticus	Ruth	I, II Chronicles
Numbers		Ezra
Deuteronomy		Nehemiah
		Esther

III. Poetry (5)	IV. Prophets (17)	B. Minor Prophets (12)	
Job	A. Major Prophets (5)	Hosea	Nahum
Psalms	Isaiah	Joel	Habakkuk
Proverbs	Jeremiah	Amos	Zephaniah
Ecclesiastes	Lamentations	Obadiah	Haggai
Song of Solomon	Daniel	Jonah	Zechariah
	Ezekiel	Micah	Malachi

D. THE CONTENTS OF THE VARIOUS DIVISIONS OF THE
   OLD TESTAMENT CANON.

Although the Old Testament canon has been variously divided
into two, three, and four sections, there is no variation in the contents of the Old Testament canon. All thirty-nine books of the Greek,
Latin, and English Bible are contained in the twenty-four books of
the Old Testament used by Philo, Christ, and Josephus, and in the
earlier twofold division of the Old Testament canon as well.

II. The primary emphasis in each section of the Old Testament.

Following the fourfold topical arrangement of the Old Testament,
we see that each section has a particular relationship to the people of Israel:

> Law—their *moral* life
> History—their *national* life
> Poetry—their *spiritual* life
> Prophecy—their *messianic* (and future) life

In the Law were laid down the fundamental *moral* principles
which were to guide them in being a holy people. The Ten Commandments are a summary of these moral principles (cf. Exod. 20 and
Deut. 5). The Israelites were never able to keep God's moral law. Only
Christ was able to keep this law and, hence, only He was able to
fulfill it and to give, by His death, the righteousness the law required
of believers (Rom. 8:1-4).

In the books of History we see the *national* life of Israel in their
quest for a land (Joshua) and a king (Samuel) as well as the final
division and destruction of their kingdom (Kings). After they returned
from the seventy-year captivity they never had another king. Instead,
they awaited the Son of David (II Sam. 7) who would one day reign
in Jerusalem (Matt. 21:9).

In the books of Poetry there is a record of the Jewish *spiritual*
life, Job, Proverbs, and Ecclesiastes are known as wisdom literature. Their
fundamental thesis is that "the fear of the Lord is the beginning of
knowledge" (Prov. 1:7). The New Testament says that Christ is the
wisdom of God (I Cor. 1:30; Col. 2:3). The Psalms record the spiritual
experiences of God's people in prayer and praise (cf. Ps. 150). The
Psalms served as both a book of spiritual poetry and a hymnal. Jesus
singled out the Psalms for their special significance, saying they spoke
of Him (Luke 24:44). The Song of Songs is a tribute to the purity
and fidelity of marital love. It pictures the love which Christ, the
Bridegroom, has for His bride, the church (cf. Eph. 5:29-32).

The books of Prophecy lay special stress on the future *messianic*
life of Israel. They tell of Christ the coming King (Zech. 9:9), who

will be the "Prince of Peace" (Isa. 9:6), the "son of righteousness" (Mal. 4:2) and the "anointed one [Messiah]" (Dan. 9:26). They speak of Christ coming both to die (Isa. 53) and to reign forever (Isa. 9:7). They announce Christ's birth by a virgin (Isa. 7:14) in the city of Bethlehem (Mic. 5:2), His crucifixion (Zech. 12:10), and His coming kingdom (Dan. 2:44; 7:13-14).

III. The structure of the Law (Torah).

A. THE NAMES OF THE BOOKS OF THE LAW.

1. *The English names.* The English names of the first five books of the Bible are derived from Latin titles which were taken from the Greek Old Testament (LXX). These books are called the Law, the Torah, the Books of Moses or the Pentateuch. They include the following:

> Genesis—origin or beginning (of the world and the Jewish people)
> Exodus—going out or departure (from Egypt)
> Leviticus—book of the Levites (who helped the priests)
> Numbers—numbering or counting (of the Israelites)
> Deuteronomy—second law or second giving of the law (by Moses to Israel)

2. *The Hebrew names.* The names of the books of the Torah in the Hebrew Bible are taken from the first words of each book as follows:

> *Bereshith*—"in the beginning" (Genesis)
> *Shemoth*—"names" (Exodus)
> *Wayyigra*—"and he called" (Leviticus)
> *Bemidbar*—"in the wilderness" (Numbers)
> *Devarim*—"words" (Deuteronomy)

B. THE TIME PERIOD COVERED IN THE BOOKS OF MOSES.

> Genesis—from the creation of the world to the bondage of Israel in Egypt (creation—1860 B.C.)
> Exodus—from the sojourn of Israel in Egypt to Mt. Sinai (c. 1860-1447 B.C.)
> Leviticus—one month between Exodus and Numbers
> Numbers—from Mt. Sinai to the end of the forty-years "wandering" (1447-1407 B.C.)
> Deuteronomy—from the end of wandering to after Moses' funeral (about two months)

C. THE THEMES OF THE BOOKS OF THE LAW.

> Genesis—the *election* of the nation
> Exodus—the *redemption* of the nation
> Leviticus—the *sanctification* of the nation
> Numbers—the *direction* of the nation
> Deuteronomy—the *instruction* of the nation

In Genesis God chose Abraham, his son Isaac, his grandson Jacob, and Jacob's twelve sons to be the channel through which He would bless the whole world (Gen. 12:1-3). Hence, the theme is God's *election* (electing or choosing).

In Exodus the chosen nation was in bondage to Pharaoh in Egypt. God delivered them under Moses and redeemed them by blood to teach them His love and power (Exod. 12:21-36). The main theme, therefore, is *redemption*.

In Leviticus God instructed the people how to be holy in both soul and body. "You shall therefore be holy, for I am holy" (Lev. 11:45) is repeated over and over again. Israel was taught that they must be sanctified (or set apart) to God. Thus the central teaching is *sanctification*.

In Numbers the people were guided through the wilderness on their way back to the promised land. Despite their disobedience, God directed them day by day using a cloud which moved before them. The chief lesson in Numbers is that the Lord gives *direction* to His people.

In Deuteronomy Moses gave his farewell speeches to Israel. They included a repetition of God's commandments. These commandments were to be the key to spiritual success in the promised land. This *instruction* of the Lord was essential to their victory.

IV. The bloodline of the coming Messiah.

From the very time of the sin of Adam and Eve God began to give predictions of the coming Messiah or Savior. On various occasions God would give new revelations of the line of descendants through which Christ would come. The main links in the messianic line are shown in Genesis, where God revealed that Christ would come through:

The Seed of the woman, or the human race (Gen. 3:15)
The line of Seth (Gen. 4:25)
The offspring of Shem (Gen. 9:26)
The family of Abraham (Gen. 12:3)
The seed of Isaac (Gen. 26:3)
The sons of Jacob (Gen. 46:3)
The tribe of Judah (Gen. 49:10)

STUDY QUESTIONS

1. List and discuss the themes of the five Books of the Law.
2. Of the different historic ways of dividing the Old Testament books, which is probably the most basic and original? Give reasons for your answer.

3. What evidence can be cited to confirm that the early twofold division of the Old Testament contained all the books we now recognize as comprising the Old Testament?
4. What is one possible explanation for the fact that the early Jews tended to divide the Prophets into two sections called the Prophets and the Writings?
5. What is the primary emphasis of each of the four sections of the Old Testament?

4

The Origination of the Nations

GENESIS 1-11

Where did everything come from? How did everything get here? These and like questions of origin are answered in the first eleven chapters of Genesis. But before we can properly understand the content of these chapters we must ask some preliminary questions: Who wrote Genesis? When was it written? To whom was it written? Why was it written?

WHO WROTE GENESIS?

There are several lines of evidence to indicate that Moses, the great lawgiver and deliverer of Israel who wrote the other four books of the Law, was the author of Genesis. (1) The earliest and continual tradition of the Jewish people, as recorded in the Talmud, attributes this book to Moses. (2) Moses is the only person we know of from this early time period who had the ability to write this book. The rest of the Israelites were a nation of uneducated slaves, whereas Moses was a highly educated son of the king (Acts 7:22). (3) Moses was the only one who had both the interest and information to write Genesis. Being Jewish Moses would have had access to the family records of his ancestors (cf. Gen. 5:1; 10:1; 25:19; etc.) which were no doubt brought down to Egypt by Jacob (Gen. 46). Since Moses was bent on delivering his people from Egypt, it is natural to assume that he was familiar with the promises of God passed down by his forefathers that God would indeed deliver them (cf. Gen. 46:3-4; Exod. 2:24). (4) Citations from Genesis show that the rest of the Old Testament regards it as part of the Law of Moses (Deut. 1:8; II Kings 13:23; I Chron. 1:1ff.). Since Moses was the author of the other "books of Moses," as we will see later, it is reasonable to attribute the first book

37

of Moses to him as well. (5) Jesus and the New Testament writers clearly regard Moses as the author of an essential part of Scripture (cf. Matt. 19:8; Luke 16:29; 24:27). We can conclude that Moses, using the family records which had been passed on to him, compiled the Book of Genesis. Although it is possible that God revealed to Moses all of this history by direct revelation when he was on Mt. Sinai (Exod. 19:20), it seems unwarranted to assume this since the Bible does not say Moses received his information in that way. As a matter of fact, it is unnecessary to make such an assertion because Jewish history shows that family records were kept and passed on to later generations. Moses could have copied his material from such records just as Hezekiah's men copied from Solomon's writings to complete the Book of Proverbs (cf. Prov. 25:1).

WHEN WAS GENESIS COMPOSED?

Moses' life extended 120 years (Deut. 34:7). The first forty years he spent as Pharaoh's son learning the wisdom of the Egyptians (Acts 7:22). Moses spent the next forty years in the desert of Midian as a shepherd (Exod. 2:15). The final forty years he spent wandering in the wilderness with the children of Israel (Deut. 8:2). According to the chronological chart (cf. p. 39), Moses lived from 1527 to 1407 B.C. His life span was as follows:

Moses in Egypt (1527-1487 B.C.)
Moses in Midian (1487-1447)
Moses in the wilderness (1447-1407)

There are three reasons for believing that Moses compiled Genesis during the first forty years of his life (before 1487 B.C.). (1) During this period Moses came to faith in God and the desire to deliver his people (cf. Exod. 2:11f.; Heb. 11:24). He must have carefully studied Israel's history and God's promises to Abraham's descendants at this time. (2) Later, while in Midian, Moses would not have had access (such as he had had in Egypt) to all the records of his people. (3) By the third period of his life, Moses was busy as a leader and writer of the other books of the Law. It is more likely, then, that Genesis was compiled while his early interest in his people's past and their deliverance gave him access to the records of their history and the promises of God to deliver them.

TO WHOM WAS GENESIS WRITTEN?

Genesis was written for a nation of Hebrew slaves in Egypt. What could be more assuring for them than to know from the records of God's revelation to their fathers that God had promised to deliver them from Egypt? There are several times in Genesis that this promise

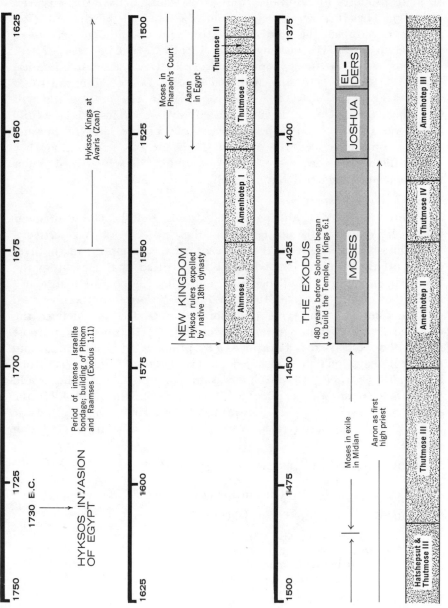

1750-1375 B.C.

is repeated (cf. Gen. 15:16; 46:4). Moses undoubtedly used the record of these promises for assurance that God would deliver the enslaved Hebrews. The Hebrew slaves were in the land of Egypt, but God had given Abraham the land of Palestine and told him to stay there in order to realize His blessings (Gen. 13:14-17). In God's *perfect* will He told Isaac, "Do not go down to Egypt" (Gen. 26:2); but because of sin God by His *permissive* will told Jacob, "Do not be afraid to go down to Egypt" (Gen. 46:3) so that one day in His *providential* will God might say, "Out of Egypt I called my son" (Hos. 11:1). While Israel was in Egypt God's people were out of the land of blessing and out of the perfect will of God. It is for this reason that they were afflicted with heavy burdens. As a result, "Israel groaned under their bondage, and cried out for help" (Exod. 2:23).

WHY WAS GENESIS WRITTEN?

Three purposes are distinguishable in each of the Old Testament books: the historical, the doctrinal, and the Christological. Respectively, these purposes include what the book aimed to accomplish in the lives of the original audience for whom it was written, main teachings the book has for the lives of all believers, and what the book tells us about Christ the coming Messiah. In Genesis the *historical* purpose was to provide comfort in suffering and hope that God would deliver the enslaved Israelites from the bondage of Egypt. The *doctrinal* purpose was to show that God is faithful to His promises (cf. Heb. 10:23) and to reveal that God's plan is based on His election (choice) (cf. Rom. 9:6-18). Its *Christological* purpose was to point to Christ, who would be the Seed of the woman (Gen. 3:15), the line of Seth (Gen. 4:25), the son of Shem (Gen. 9:27), the offspring of Abraham (Gen. 12:3), Isaac (Gen. 21:12), and Jacob (Gen. 25:23), and from the tribe of Judah (Gen. 49:10).

WHAT IS THE BOOK OF GENESIS ABOUT (CHS. 1-11)?

I. The outline of Genesis.

A. THE ORIGIN OF NATIONS (CHS. 1-11).

1. The creation of man (1-2).
2. The corruption of man (3-5).
3. The destruction of man (6-9).
4. The dispersion of man (10-11).

B. THE ELECTION OF THE CHOSEN NATION (CHS. 12-50).

II. The content of Genesis 1-11.

The main theme of Genesis is the election or choice of a nation through whom God would bless all nations. The first eleven chapters

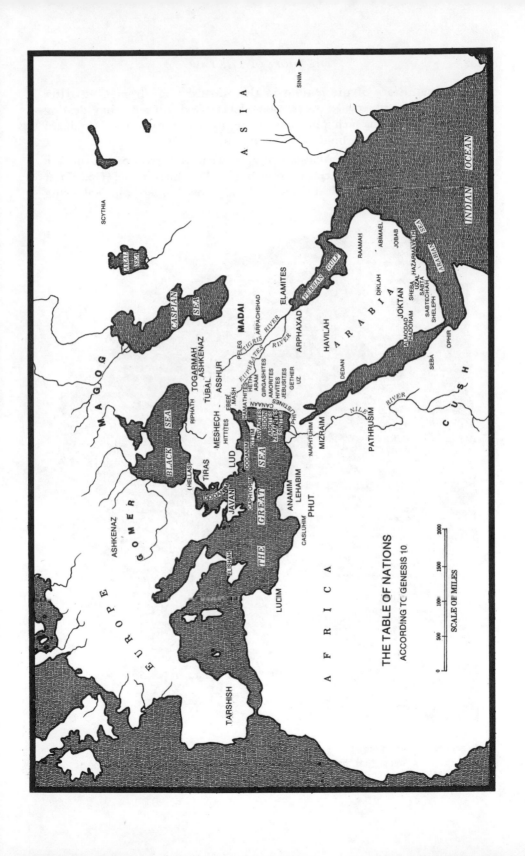

THE TABLE OF NATIONS
ACCORDING TO GENESIS 10

SCALE OF MILES

0   500   1000   1500   2000

trace the history of the nations as they turned away from God. After the nations had turned from God (1-11), God turned from dealing with the nations as such and chose one nation (beginning with Abraham) through whom He would bless all nations (12-50).

The origin of the nations begins with the creation of heaven and earth (1) and especially of man (2). But man failed God's test and sinned, bringing death and judgment on himself (3). Following

A portion of the Gilgamesh Epic from Nineveh ca. 650 B.C. The Epic contains an account of a flood that has remarkable parallels to the account in Genesis. The British Museum

in his father Adam's steps, Cain started an evil civilization (4) which ultimately brought wickedness and violence which filled the earth and precipitated the Flood (6-9). Meanwhile, God was fulfilling His promise to bring a Savior (3:15) by developing a godly line of people through Seth, from whom came Noah and his blessed son Shem (9). After the Flood descendants of Noah through Ham developed a wicked kingdom centered around the tower of Babel, which God had to judge by scattering them abroad (10-11). Thus the history of the nations ends in their abortive attempt to unify without God and to forge a world kingdom motivated by their own vanity.

HOW CAN GENESIS BE RECONCILED WITH MODERN SCIENCE?

Some general principles of reconciliation between science and Scripture. There is no contradiction between the facts of Genesis and the facts of science. There is a difference between *some interpretations* of Genesis and *some theories* of science. Since God is revealed in both His *Word* (Scripture) and His *world* (science) (Ps. 19:1; Rom. 1:19), there is *really* no contradiction between them. When the Bible and science *appear* to be in conflict, we must remember that scientific theories change, and they may be wrong today. In addition, there is more than one way to interpret the early chapters of Genesis. Finally, through the years science has come to support many things in the Bible which it once taught were untrue.

Some areas where science supports the Bible. Archaeology has discovered thousands of things which prove the historical accuracy of the Bible. Astronomy agrees with Genesis that the world had a beginning. Geology supports the order of creation presented in Genesis 1, following its approach that the universe came first, the world was formed next, that life began in the sea, with the lower forms of life appearing first, and that man is the highest and latest form of life to appear. Physics (the second Law of Thermodynamics) shows the world is running out of available energy. Hence the world cannot be eternal but must have had a beginning. Mathematics (the Law of Probability) shows that the world did not happen by chance but was designed by an intelligent power. Biology teaches that each creature reproduces its own kind, and Anthropology shows that there is only one race of mankind (cf. Acts 17:26) with different ethnic groupings within it. This indicates a common ancestor for all men.

Evolution and creation are a serious area of conflict between science and the Bible. The Bible teaches that God created matter, life, and man (Gen. 1:1, 21, 26). It also teaches that God made the basic kinds of organisms like fish, fowl, plants and beasts (Gen. 1) and that each organism reproduces after its own kind (Gen. 1:11, 12, 21). Finally, the

Bible says that man and woman were specially created by God from the earth (Gen. 2:7f.). What the facts of science indicate about the origin of life and man is that the most basic forms of life began suddenly and abundantly and that new forms of life began in the fossil record in the same way. Science reveals that there are different kinds of life forms in which small developments and changes may occur by means of limited cross-breeding and mutations (called *micro-evolution*). But science also reveals that no large changes are observable (called *macro-evolution*) and that at the known rate of mutation over the estimated scientific time scale of a half billion years, the odds against things happening by chance alone are 1 followed by 3 million zeros to 1 (this is admitted by the famous evolutionist Julian Huxley in his book, *Evolution in Action*). Our conclusion in the light of the facts of Scripture and science is that although evolution is *theoretically* possible, it is *scientifically* highly improbable and *biblically* untenable (since the Bible clearly teaches that God created the different kinds of organisms, including man).

The age of the world and of mankind is another area of conflict between the Bible and modern science. Science says the world is billions of years old while some Bible scholars say the world was created about 4004 B.C. The facts of the matter are simply these: the Bible does not say how old the world or mankind is; there are gaps in the genealogical tables of Genesis 5 and 11 of such a nature that one cannot simply add up all the ages and get 4000 years B.C. (cf. I Chron. 3:11f. and Matt. 1:8); and scientific methods of dating are not absolute but subject to change. Therefore, the so-called contradiction between the Bible and modern science is only a conflict in opinion and not a contradiction in fact.

STUDY QUESTIONS

1. For what reasons do we believe that Moses is the author of Genesis?
2. Discuss the three purposes for which Genesis was written.
3. Respond to the statement: scientific facts contradict the facts of Scripture.
4. Discuss areas in which science supports the Bible.
5. What is the purpose of Genesis 1-11 and how do these chapters relate to the theme of the whole book?

5

The Election of the Jewish Nation
GENESIS 12-50

THE ORIGIN OF THE NATIONS (Gen. 1-11).

We have already seen that Genesis 1-11 deals with the origin of the universe, man, and the nations. In these chapters we can trace the creation of man, his subsequent fall and destruction through the Flood, as well as the eventual dispersion of the nations which rejected God. However, in contrast to this dark picture of mankind, these chapters also offer a glimmer of hope. For God's promise to bring a Savior (3:15) begins to develop. It can be seen in the preservation of a godly line through Noah's blessed son Shem (9). What was begun in chapters 1-11 is further developed in Genesis 12-50, which record God's selection of Israel to carry out His redemptive plans.

THE ELECTION OF THE CHOSEN NATION (Gen. 12-50).

The history of the nations given in Genesis 1-11 ends with the dispersion of the nations which rejected God. The attention of God now turns from the scattered nations to His dealings with one nation through which He will fulfill His promise to bless the peoples of the earth. The beginning of this chosen nation is found in God's call of Abraham.

I. Abraham (12-25a).

A.   THE CALL OF ABRAHAM (Gen. 12:14).

The focus of God's plan of blessing and redemption for the human race now shifts to one man from the line of Shem—Abram. In the opening verses of Genesis 12, Abram received the specific call from God to leave his homeland and go forth to the land of Canaan. However, along with this command came a most important promise to

Abram. God promised that He would make a great nation out of Abram's descendants, and God changed Abram's name to Abraham— "father of a multitude" (Gen. 17:5). Furthermore, this nation would be the means through which God would bless all the nations of the earth (Gen. 12:3). In short, in Abraham's descendants God selected a people through whom He would carry out His promise of redemption. Abraham, heeding God's call, journeyed to the land of Canaan with his wife (Sarah) and nephew (Lot). This land was promised to Abraham's descendants as their future possession (Gen. 13:14-15).

B. THE COVENANT WITH ABRAHAM (Gen. 15-16).

In Genesis 15, the promise to Abraham is dramatically reaffirmed, even though Abraham is still without an heir. God now states that Abraham's descendants shall be as numberless as the stars. Then God reveals a bit of His future plan for Abraham's descendants. He says that they will be enslaved in *another land* for 400 years. Nevertheless, God affirms that the descendants will return to and possess the land of Canaan. Thus God made a covenant with Abraham which stated that the land of Canaan would be his descendants' possession. Still, even though God had promised an heir, Abraham and Sarah did not have a son. In unbelief, Sarah offered to Abraham her maid Hagar. It was her attempt to help God fulfill His promise, and through the union of Abraham and Hagar a son named Ishmael was born. Abraham finally had an heir, although it was a result of his own work rather than the fulfillment of God's promise.

C. THE CONFIRMATION TO ABRAHAM (Gen. 17-21).

In Genesis 17 the covenant God made with Abraham is reaffirmed. On this occasion, circumcision is initiated as the sign of the covenant between God and Abraham. Moreover, at this point, God makes a further promise to Abraham. He promises to Abraham a son, Isaac, through his wife Sarah. Such a thing seemed both humorous and impossible to Abraham and Sarah, for he was one hundred and she was ninety years of age. Abraham felt that Ishmael could continue his line, but God had different plans and affirmed that His covenant with Abraham would be continued by his future son, Isaac. God's promise, in spite of Abraham's and Sarah's doubts, is fulfilled: at the age of ninety, Sarah bears a son, Isaac (meaning "laughter"). God has now confirmed His covenant and designated through whom His plan of redemption would be carried.

D. THE CONFIDENCE OF ABRAHAM (Gen. 22-23).

With the birth of Isaac God's covenant with Abraham is literally fulfilled. Through Isaac the elected nation is to come. However, the

ABRAHAM'S FAMILY TREE

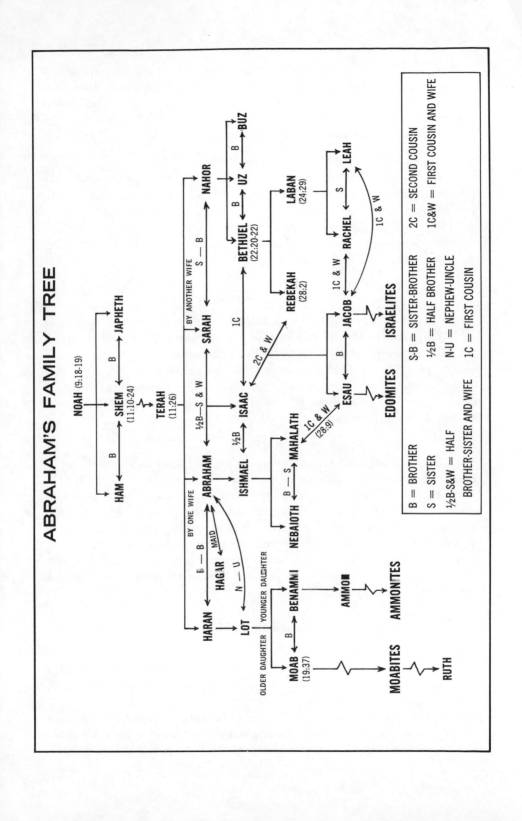

faith of Abraham is dramatically tested (Gen. 22:1). He is commanded by God to offer Isaac as a burnt offering. Abraham obeys God and is about to slay Isaac when God stops him. Abraham's faith and commitment to God are proven, and God again promises to make a blessed nation of Abraham's descendants (Gen. 22:18).

E.   THE CONCERN OF ABRAHAM (Gen. 24-25a).

God blesses the life of Abraham in every way (Gen. 24:1). As Abraham advances in age, his attentions turn toward obtaining a wife for his son Isaac. He sends a servant to his home country to find a bride for Isaac. Moving clearly by the providential leading of God, Abraham's servant finds Rebekah and brings her to be Isaac's wife. Abraham then dies at the age of 175 (Gen. 25:7-8).

II. Isaac (25b-27).

A.   THE BLESSING CONFIRMED (Gen. 25b-26).

We have already seen that God's promise to Abraham is to be fulfilled through Isaac (Gen. 17:19). This promise to Abraham becomes a reality as God establishes the covenant with Isaac in two separate instances (Gen. 26:3-5; 24-25). God promises that Isaac's descendants will number as the stars, inherit the land of Canaan, and be the source of blessing for the whole world.

B.   THE BLESSING CONFERRED (Gen. 27).

Just as the blessing and promise of God pass from Abraham to Isaac, they must also pass from Isaac to his son. But Isaac had twin sons, Esau and Jacob. Esau is born first and Isaac's blessing therefore rightfully belongs to him. However, when the time comes for Isaac to confer his blessing on Esau, he is deceived into blessing Jacob instead. Rebekah plots the whole incident and prods Jacob into disguising himself as Esau in order to deceive the dim-sighted Isaac. With this trick, Jacob ("the supplanter") receives Isaac's blessing, much to the dismay of his brother Esau.

III. Jacob (28-36).

A.   JACOB'S CALL (Gen. 28).

Having blessed Jacob, Isaac sends Jacob to Paddan-aram to find a wife from among the daughters of Laban. While on his journey, Jacob stops to sleep and has a vision. In it he sees the Lord standing at the top of a ladder reaching to heaven. The Lord speaks to Jacob and in a dramatic way reaffirms to him the original covenant made with Abraham and Isaac. Through Jacob's descendants God promises to bless all nations.

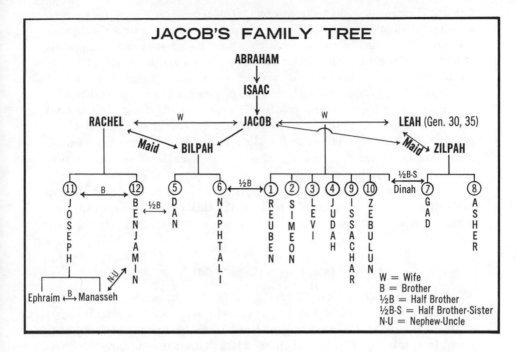

JACOB'S FAMILY TREE

Jacob now becomes the vital link through which God's plan to redeem the world is to be fulfilled.

B. JACOB'S MARRIAGE (Gen. 29-31).

Jacob, honoring his father's wish, arrives at Paddan-aram to find his wife. Here he finds Rachel, daughter of Laban, and falls in love with her. Desiring to marry her, he pledges to serve Laban seven years for the right to marry Rachel. After the seven years, however, Laban tricks Jacob by giving him Leah, his older daughter, on the wedding night. Jacob still wants to marry Rachel, and agrees to work another seven years if Laban will give him his daughter Rachel in marriage as well. From these two wives and their concubines twelve sons are born to Jacob.

Following the birth of Joseph, Jacob decides to leave Laban's land and return to Canaan. After a considerable amount of difficulty over the rightful ownership of property (Gen. 30b-31) Jacob and his family depart from Paddan-aram.

C. JACOB'S RETURN TO CANAAN (Gen. 32-35).

After leaving Laban, Jacob encounters immediate trouble. Jacob had learned that Esau was coming to him with four hundred men. This of course strikes terror into Jacob's heart for he thinks that Esau is coming to seek revenge for the trick by which Jacob had stolen Isaac's blessing. Fearful of Esau's intentions, Jacob sends messengers to Esau in an attempt to appease him. On the night before Esau is to arrive, Jacob encounters an angel of the Lord with whom he wrestles until daybreak. During that incident, the angel changes Jacob's name to Israel ("contender with God"). When Esau arrives Jacob is surprised to find that Esau carries no grudge. In fact, he is happy to see his twin brother.

Upon reaching Canaan, Jacob first settles in Shechem. When God directs he moves to Bethel, the place where he had first received God's promise in the vision. Here God again affirms to Jacob that his name is now Israel. God also reaffirms the promise to make Jacob a great nation which will possess the land.

On the way to Ephrath, Rachel gives birth to Jacob's twelfth son, Benjamin, and she dies in the process. At this point, the narrative of Genesis shifts to follow the life and career of Joseph, Benjamin's only full brother.

IV. Joseph (Gen. 37-50).

A. JOSEPH AS A SLAVE (Gen. 37-39).

Joseph is Jacob's first son by his favorite wife, Rachel. Jacob shows his favor by giving Joseph a multicolored robe. As a result of this favoritism, Joseph is hated by his brothers. Their hatred is compounded when Joseph tells of his dreams which depict his brothers bowing down before him as though he were a ruler. Finally, this hatred and jealousy result in Joseph's brothers conspiring to get rid of him. They plot to kill him but instead they decide to sell Joseph to a group of Ishmaelite traders who are going to Egypt. Joseph is there sold as a slave to Potiphar, an officer of Pharaoh. Meanwhile, the brothers take Joseph's robe to their father after soaking it in goat's blood. The brothers thus leave Jacob with the impression that Joseph is dead.

Down in Egypt, Joseph is soon elevated to a high position with Potiphar because of his trustworthy and hard-working nature. He is made the overseer of all Potiphar's possessions. Then, suddenly, his place of high favor is lost. Potiphar's wife, having been continually rejected in her efforts to seduce Joseph, falsely accuses him of immoral attentions and Joseph is confined to prison.

B. JOSEPH AS THE SERVANT TO EGYPT (Gen. 41-45).

Two years later, the Pharaoh has a dream which none of his wise men can interpret. Having heard of Joseph's past success in interpreting dreams, he sends for Joseph in prison. Joseph relates that the dreams speak of an impending seven years of prosperity followed by seven years of severe famine. He warns Pharaoh to be prepared and Pharaoh takes his advice. Since Joseph was able to interpret the dream, he is made the ruler over all Egypt for the purpose of preparing for the coming famine.

When the famine comes, it also affects Canaan where Jacob and his eleven other sons still live. Therefore, Jacob sends all his sons except Benjamin to Egypt to get grain. Since Joseph is now the ruler over Egypt they have to make their appeal before him, and the dreams of the young Joseph are now fulfilled. While the brothers do not recognize Joseph, he recognizes them but does not reveal his identity. Only after a series of interviews together with various tests and commands (Gen. 43-44) does Joseph finally and joyfully reveal his identity to his brothers. He is quick to assure them that he has no contempt in his heart, for he knows God has used him to save and preserve the family of Jacob in this time of famine (Gen. 45:4-7).

C. JOSEPH THE SAVIOR OF ISRAEL (Gen. 46-50).

Joseph brings the whole family of Jacob into Egypt at this time. While they are on their way to Egypt, God tells Jacob not to be afraid to enter Egypt, for He will make Israel a great nation there and bring that nation back into Canaan again: God's covenant with Abraham is still valid. Having been saved from the famine through Joseph, the children of Israel (Jacob) are now to become a great nation in Egypt. The family of Jacob is welcomed in Egypt and given possession of the land of Goshen. At the age of 147, Jacob dies in Egypt. He leaves his twelve sons, the twelve tribes of Israel (Gen. 49:28), to grow and prosper in the land of Egypt. Knowing that they will return to Canaan, he requests that they remember to take his body back with them when they depart from Egypt.

STUDY QUESTIONS

1. On what basis did Abraham, Isaac, and Jacob receive the promise of God?
2. What did this promise have to do with the land of Palestine?
3. Why was Jacob (the younger son) chosen by God over Esau (the older)?
4. How do you explain the apparent contradiction between the command not to go to Egypt (Gen. 26:2) and the command not to fear going to Egypt (Gen. 46:3)?
5. In what way is Joseph a picture of Christ?

6

The Redemption of the Nation
EXODUS

Genesis ends with the chosen nation in bondage outside the promised land of blessing. Exodus begins with a description of that bondage. Nevertheless, in the midst of their suffering God wrought a great deliverance for the chosen nation through Moses. The theme of Exodus is the story of their *redemption* from bondage.

WHO WROTE EXODUS?

Moses the great deliverer and lawgiver of Israel is the author of Exodus. There are several lines of evidence to support his authorship of the book.

Possible evidence.

The evidence which supports the Mosaic authorship of Genesis (see ch. 4) also applies to Exodus. No other known person from that period had the time, interest, and ability to compose such a record. In addition, Moses was an *eyewitness* of the events in Exodus and as such was qualified to be the author of the book.

Probable evidence.

Three other lines of evidence support the probability that Moses wrote Exodus. (1) The earliest Jewish teaching ascribes this book, along with the other four books of the Torah, to Moses. (2) The vividness of the accounts of crossing the Red Sea and the giving of the Law at Sinai strongly suggests that the author had a firsthand acquaintance with those events. Some of the conversations and events involved were known directly only by Moses. (3) The detailed knowledge of the geography of the wilderness (see Exod. 14) is incomprehensible apart from firsthand experience gained from living there for many years. The same is true of the author's knowledge of the ancient customs and practices described in Exodus.

Positive evidence.

That Moses wrote Exodus is supported by positive testimony beginning in his day and continuing into modern times through an unbroken chain. In Moses' day it was recorded in the Bible that "Moses wrote all the words of the Lord" (Exod. 24:4). In Joshua's day Moses' law was enjoined to the people (Josh. 1:7). In David's day the king referred to "his commandments . . . written in the law of Moses" (I Kings 2:3). King Josiah discovered "the book of the law" in the Temple (II Chron. 34:14). During the Babylonian exile, Daniel read of the curse "written in the law of Moses" (Dan. 9:11). Ezra the priest set up Passover observances for the returning remnant "as it is written in the book of Moses" (Ezra 6:18). The Old Testament ends with Malachi's exhortation, "Remember the law of my servant Moses" (Mal. 4:4). Definitive for a Christian is the fact that Jesus quoted from Exodus 20:12 using the introduction, "For Moses said" (Mark 7:10; cf. Luke 20:37). The apostle Paul noted, "Moses writes that the man who practices the righteousness which is based on the law. . ." (Rom. 10:5f.; cf. Exod. 20:11). Finally, the testimony of both the Jewish community and the Christian church throughout history has been to the effect that Moses wrote the Book of Exodus. The weight of this ancient and enduring testimony cannot be overthrown by the mere speculations of "Johnny-come-lately" skepticism.

WHEN WAS EXODUS WRITTEN?

The events of Exodus cover the period between 1445 and 1405 B.C. During that time the Israelites wandered forty years in the wilderness of Sinai (Exod. 40:38). The record may be divided into three parts. (1) Some events occurred *before* Sinai, namely, the exodus from Egypt and the trip to Sinai. (2) Some of the teaching was given *at* Mt. Sinai (Exod. 20) after Moses' first ascension to the top (Exod. 24:4). Most of the revelation was given *on* Mt. Sinai during the forty days of Moses' second ascension (Exod. 34:27, 28). (3) The rest of the events occurred *in* the Sinai wilderness and on the plains of Moab where "Moses had finished writing the words of this law in a book" (Deut. 31:24).

TO WHOM WAS EXODUS WRITTEN?

Exodus was written to the twelve tribes of delivered Hebrew slaves who had now become a theocratic nation. A theocracy is the rule of God. At Mt. Sinai the delivered Israelites said, "All that the Lord has spoken we will do" (Exod. 19:8). By this act they bound themselves to God as "a holy nation" (Exod. 19:6). This holy (i.e., "set apart for God") nation needed God's holy laws to perform their duty to Him. Through the laws given in Exodus, God ruled His people.

WHERE WERE THE ISRAELITES LOCATED?

There are three basic stages indicated within Exodus. In the early chapters the Israelites were slaves in Egypt (1-14). Then they journeyed from Egypt into the wilderness of Mt. Sinai (15-18). When they reached Mt. Sinai they set up a camp and there the law was given to them (19-40).

WHY WAS EXODUS WRITTEN?

There are three purposes revealed in the writing of Exodus.

The historical purpose.

The aim of Moses in writing Exodus is to show how the family of Jacob (totaling some seventy souls) developed into the nation of Israel (estimated at over two million). This estimate is based on the fact that the men age twenty and above (say, a quarter of the population) numbered over six hundred thousand (Num. 1:46).

The doctrinal purpose.

Several important lessons are taught through the Book of Exodus. First, there is the obvious overall theme of redemption and deliverance pictured by the Passover Lamb and the Red Sea experience. Then there is the ever-present truth that obedience to God is necessary for a holy people. Finally, there is clear evidence of God's faithfulness to the Abrahamic covenant in which He promised to bless Israel and to bring them into the land of promise (cf. Gen. 13:14f.; Exod. 3:7f.).

The Christological purpose.

Christ is depicted in Exodus in many ways. Like Moses He is the great deliverer of His people (cf. Deut. 18:15). Christ is also pictured in the Passover Lamb. The lamb was without flaw or blemish and was sacrificed for the sins of God's people (Exod. 12; cf. I Cor. 5:7). In the Tabernacle (a portable temple) Christ is again prefigured. According to the apostle John, this portrays Christ as He "dwelt [literally, 'pitched His tent'] among us" (John 1:14). Finally Christ is presented as our high priest who makes intercession for us (cf. Heb. 7:25).

WHAT IS THE BOOK OF EXODUS ABOUT?

The overall theme of Exodus is redemption. It tells how God buys back His people from the slavery of sin and brings them into His presence. This redemption is revealed in two ways in Exodus: first, by deliverance from Egypt (1-18) and then by the duties enjoined upon God's people as His redeemed people (19-40). The following outline and summary will serve as a guide in understanding the Book of Exodus.

I. The deliverance of the nation from bondage (1-18).

A. THE DEPRESSION OF THE PEOPLE (1).

The book begins, "There arose up a new king [probably Thut Mose III] over Egypt, who knew not Joseph" (Exod. 1:8, KJV). Not only did this new king show no special favor to the Israelites, he in fact began to oppress them (1).

B. THE DELIVERER FOR THE PEOPLE (2-6).

God heard the cry of His suffering people and raised up Moses to deliver them. Moses had been trained as a prince for forty years. Then, after an abortive attempt to deliver his enslaved brothers by his own strength, Moses received *preparation* under God as a shepherd in the desert of Midian (2). At eighty years of age, and after another king of Egypt (probably Amen Hotep II) ascended to the throne (2:23), Moses received the *commission* of God to return to Egypt. Upon his return Moses requested that Pharaoh let Israel go (3-4). The reluctant but supernaturally armed Moses made *intercession* for his people before a hardhearted king (5). With the reinforcement of a further *revelation* of who God is (6), Moses began his contest with the gods of Egypt. Moses was the representative of the God of Abraham, the Great "I AM" (3:14). This God had revealed His name as Jehovah, the Lord (6:3).

C. THE DELIVERANCE OF THE PEOPLE (7-18).

1. *The plagues of Egypt* (7-11). Moses called down ten plagues on Egypt because Pharaoh refused to let Israel go. Each plague seems to have been directed against a specific Egyptian god in order to show that Jehovah is the true God.

a. Bloody water (7:12)—against the god *Nilus,* the sacred river god.
b. Frogs (8:6)—against *Hekt,* the goddess of reproduction.
c. Lice (gnats) (8:17)—against *Seb,* the god of the earth.
d. Flies (beetles) (8:24)—against *Khephera,* the sacred scarab.
e. Murrain (plague) on Egyptian cattle (9:3)—against *Apis* and *Hathor,* the sacred bull and cow.
f. Boils on man and beast (9:10)—against *Typhon,* the evil-eye god.
g. Hail (9:23)—against *Shu,* the god of the atmosphere.
h. Locusts (10:14)—against *Serapis,* the protector from locusts.
i. Darkness (10:22)—against *Ra,* the sun god.
j. Death of the first-born of man and beast (11:5)—against *Ptah,* the god of life. Perhaps this was a blanket attack against all the gods of Egypt.

2. *The passover in Egypt* (12:13). To ward off the last plague from their households the children of Israel were instructed to take a lamb and put its blood on their doors so the angel of the Lord would pass over them and spare the lives of their first-born. Those who did not take shelter under the blood of the passover lamb would be visited by the

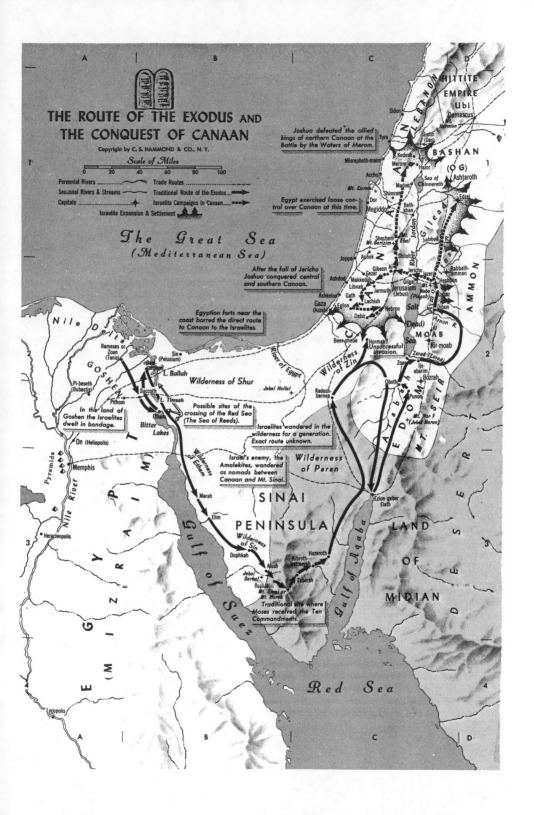

THE ROUTE OF THE EXODUS AND THE CONQUEST OF CANAAN

Copyright by C. S. HAMMOND & CO., N.Y.

Scale of Miles

0   20   40   60   80   100

Perennial Rivers .... Trade Routes ....
Seasonal Rivers & Streams ～～～ Traditional Route of the Exodus ➤
Capitals .... Israelite Campaigns in Canaan ➤➤➤
Israelite Expansion & Settlement

Joshua defeated the allied kings of northern Canaan at the Battle by the Waters of Merom.

Egypt exercised loose control over Canaan at this time.

The Great Sea
(Mediterranean Sea)

After the fall of Jericho Joshua conquered central and southern Canaan.

Egyptian forts near the coast barred the direct route to Canaan to the Israelites.

In the land of Goshen the Israelites dwelt in bondage.

Possible sites of the crossing of the Red Sea (The Sea of Reeds).

Israelites wandered in the wilderness for a generation. Exact route unknown.

Israel's enemy, the Amalekites, wandered as nomads between Canaan and Mt. Sinai.

Wilderness of Shur

Wilderness of Etham

Wilderness of Sin

Wilderness of Paran

Wilderness of Zin

SINAI PENINSULA

Hormah Unsuccessful invasion.

Traditional site where Moses received the Ten Commandments.

Gulf of Suez

Gulf of Aqaba

Red Sea

LAND OF MIDIAN

DESERT

angel who would pass *through* their homes with the plague of death (12:13).

3. *The passage from Egypt* (14-18). By a mighty miracle God drove back the waters of the Red Sea, drowned the pursuing armies of Egypt, and safely delivered His people on the Sinai peninsula (14). Here they burst forth into the first "song of redemption" recorded in Scripture (15). There followed a series of testing experiences. Among them were the bitter waters at Marah which Moses turned sweet (15b) as well as the manna (bread) from heaven (16a) and the quails (16b) to satisfy their hunger. At Rephidim Moses brought forth water out of a rock to quench their thirst (17a), and Joshua led them in victory over the attacking Amalekites (17b). At the advice of his father-in-law, Jethro, Moses chose able men to be heads and rulers over the people to assist him in settling their disputes (18).

II. The duty of the people (19-40).
A. THE TABLES OF THE LAW—TEACHING OBEDIENCE TO GOD (19-24).

Duty follows deliverance. Complete redemption involved more than getting Israel out of Egypt. It also involved getting "Egypt" (i.e., the world) out of them. Not unlike believers of today, the Israelites often lusted for the things of Egypt (16:3) instead of fulfilling their duty. Their duty was to follow God's law in order to receive God's blessing.

1. *The covenant sealed* (19). Freely and repeatedly Israel assured Moses, "All that the Lord has spoken we will do" (v. 8). Thus the redeemed people of God accepted the Mosaic covenant (agreement) and on many occasions bound themselves with one accord to live by it.

2. *The commandments revealed* (20). A divinely revealed summary of their moral duties to God and their fellow man was given to God's people in the Ten Commandments written on two tables of stone. These duties are both positive and negative in tone because they speak for God and against His enemies.

    a. Duties to God (Commandments 1-4).

        1) Supremacy of God—against polytheism: "have no other gods before me."

        2) Similitude of God—against idolatry: "make no graven images."

        3) Sacredness of God—against profanity: "do not take the name of the Lord in vain."

        4) Service of God—against secularism: "remember the sabbath day to keep it holy."

    b. Duties to man (Commandments 5-10).

        1) Supremacy of man—against disrespect for parents: "honor your father and your mother."

Moses' Peak on Mount Sinai, the traditional site where Moses received the Ten Commandments. Photo by Charles F. Pfeiffer

2) Similitude of man (to God)—against murder: "you shall not kill."

3) Sacredness of man—against adultery: "you shall not commit adultery."

4) Service of man (his property)—against theft: "you shall not steal."

5) Service of man (his person)—against lying: "you shall not bear false witness."

6) Service of man (his possessions)—against coveting: "you shall not covet."

Almost a millennium and a half later, Jesus summed up these duties when He said, "You shall love the Lord your God with all your heart..." (commandments 1-4) and "You shall love your neighbor as yourself" (commandments 5-10) (Matt. 22:37, 39). Man has a twofold moral duty: to love God and to love others. No moral code has ever surpassed these rules. Jesus said He came to fulfill them (Matt. 5:17) and to extend them by showing the greatest act of love one can for a fellow man (John 15:13). He did not come to destroy them. It has been well said that he who breaks God's laws will in the end be broken by God's laws.

3. The civil laws stated (21-23). The laws of civil society should be based on God's moral laws. They include the rights of persons such as slaves, parents, and pregnant women (21). There are also rights of property (22) and personal integrity (23).

4. The covenant confirmed (24).

B. THE TABERNACLE OF WORSHIP—TEACHING ON HOW TO APPROACH GOD (25-40).

1. *Directions from God* (25-31). In this section, God provided instructions for building the Tabernacle. The Tabernacle was a demonstration on how to worship God. Jesus Christ is the fulfillment of its typology, for it sets forth a picture of His earthly ministry. The following chart will illustrate the teaching of the Tabernacle.

PART OF THE TABERNACLE	WHAT IT TAUGHT	HOW CHRIST FULFILLED IT
1. Door (gate)	There is only one way to God.	"I am the door" (John 10:9).
2. Brazen altar	Substitution is necessary for atoning sins.	"I give my life a ransom for many" (Mark 10:45).

3. Laver	Purification is needed for God's presence.	"If I do not wash you, you have no part in me" (John 13:8).
4. Lamps	Illumination is needed to do God's work.	"I am the light of the world" (John 8:12).
5. Bread	Sustenance is needed for God's people.	"I am the bread of life" (John 6:48).
6. Incense	Intercession is needed for God's people.	"I am praying for them" (John 17:9).
7. Veil	There is separation between God and His people.	"Behind the curtain [veil] where Jesus has gone . . . for us" (Heb. 6:19, 20; cf. 10:20).
8. Mercy Seat	Only blood can make atonement for sin.	"He is the expiation [satisfaction] for our sins" (I John 2:2).
9. Priest	God must be approached through representation.	

AARON AS PRIEST	CHRIST AS PRIEST
Entered the earthly Tabernacle.	Entered the heavenly Temple (Heb. 6:19).
Entered once a year.	Entered once for all (Heb. 9:25).
Entered beyond the veil.	Rent the veil (Heb. 10:20).
Offered for his own sins.	Offered only for our sins (Heb. 7:27).
Offered the blood of bulls.	Offered His own blood (Heb. 9:12).

Just like the Tabernacle, the Aaronic priesthood prefigured the life of Christ. Aaron, Moses' brother, was the first high priest of Israel. As a Levite, he was the ministering agent to God in behalf of the people.

2. *Disobedience to God* (32-34). While God was providing instructions for worship by His people, they fell into idolatry by worshiping the golden calf. This is a sad interlude for a people who had just pledged to have no other gods before Jehovah and to make no graven images. It shows how easily men can turn away from God.

3. *Dedication to God* (35-40). The moral law demands duty just as worship demands dedication. In order to build the Tabernacle, the

PLAN OF
THE TABERNACLE COMPLEX

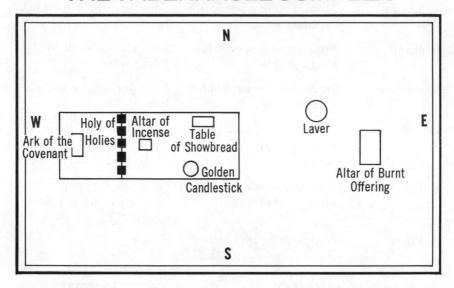

Israelites needed to dedicate their treasures to God (35). In addition certain capable men, such as Bezalel and Oholiab, dedicated their talents to the Lord for building the Tabernacle (36-39). Finally, the Tabernacle itself was dedicated to God. God accepted it and filled it with His glorious presence (40).

There are several purposes for the Tabernacle in the life of Israel. It was given to God's people as a means of teaching them about Him.

1. It was an *identification* of the presence of God for Israel (Exod. 40:34).
2. It was an *illustration* of God's plan of salvation for the world (Heb. 9:9-11).
3. It was an *incarnation* of the person of God for His people (John 1:14).
4. It was a *prefiguration* of the pattern of God in heaven (Heb. 9:23, 24; cf. Rev. 4-5).

STUDY QUESTIONS

1. What reasons are there for believing Moses is the author of Exodus?
2. What is the main doctrinal emphasis of Exodus? How does it compare to that of Genesis?

3. In what ways can Christ be seen in Exodus?
4. What was Christ's attitude toward the Ten Commandments given in Exodus?
5. Discuss specifically how the Tabernacle typifies the life and work of Christ.

7

The Sanctification of the Nation

LEVITICUS

Exodus is a book of deliverance; Leviticus is a book of purification. Exodus tells of the *redemption* of the Jewish people; Leviticus relates their *sanctification*. It has been well said that it took God only one night to get Israel out of Egypt but it took forty years to get Egypt out of them. The former is an *act* of salvation; the latter is a lifelong *process* of sanctification. The initial act of salvation (called justification) is that by which God *declares* a man righteous. This is illustrated in Exodus. Leviticus, on the other hand, is concerned with the process of *making* men righteous (called sanctification). "You shall be holy; for I the LORD your God am holy" is the theme of the Book of Leviticus (19:2).

WHO WROTE LEVITICUS?

According to the book itself, Moses, the great leader and lawgiver of Israel, was the author of Leviticus. There are two lines of evidence to support this contention. First, the same kind of arguments that indicate Moses wrote Exodus also support his authorship of Leviticus (see ch. 6). But there is additional evidence — both internal and external — to support the Mosaic authorship of Leviticus. (1) Some fifty-six times the Book of Leviticus says something to the effect that "the Lord spoke unto Moses" (cf. 1:1; 4:1; 5:14; 6:1, 8, 19; 7:22). (2) There are many references in the New Testament to the Mosaic authorship of Leviticus (Matt. 8:4; Luke 2:22; Heb. 8:5), some of which come from the lips of Christ. (3) The Ras Shamra Tablets (c. 1500-1300 B.C.), found along the Syrian coast, indicate that the antiquity of the Levitical system of trespass offering extends to the time of Moses. This evidence answers the criticism that the Book of Leviticus was written during a period much later than Moses' day.

WHEN WAS LEVITICUS WRITTEN?

According to Leviticus, its revelations were given to Moses at Mt. Sinai (25:1, 2; 26:46; 27:34) and in the wilderness of Sinai. This would indicate that they were given about 1445 B.C. It is possible, however, that those revelations were not written down in their completed form until just before Moses' death. That means that Leviticus was possibly written at the end of the forty years of wandering (Deut. 31:24), which would be 1405 B.C.

WHERE WERE THE ISRAELITES LOCATED?

The revelations recorded in Leviticus were first given to the people at Mt. Sinai where God spoke from the mount (25:1) and from the "tent of meeting" (1:1). Though they were given subsequent to the Ten Commandments (Exod. 20) the Israelites were still in the same area of Mt. Sinai. These instructions taught the delivered slaves how to be "a kingdom of priests and a holy nation" (Exod. 19:6).

WHY WAS LEVITICUS WRITTEN?

We may divide the purposes of Leviticus into three categories.

The historical purpose.

Leviticus was given to show the redeemed people how to live holy lives. It was to be a handbook on holiness for the priests. Included in it were both the kinds and the manner of offerings which should be used to approach God.

The doctrinal purpose.

There are two central teachings in Leviticus. The first is that God is holy. Second, since God is holy, He must be approached in a prescribed way through offerings made by a priest. According to Leviticus both priestly mediation and sacrificial offerings are necessary parts of a proper worship and approach to God.

The Christological purpose.

Leviticus teaches us much about Christ by way of types. In the New Testament, Christ is shown as the fulfillment of both the sacrificial system and the priestly meditation (cf. Heb. 8:10).

WHAT IS THE BOOK OF LEVITICUS ABOUT?

Leviticus can be neatly divided into two sections: the way to the Holy One (1-10) and the way of holiness (11-27). The first section describes the meaning of the Lord's statement, "I am holy." The second section prescribes the manner of obeying the command, "You shall be holy." The former outlines the way to God (judicial) and the latter sketches the walk with God (practical). The following outline and summary will help us understand the Book of Leviticus.

1. The way to the Holy One (1-10).

According to these chapters, God must be approached by two means: sacrifice and the priesthood. The first is called oblation and the second involves mediation.

A. BY SACRIFICE (1-7).

1. *The revelation of the offering* (1-5)—what must be offered. There were five different kinds of offering. The first three were voluntary and the last two compulsory. The former were for acceptance by God; the latter were as atonement to Him.

Offerings of Dedication (Godward)	Offering of Expiation (manward)
1) Burnt offering (1)	4) Sin offering (4)
2) Cereal (meal) offering (2)	5) Guilt (trespass) offering (5)
3) Peace offering (3)	

2. *The ritual of the offering* (6-7)—how it must be offered. There were three aspects to the ritual of presenting an offering to God.

The *reason* for the offering—man is *sinful.*

The *rule* of the offering—the sacrifice is *substitutional* for man's sin.

The *ritual* of the offering—the process was *ceremonial* illustration of how God is to be approached through Christ.

The key thought is expressed in the verse: "For the life of the flesh is in the blood; and I have given it for you upon the altar to make atonement for your souls; for it is the blood that makes atonement..." (Lev. 17:11). The Book of Hebrews says, "Without the shedding of blood there is no forgiveness of sins" (9:22).

B. BY THE PRIESTHOOD (8-10).

Not only was a sacrifice necessary in approaching God, but more specifically the sacrifice had to be administered by a priest or mediator. A priest is someone who represents man before God. He serves as a mediator before God on behalf of man. He is unlike a prophet, who represents God before men and proclaims His Word to them.

1. *The consecration of the order of Aaron* (8). God chose Aaron and his sons instead of all the first-born sons in every Israelite family to be priests. The Aaronic priesthood was established in their order by *water* (symbol of purification), *oil* (symbol of sanctification), and *blood* (symbol of consecration).

2. *The inauguration of the office* (9). The initiation of their priestly duties was accompanied by a manifestation of the glory of God and the approbation (approval) of God in the consummation of the sacrifice by fire (vv. 23, 24).

3. *The transgression of the ordinance* (10). Nadab and Abihu were sons of Aaron. They became sad object lessons because of their presumptuous attempt to perform God's work in a human way.

II. The way of holiness (11-27).

The second half of the Book of Leviticus deals with the divine demand to live a holy life by both separation and sanctification. It is practical in its approach to the daily lives of God's redeemed people.

A.   HOLINESS DEMANDS SANITATION (PURITY OF BODY) (11-16).

In this section the children of Israel are told to maintain clean food (11), clean bodies (12-13), clean clothes (14), clean contacts (15), and to be a clean nation (16). The first part shows God's requirements (11-15); the last part His provision (16). The cleansing of the nation (16) occurred once each year on the Day of Atonement (Yom Kippur). That day is a prefiguration of the work of Christ.

B.   HOLINESS DEMANDS SANCTIFICATION (PURITY OF SOUL) (17-27).

The final section of Leviticus is concerned with both the requirements and provision for purity of life. The requirements call for holiness in diet (17), social contacts (18-20), the priesthood (21-22), as well as in worship (23) and conversation (24). Because of man's failure in these areas, there were social provisions—the year of Jubilee (25), national provisions—the Covenant (26), and personal provisions—instructions on the use of vows (27). The entire system of national worship through these feasts is a type of Christ and the coming messianic kingdom (cf. Lev. 23). The following chart will indicate this relationship.

FEAST	TYPE OF	TIME OF YEAR
Passover	Death of Christ (I Cor. 5:7)	April
Unleavened bread	Holy walk of believers (I Cor. 5:8)	April
First fruits	Resurrection (I Cor. 15:23)	April
Pentecost	Descension of Spirit (Acts 2:4)	June
Trumpets	Regathering of Israel (Matt 24:31)	September-October
Atonement	National cleansing (Rom. 11:23)	September-October
Tabernacles	Messianic kingdom rest (Zech. 14:16; Matt. 17:4)	September-October

The five main feasts may be subdivided into pilgrimage (1-3) and non-pilgrimage (4-5) feasts.

1. Passover (pilgrimage)—Barley offered as a feast of *Remembrance* (of deliverance from Egypt).

2. Pentecost (pilgrimage)—Wheat offered as a feast of *Reaping*.
3. Tabernacles (Booths) (pilgrimage)—Oil and wine offered as a feast of *Rejoicing*.
4. Atonement (Yom Kippur) (non-pilgrimage)—Bull and ram offered as a feast of *Redemption*.
5. Trumpets (non-pilgrimage)—Bull and ram offered as a feast of *Reunion*.

During the course of Jewish history, two more feasts were added. The feast of *Purim* was celebrated in February (Esther 3:7; 9:21) and recalled Israel's deliverance from the Persians. The feast of *Dedication* (**Lights**) was celebrated in December (Dan. 11:31; cf. I Macc. 4:52) in remembrance of Israel's deliverance from the Greeks. The last feast is known as Hanukkah and is celebrated about the time of Christmas.

Another interesting aspect of the Jewish festal system is its septenary (seven) structure. It is readily arranged into groupings of seven. On the seventh *day* (the Sabbath) the people rest. Following the seventh *week* (after Passover) is Pentecost, when harvesters rest. During the seventh *month* at the feast of Trumpets, the nation rests. Every seventh *year* is a sabbatical, during which the land rests. Finally, following the seventh *seven of years* (forty-nine years) comes the year of Jubilee when everything rests.

The symbolical significance of the number seven is that it is the number of earthly perfection and rest. There are seven days in a perfect or complete week and God rested on the seventh day after creating the world in six. Man too was asked to rest on the seventh day, week, month, year and seventh seven of years.

STUDY QUESTIONS

1. Compare the respective themes of Exodus and Leviticus.
2. What is the messianic significance of the feasts in Leviticus?
3. Compare and contrast the emphasis of the two main sections of Leviticus.
4. "The life of the flesh is in the blood . . . ." Discuss the importance of this phrase to the overall theme of Leviticus.
5. How does the number seven fit into the festal system of the Book of Leviticus?

8

The Direction of the Nation
NUMBERS

Numbers is the book of the numbering and wandering of the children of Israel. The title of the book in the Hebrew Bible is taken from its first three words: "In the wilderness." Numbers covers the time period between thirteen months after the Exodus and the end of the forty years of wandering (Num. 1:1; Deut. 1:3). The spiritual lesson taught in the book is that God's people cannot get into the promised land of His blessing without going through the wilderness of testing.

In Genesis we observed the *election* of the nation. In Exodus their *redemption* was accomplished. In Leviticus God made provision for their *sanctification*. In Numbers the lesson is their *direction* by God. As Israel journeyed through the wilderness, God directed them by a pillar of cloud that illuminated at night. When the cloud moved they moved; when the cloud stayed they encamped. Whether it was for a day or a year (9:15-23), the cloud provided direction for God's people. A number of Christian songs sound the theme of Numbers: "My Lord Knows the Way Through the Wilderness" tells us that all we have to do is to follow. The famous spiritual "Walk Together, Children" tells us not to get weary.

WHO WROTE LEVITICUS?

The evidence that Moses was the author of Numbers is similar to that for Exodus and Leviticus. In addition, there are several lines of evidence that are distinctive to Numbers. (1) The book claims to be written by Moses (1:1; 33:2). (2) Numbers also gives a detailed, accurate, eyewitness account which could be provided only by someone as familiar with the desert as was Moses. (3) A number of New Testament quotations directly cite events in Numbers and associate them with Moses (Acts 7,

13; I Cor. 10:1-11; Heb. 3). (4) Our Lord quoted from Numbers and verified that it was indeed Moses who lifted up the serpent in the wilderness (John 3:14; cf. Num. 21:9).

WHEN WAS NUMBERS WRITTEN?

The events of the Book of Numbers cover thirty-eight years—the period between thirteen months after the Exodus (1:1) and the end of the forty-years wandering. It could not have been completed until then (1405 B.C.). But it was completed sometime before Moses died (cf. Deut. 31:24).

TO WHOM WAS NUMBERS WRITTEN?

It is important to notice that there are at least two groups included in the Book of Numbers. The first group is the disobedient older generation who died in the wilderness because of their sin of unbelief. At the beginning of the book this group numbered 603,550 males twenty years and above (1:45, 46). A second group, those under twenty years of age at the beginning, grew up in the wilderness and later entered the promised land. By that time 601,730 males were twenty years of age and older (26:51). Those under twenty years old were not included in the numbering (census). The book as a whole, with its review of the sins of the fathers, stands as a message to the younger generation not to imitate their parents in unbelief. Instead, they should go into the land and take hold of their possessions which God had long ago promised to Abraham (Gen. 12:1; 13:14-17).

WHERE WERE THE PEOPLE LOCATED?

The overall location of the wandering Israelites was the Sinai peninsula (see map of wilderness wanderings). Most of their time, however, was spent in and around Kadesh-barnea, an oasis on the way to the promised land (cf. Num. 13). Finally, they found themselves on the plains of Moab near Jericho (35:1; 36:13). What was normally a trip of only a few weeks took them forty years to accomplish because of their unbelief.

WHY WAS NUMBERS WRITTEN?

There are three purposes evident in the writing of Numbers.

The historical purpose.

The Book of Numbers provides a history of Israel's wanderings from Mt. Sinai to Mt. Nebo. It accounts for most of the forty years in which God punished the faithless generation that experienced His redemption from Egypt. During that time He also prepared a faithful generation to inherit the land.

The doctrinal purpose.

There are several important truths taught in Numbers. First, the

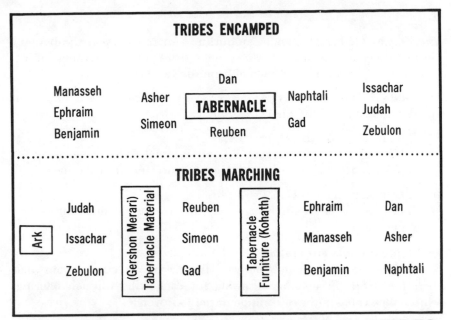

ARRANGEMENT OF THE TWELVE TRIBES AROUND THE TABERNACLE

providential direction of God is clearly manifest—it is God who leads His people. Second, God's perseverance for His people is shown. There are no shortcuts to God's blessings. Trials and testings are used to temper the faith of God's children. The hymn writer aptly says, "Trust and obey, for there's no other way...."

The Christological purpose.

There are several types or pictures of Christ in Numbers. The New Testament indicates that the Rock from which the thirsting multitude drank was Christ (I Cor. 10:4). Jesus said the serpent on the stake portrayed His crucifixion (John 3:14). The daily manna pictured the Bread of Life who came down from heaven (John 6:32). Balaam foresaw that "a star shall come forth out of Jacob" (Num. 24:17). The overall presence of Christ is symbolized in Numbers by the pillar of cloud. Through this symbol He is shown as the Director or Leader of His people.

WHAT IS THE BOOK OF NUMBERS ABOUT?

In contrast to Leviticus, the book of *worship,* Numbers is a book of the people's *walk* with God. Leviticus stresses their *purity;* Numbers their *pilgrimage.* Leviticus is *ceremonial* while Numbers is *historical.* Leviticus gives a call to *fellowship* with God; Numbers is a call to *faithfulness* to God. The emphasis shifts from *sanctification* before God to *direction* by God. Let's look at an outline and summary of the Book of Numbers.

I. Israel's direction from the Lord (1-10).

God's directions to His people were very explicit. He was concerned about every aspect of their lives.

A.   THE POSITION OF THE PEOPLE (1-4).

There was a highly organized and symmetrical arrangement for encampment around the center of His presence in the Tabernacle.

B.   THE PRECEPTS FROM GOD (5-6).

These precepts taught His people how to handle uncleanness and sin in the camp.

C.   THE PROVISION FOR CLEANSING (7-9a).

Before the people moved forward there were directions about their cleansing. God effected this cleansing for each tribe through offerings which culminated in the celebration of the Passover.

D.   THE PILGRIMAGE TOWARD THE PROMISED LAND (9b-10).

God prepared His people to move forward as He led them to their place of blessing.

II. Israel's disbelief in the Lord (11-14).

A.   DISCONTENT WITH THE PROVISIONS OF GOD (11-12).

Even before Israel's fatal disbelief in God's promise that they would enter the land, the "mixed multitude" cried to return to Egypt because they were displeased with the food (manna) God had provided (11). Miriam and Aaron were discontent with Moses' leadership, and this aroused God to speak in angry vindication of Moses (12).

B.   DISBELIEF OF GOD'S PROMISE (13-14).

This came at Kadesh-barnea when the spies returned with a discouraging report about the giants in the land. The people failed to believe that "faith is the victory that overcomes the world." For their disbelief, God pronounced on them one year of judgment for every day the spies were in the land. Since they were there for forty days, the judgment on their disbelief caused them to spend forty years in the wilderness.

III. Israel's discipline from the Lord (15-36).

God's discipline is the consequence of man's disbelief. For forty years they wandered because of their fearful unbelief. This period is divided into two sections.

A. THE PASSING OF THE OLD GENERATION (15-26).

The first section witnesses the death of the disobedient generation. They had received a revelation from the Lord to remember His commandments and to be holy (15). Korah led an abortive revolt against Moses, the servant of the Lord (16). God vindicated His servant by causing Aaron's rod to bud (17). There followed a series of regulations for Aaron (18) and for the people (19). Because of further disobedience, a series of retributions came upon the people (20-21). Nonetheless, when Balaam tried to curse God's chosen people, they were pronounced righteous in God's redemptive eyes (22-24). Finally, with the old generation's passing, there was a renumbering of the Israelites (25-26).

B. THE PREPARATION OF THE NEW GENERATION (27-36).

Following the discipline of the faithless fathers by death, God begins the final preparation of the new generation to possess the land. Moses begins with some instructions on rights to the land they are about to possess (27). He continues by laying down some rituals of the law to be performed when they live in the land (28-30). There follows the revenge on the Midianites who had corrupted Israel previously (31). The request of the Reubenites to live east of the Jordan River is granted, provided they first go west to fight against the inhabitants of the land (32). Moses then reviews the wanderings of Israel stage by stage (33). The regulations for the boundaries of their lots are given in advance (34). Finally, the cities of refuge are provided for the Levites and for those who commit involuntary manslaughter (35-36).

The old generation had passed; the new generation was prepared. All that remained to be accomplished was for Moses to give the great farewell instructions of Deuteronomy. Then the people would realize God's ancient promises to Abraham, Isaac, and Jacob: "Arise, walk through the length and breadth of the land, for I will give it to you" (Gen. 13:17).

STUDY QUESTIONS

1. In what ways can the person of Christ be seen in Numbers?
2. Compare the two groups of people discussed in Numbers.
3. Discuss the various forms of unbelief expressed by the Israelites. What was the result of this unbelief?
4. What are the purposes for which Numbers was written?

9

The Instruction of the Nation

DEUTERONOMY

Deuteronomy means "second law," that is, the second giving of the law. The law was given the first time at Mt. Sinai to the older generation before they entered the wilderness for forty years. The law was given the second time by Moses on the plains of Moab to the new generation before they entered the promised land. The Book of Deuteronomy consists of a series of farewell speeches by Moses as he prepared the people of Israel to enter, conquer, and possess the land. Deuteronomy is the fifth and final book of Moses and it completes the Pentateuch. The following comparison of the five books of Moses will help us to understand the distinctive role each plays in the Torah.

BOOK	ROLE	ASPECT
Genesis	God's sovereignty	the plan of God
Exodus	God's charity	the redemptive power of God
Leviticus	God's sanctity	the person of God
Numbers	God's severity	the providence of God
Deuteronomy	God's solemnity	the principles of God

WHO WROTE DEUTERONOMY?

Besides the general evidence for the Mosaic authorship of the Pentateuch as a whole, there are several arguments that specifically support the claim that Moses wrote Deuteronomy. (1) The distinct claim of the book itself is that Moses wrote it (1:1; 4:44; 29:1). (2) Deuteronomy is the book of the Law most quoted in the New Testament, being cited over eighty times (cf. Acts 3:22; Rom. 10:19; I Cor. 9:9). (3) Jesus quoted the Book of Deuteronomy as the Word of God by which He resisted Satan (Matt. 4:7, 10) and directly attributed it to the hand of Moses (Matt. 19:7; Mark 7:10; Luke 20:28). (4) Joshua, Moses' immediate successor, attributed the Book of Deuteronomy to Moses (Josh. 1:7). (5) The remainder of the Old Testament attributes Deuteronomy and the rest of the Law to Moses (cf. Judg. 3:4; I Kings 2:3; II Kings 14:6; Ezra 3:2; Neh. 1:7; Ps. 103:7; Dan. 9:11; Mal. 4:4). (6) The unity and integrity of thought are Mosaic. (7) The geographical and historical details of the book display a firsthand, informed acquaintance such as Moses would have had. The final chapter of Deuteronomy deals with the death of Moses. It was probably not prophetic. Rather, it is likely that it was written by Joshua, who succeeded Moses (cf. Deut. 34:9 and Josh 1:1f.). (8) Finally, recent studies of the form and content of Near Eastern covenants indicate that Deuteronomy is from the period of Moses (see Meredith Kline, *Treaty of the Great King*, Eerdmans, 1963).

WHEN WAS DEUTERONOMY WRITTEN?

Deuteronomy was written at the end of the forty-years wandering in the wilderness. Just before Israel entered the promised land in 1405 B.C., they needed to have the law reviewed and their commitment to God reinforced.

TO WHOM WAS DEUTERONOMY WRITTEN?

This book was written to the new generation, those under twenty years of age when they came out of Egypt. This second giving of the law was a renewal of the covenant that God had made with their fathers. This new generation received God's charge to inherit their promised blessings.

WHERE WERE THE PEOPLE OF ISRAEL LOCATED?

According to the Book of Deuteronomy, the Israelites were located on the east side of the Jordan River. There, on the Plains of Moab, they were encamped due east of the city of Jericho (1:1; 29:1; cf. Josh. 1:2).

WHY WAS DEUTERONOMY WRITTEN?

There are three distinct purposes served by the Book of Deuteronomy.

The historical purpose.

The Book of Deuteronomy provides a review of the nation's history as well as a renewal of the covenant made between God and the fathers of the nation concerning the land of Canaan.

The doctrinal purpose.

Deuteronomy provides a restatement and reinterpretation of Israel's national laws and ordinances. It is God's instructions on how to live a victorious life in the land of blessing. The manifest lesson is that obedience to God's laws is necessary for the blessing and well-being of His people.

The Christological purpose.

The main messianic predictions of Deuteronomy concern the scattering and restoration of Israel (30) and the Prophet like Moses (Christ) whom God will raise up (18:15; cf. Act 7:37).

WHAT IS THE BOOK OF DEUTERONOMY ABOUT?

There are three basic divisions in Deuteronomy: the historical (retrospective) look at Israel's past (1-4), the legislative (introspective) look at the present (5-26), and the prophetical (prospective) look at the future (27-34).

I. The review of Israel's wanderings (1-4).

Moses first reminds the people of their past. He points out their murmuring at Kadesh-barnea (1), and their years of wandering in the wilderness as a result of their sin (2-3); then he gives them a warning before entering the land of Canaan (4). He urges them to "give heed to the statutes and the ordinances which I teach you, and do them; that you may live, and go in and take possession of the land which the LORD, the God of your fathers, gives you" (4:1).

II. The rehearsal of God's laws (5-26).

From a look at their past deeds Moses turns to a look at Israel's present duty toward the law of God. He rehearses and reinterprets the general Sinaitic laws as well as the special ceremonial and civil laws.

A. RESTATEMENT OF THE SINAITIC LAWS (5-11).

The Decalogue or Ten Commandments is recited (5a) and then reinterpreted to meet the new conditions of the new generation (5b-11). Moses is presented as the mediator of the law (5b) who gives its meaning to the people (6-8) and then appeals to their memory of how God graciously redeemed them and revealed Himself to them despite their stubborn disobedience (9-11).

B. RESTATEMENT OF THE SPECIAL LAWS (12-26).

Besides their general moral duty, specific ceremonial and civil obligations are enjoined on the people by the law. First, the ceremonial duties are set forth in statutes and ordinances related to sacrifices, tithes, and feasts (12-16a). Next, the civil duties with regard to judges, strangers, landowners, and soldiers (16b-20) are given. Last, the social duties to one's own family (21), friends (22), and the whole fraternity (brotherhood) of Israel and strangers (23-25) are declared.

III. The revelation of Israel's future (27-34).

The final section of Deuteronomy is a prospective look to Israel's near and distant future.

A.   ISRAEL'S NEAR FUTURE   (27-28a).

Moses sees two things in store for God's people: cursings if they disobey God (27) and blessings if they obey Him (28a). These promises were to be repeated in an antiphonal choir from Mt. Ebal and Mt. Gerizim when they entered the land.

B.   ISRAEL'S DISTANT FUTURE   (28b-30).

Moses makes an amazing prediction about Israel's captivity or dispersion into all the world (28b-29) as well as a promise of their return (30). The repatriation of Israel to their land in 1948 was an amazing fulfillment of this prophecy made more than three thousand years earlier.

C.   FAREWELL OF MOSES TO ISRAEL (31-34).

Because of his sin Moses was not allowed to enter into the promised land. He gave his parting words on the east side of the Jordan River and was buried in an unknown location by God. Before his departure, however, Moses indicated that Joshua was to be his successor, and that he would lead the people across the Jordan (31). Moses then composed a song about the Lord's dealings with Israel (32) before giving his final sermon (33). Moses was taken up to Mt. Nebo where he died. The separation was complete. Moses does not appear again until we see him in glory with Jesus on a different mountain, the Mount of Transfiguration—which is in the promised land (Matt. 17:3)!

STUDY QUESTIONS

1. In what way does the meaning of the word *Deuteronomy* reveal the theme of this book?
2. What are some of the specific evidences pointing to the Mosaic authorship of Deuteronomy?
3. Briefly discuss the respective emphases of the three basic divisions of Deuteronomy.
4. In the repetition of the law (Deut. 5; cf. Exod. 20) what are some of the differences that occur? What reason can you give for these differences? Are there any changes in the essence of the laws themselves?
5. What specific predictions are made in Deuteronomy concerning the future of Israel?

PART THREE
The Books of History:

The Preparation for Christ

10

Introduction to the Books of History

The Old Testament can be divided into four basic sections. Each of these sections has a particular emphasis in its teaching about Christ. A review of the first section, the Law, will reveal how each book filled its role.

LAW: THE FOUNDATION FOR CHRIST.

Genesis—the election of the nation
Exodus—the redemption of the nation
Leviticus—the sanctification of the nation
Numbers—the direction of the nation
Deuteronomy—the instruction of the nation

An overview of the second section, History, will reveal its particular position in the disclosure of Christ. Each book plays an important role in presenting that overall message.

HISTORY: THE PREPARATION FOR CHRIST.

Joshua—the possession of the nation
Judges-Ruth—the oppression of the nation
I Samuel—the stabilization of the nation
II Samuel—the expansion of the nation
I Kings 1-10—the glorification of the nation
I Kings 12-22—the division of the nation
II Kings 1-17—the deterioration of the northern nation
II Kings 18-25—the deportation of the southern nation
I Chronicles—the preparation of the nation's Temple
II Chronicles—the destruction of the nation's Temple
Ezra—the restoration of the nation's Temple

Nehemiah—the reconstruction of the city
Esther—the protection of the nation's people

Later we will look at the other two Old Testament sections in detail. For the present, we need only to show their place in the general scope of the disclosure of Christ.

POETRY: THE ASPIRATION FOR CHRIST.

PROPHECY: THE EXPECTATION OF CHRIST.

Whereas the Law deals with the moral life of Israel and History with their national life, Poetry will be concerned with their spiritual life and Prophecy their future life. The unfolding of Israel's national life in preparation for their Messiah is the concern of this chapter. There are many ways to view the development of the nation. We will emphasize the historical, biographical and chronological aspects of it. A more detailed historical description will be provided in the succeeding chapters as each book in the History section is discussed.

I. A historical sketch of Israel's history.

There are five great periods in Israel's history. The biblical record corresponds to these periods, as is clear from the following survey:

A. THE PATRIARCHAL PERIOD (Gen. 12-50) —c. 2000 to 1875 B.C.

This period began when Abraham entered the promised land. It includes the life span of his son Isaac, his grandson Jacob, and Jacob's entire family (seventy persons) who entered Egypt about 1875 B.C. Following this emigration from the promised land, Israel's history experienced an interim of over four hundred years which ended in bondage in Egypt. Then in about 1450 B.C. God raised up Moses to deliver His people.

B. THE THEOCRATIC PERIOD (Exod.-Ruth)—1445-1043 B.C.

A theocracy is a nation ruled by God. The term is derived from the Greek words *theos* ("god") and *archos* ("ruler"). At Mt. Sinai (Exod. 19), after their deliverance from Egypt, Israel became a theocracy. From that time on God ruled directly over Israel by way of His law and through His prophetic spokesmen. Beginning with Moses this form of rule continued through Joshua and concluded with Samuel. There was no king in Israel since God was their king and they were His kingdom (cf. Exod. 19:6).

C. THE MONARCHICAL PERIOD (I Sam.-II Chron.) —1043-586 B.C.

The people of Israel clamored for a king so they could be like the surrounding nations. God acceded to their demands and permitted

Israel to have a king. Israel's first three kings, Saul, David, and Solomon, brought the nation to its period of greatness. At Solomon's death (931 B.C.), his kingdom was divided into two unequal realms. Jeroboam, Solomon's captain, took the northern ten tribes (known as Israel) and Rehoboam, Solomon's son, became king of the southern two tribes (known as Judah). These kingdoms gradually deteriorated until Israel was taken captive by the Assyrians in 722 B.C., Judah was conquered by the Babylonians in 605 B.C., and Jerusalem was razed in 586 B.C. In principle, however, Israel never had an unqualified monarchy (one ruler) since the rulers were to be subject to God's law and to the words of the prophets. In practice, their failure to heed God's voice and to adhere to His law led to their ultimate downfall.

D. THE EXILIC PERIOD (no historical book) —605-536 B.C.

The captivity or exile was seventy years in duration (Jer. 25:11). The break in the historical narrative during this period is filled in by three prophets: Jeremiah (in Lamentations), Ezekiel, and Daniel. The period of Babylonian capitivity ended after the fall of Babylon to the Medo-Persians in 539 B.C., when Cyrus made the proclamation that permitted the remnant of Israel to return in 536 B.C. (Ezra 1:1f.).

E. THE RESTORATION PERIOD (Ezra-Esther)—536-420 B.C.

The priest Zerubbabel led a remnant of nearly fifty thousand people back to the land to rebuild the Temple in Jerusalem. With the encouragement of the prophets Haggai and Zechariah, he began his project in 536 B.C. In 458 B.C. Ezra the priest returned with less than two thousand Jews. He was followed by Nehemiah (445 B.C.), who undertook the reconstruction of the city. His work was encouraged by the reforms of Malachi (433-420 B.C.). The restored remnant never again became a monarchy. They were ruled by governors, but had no king. When their King did come, some four hundred years later, He was rejected and crucified with the following inscription on His cross: "This is Jesus of Nazareth, the King of the Jews."

II. A biographical survey of Israel's history.

The history of Israel is in a real sense the story of great leaders. In the patriarchal period there were four great figures: Abraham was the father of the faithful, Isaac was the promised seed of God, Jacob became the father of the twelve tribes, and Joseph his son was protected by God so he could be the preserver of his people.

The theocratic era began with Moses the great deliverer. He was followed by Joshua, who led the people into the promised land, and by great judges such as Gideon, Samson, and Samuel, who served as leaders until the first kings of Israel were anointed.

The monarchy began with wrong motives and the choice of the wrong man (Saul), but the kingdom was blessed of God and expanded by Saul's successor, David. David's son Solomon was the most glorious of all Israel's kings. Of the wisdom and riches of his reign only "the half has been told." Following Solomon there were only a few notable leaders among the kings of Judah. These included Joash, Hezekiah, and Josiah. All of Israel's kings, and most of the remainder of Judah's, were conspicuously lacking in spiritual leadership. Nevertheless, what the kings lacked in moral influence was made up for by the great prophets. Most notable among them were Elijah, Elisha, Isaiah, and Jeremiah before the exile, Ezekiel and Daniel during the exile, and Zechariah and Malachi after the exile. Ending with Ezra and Nehemiah, who led in the repatriation, Israel's redemptive history is a parade of men of God who were instruments in His-story.

III. A chronological outline of Israel's history.

The following chart should be consulted in order to get a clear chronological picture of contemporary kings and prophets in Israel and Judah as well as of events in the surrounding nations. Certain dates should be committed to memory because of their importance. These include the death of Solomon and division of the kingdom (931 B.C.), the captivity of Israel by Assyria (722 B.C.), the captivity of Judah by Babylon (605 B.C.), the destruction of the Temple in Jerusalem (586 B.C.), and the return of the remnant to the land (536 B.C.). One can become familiar with other dates throughout the study of the rest of the Old Testament by making constant reference to this chronological table.

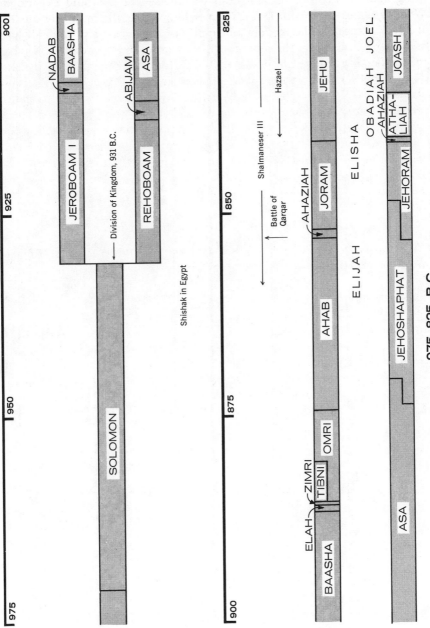

975-825 B.C.

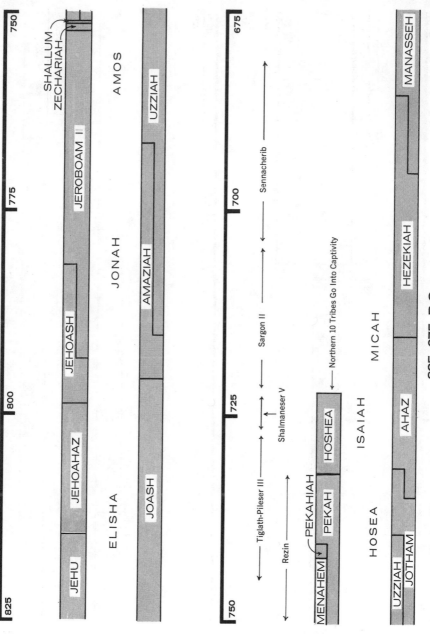

825 - 675 B.C.

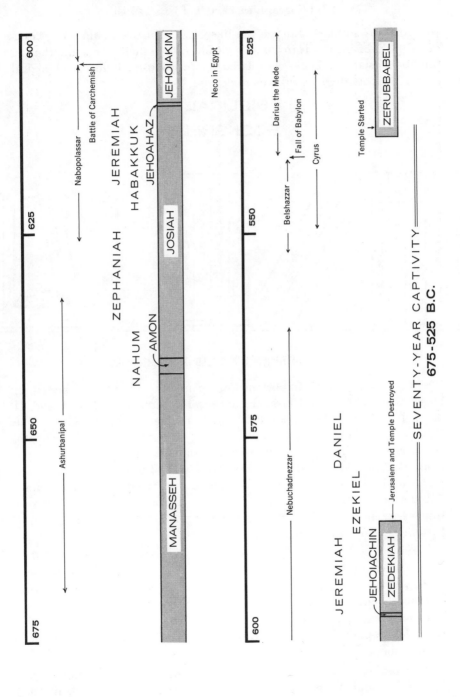

675   650   625   600

Ashurbanipal

Nabopolassar

Battle of Carchemish

ZEPHANIAH   NAHUM   HABAKKUK   JEREMIAH

AMON   JOSIAH   JEHOAHAZ   JEHOIAKIM

MANASSEH

Neco in Egypt

600   575   550   525

Nebuchadnezzar

Belshazzar   Darius the Mede

Fall of Babylon

Cyrus

Temple Started

JEREMIAH   EZEKIEL   DANIEL

JEHOIACHIN   ZEDEKIAH

Jerusalem and Temple Destroyed

ZERUBBABEL

SEVENTY-YEAR CAPTIVITY
675-525 B.C.

IV. A bibliographical sketch of Israel's history.

One way to help visualize the historical sequence of the Old Testament books of history is to use this "biblical bookshelf." Imagine that all the Old Testament books are placed on this bookshelf in chronological order. The bookshelf would look something like this:

BIBLICAL
BOOKSHELF

HISTORICAL LINE OF OLD TESTAMENT BOOKS

There are several important things to note about this bookshelf chart. The Book of I Chronicles covers the same period as I and II Samuel. II Chronicles covers the same period as I and II Kings. The history of the kings in Samuel and Kings was written from a prophetic point of view whereas the Chronicles record the history of the Temple from a priestly viewpoint. The Book of Esther fits between chapters 6 and 7 of the Book of Ezra. Old Testament history ends with Nehemiah. All the rest of the Old Testament books (the Poets and Prophets) fit somewhere into the historical context represented by Samuel, Kings, Chronicles, Ezra, and Nehemiah.

Job probably fits into the latter part of Genesis. Many of the Psalms were written by David during the time of II Samuel. Proverbs, Ecclesiastes, and the Song of Solomon fit into I Kings. Most of the writing prophets fit into II Kings. Jeremiah's Lamentations, Ezekiel, and Daniel, however, come during the seventy-year captivity; Haggai, Zechariah, and Malachi prophesied after the captivity during the time of Ezra and Nehemiah.

According to this overview, the history of the Old Testament ends some four hundred years before Christ. During the so-called silent years,

God did not speak through prophets to Israel. Instead He worked preparing the Gentile world politically, culturally, linguistically, and religiously so that "when the fulness of the time was come, God sent forth His Son" (Gal. 4:4, KJV).

STUDY QUESTIONS

1. Define the terms *theocracy* and *monarchy*, and indicate the difference between them.
2. Briefly trace Israel's development from a theocracy to a monarchy.
3. Name the significant events to which the following dates refer: 931 B.C., 722 B.C., 605 B.C. and 586 B.C.
4. What are the five great periods of Israel's history?
5. Name the men who played a significant role in each period.
6. Name the prophets who wrote before the exile, during the exile, and following the exile.

11

The Possession of the Nation

JOSHUA

Moses led Israel out of bondage, but it was Joshua who took them into blessing. Moses brought them through the Red Sea, but Joshua took them over Jordan. Moses is the symbol of deliverance and Joshua the emblem of victory. It is one thing to be redeemed from Egypt (the world) but quite another thing to be victorious over the world. Joshua teaches us the lesson that faith is "the victory that overcomes the world" (I John 5:4).

WHO WROTE JOSHUA?

The evidence indicates that the basic composition of the Book of Joshua was by Joshua, the successor of Moses. Perhaps some supplementary material was added by those who outlived him, such as Eleazar or his son Phinehas (Josh. 24:33). Nevertheless, early in the book there is the use of the first person plural "we" (Josh. 5:1, 6). This clearly indicates that Joshua is witnessing and writing of the events. Joshua 24:26 records that "Joshua wrote these words in the book of the law of God." This passage refers at least to his farewell charge, if not to the book as a whole. The book was probably written before Saul's day, for the Gibeonites were still alive" (Josh. 9:27; cf. II Sam. 21:1-9). The book was definitely written before David's day, since the Jebusites still inhabited the city of Jerusalem (Josh. 15:63; cf. II Sam. 5:6). The book was written before the death of Rahab, since she is referred to as one who "dwelt in Israel to this day" (Josh. 6:25). The author of the book had the genius of a general and provides detailed information of Israel's campaigns (6-12). All this evidence points toward Joshua as the basic composer of the book that bears his name.

There are, however, some indications that others made additions to the Book of Joshua. The last portion of the final chapter (the death of Joshua) was apparently written by someone else. Just as Joshua probably wrote the last chapter of Deuteronomy (about the death of Moses), someone who outlived Joshua probably wrote the passage on Joshua's death (Josh. 24:31). There are also some allusions to events that occurred later in the Book of Judges, such as Othniel's capture of Kirjath-sepher (Josh. 15:13-17; cf. Judg. 1:9-13) and Dan's migration to northern Israel (Josh. 19:47; cf. Judg. 18:27-29). These later additions may have been made by someone like Eleazar or Phinehas (cf. 24:33).

When Was Joshua Written?

The Book of Joshua was written by about 1380 B.C., at the conclusion of the conquest of the land of Canaan and just prior to Joshua's death. Several pieces of evidence provide the foundation for this view. Moses died in 1405 B.C. and Joshua became Israel's leader (see chronological chart). Caleb was forty years of age at the beginning of the thirty-eight years Israel wandered in the wilderness and seventy-eight at the end (Josh. 14:7). Joshua died at age one hundred ten after the conquering of the land (Judg. 2:8). Joshua was about the same age as Caleb, probably a few years older (since he was the leader), and died sooner. Assuming Joshua to be about six years older than Caleb, Joshua died when Caleb was one hundred and four. Since Caleb was seventy-eight at the beginning of the conquest there were twenty-five years between the beginning of the conquest of Canaan and the death of Joshua. This means that Joshua died c. 1379 B.C.

To Whom Was Joshua Written?

The Book of Joshua is addressed to the victorious Israelites who were settling the promised land. They had just conquered that land as a whole, but were reminded that "there remains yet very much land to be possessed" (Josh. 13:1).

Where Were They Located?

The twelve tribes of Israel were now located in the land of Canaan. They had completed their wilderness wanderings. Reuben, Gad, and half the tribe of Manasseh chose to settle on the east side of the Jordan. The remainder of the tribes settled on the west side as the following map indicates.

It should be noted that the sections indicate only the areas allotted to the various tribes. It was their responsibility to complete the specific conquest of their area. As their immediate history reveals, many of the tribes never drove out the enemies who remained in the land. As a result, they never really possessed all of their allotted land.

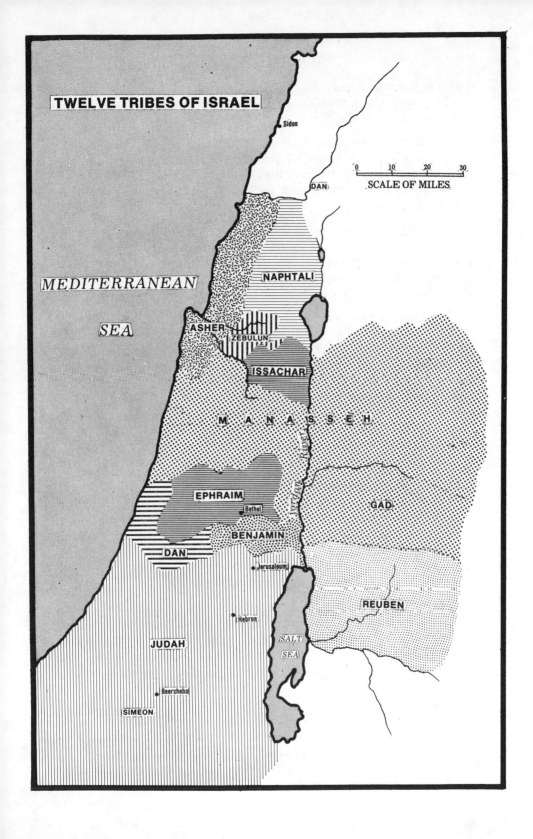

TWELVE TRIBES OF ISRAEL

Sidon

DAN

SCALE OF MILES
0   10   20   30

MEDITERRANEAN

SEA

NAPHTALI

ASHER

ZEBULUN

ISSACHAR

M A N A S S E H

EPHRAIM

Bethel

GAD

BENJAMIN

DAN

Jerusaleum

REUBEN

Hebron

SALT
SEA

JUDAH

Beersheba

SIMEON

WHY WAS JOSHUA WRITTEN?

The purposes of the Book of Joshua are historical, doctrinal, and Christological.

The historical purpose.

This book reveals how God brought the holy nation into the Holy Land in fulfillment of His promises to the patriarchs Abraham, Isaac, and Jacob. It shows how Joshua and Israel conquered and settled the promised land.

The doctrinal purpose.

There are a number of significant teachings in Joshua. The book manifests God's faithfulness to His promises. It shows that the victorious life must be lived by faith in God. It indicates that although God's gifts are free, we must struggle by faith to take hold of our possessions.

The Christological purpose.

The name *Joshua* means "Jesus" or "savior." This is how the Greek Old Testament (Septuagint or LXX) translates the title of this book. The role of Joshua as captain of his people and the one who leads them into their possessions certainly foreshadows Christ. Christ is also portrayed in the Book of Joshua in the person of the "commander of the army of the LORD (Josh. 5:14). The context of this passage shows that it is indeed the "angel of the Lord," or the preincarnate Christ Himself, whose holy presence demands worship on Joshua's part (cf. Exod. 3:2a). Finally, Christ is the inheritance of the saints (cf. Eph. 1:14).

WHAT IS THE BOOK OF JOSHUA ABOUT?

The Book of Joshua divides rather neatly into three parts: entering, conquering, and possessing the land. It is a book of triumph for faithful obedience to God. The following review of its contents will help in understanding this lesson.

I. Entering the promised land (1-5a).

A. THE PREPARATION OF THE PEOPLE (1-3a).

After nearly forty years of unbelief and divine judgment, Israel was ready to enter the promised land. But before Israel entered the land, Joshua encouraged them to "be strong and of good courage" (1:6). They had to be prepared for the battles ahead. Their *inward* preparation was to be in obedience to the law as stated in the words, "This book of the law shall not depart out of your mouth" (1:8). Their *outward* preparation for conquering the land was to send out two spies to look over the land (2). In contrast to the spies Moses sent out at the beginning of the wanderings, these spies came back with a good report. They said, "All the inhabitants of the land are fainthearted because of us" (2:24). Their final preparation was to move onward behind the ark, the symbol of God's presence, which led the way (3a).

B. THE PASSAGE OF THE PEOPLE (3b-4).

As the waters of the Red Sea were divided for their deliverance from Egypt, so the waters of the Jordan River dried up through a miracle for their entrance into the promised land (3b). Joshua then erected stones as a memorial of this monumental event (4).

C. THE PURIFICATION OF THE PEOPLE (5a).

Circumcision was given by God to Abraham as a sign of the covenant. By that sign Abraham's descendants were identified as a holy people (cf. Gen. 17:10f.). Joshua renewed this act of purification by circumcising the new generation just as Moses had done with their fathers who came out of Egypt.

II. Conquering the promised land (5b-12).

A. THE REVELATION OF THE VICTORY—THE LORD IS IN THE CAMP (5b).

The most fundamental fact of Israel's victory formula was the recognition that the Lord was their commander (v. 14). Their victory would come from God as they obeyed His orders.

B. THE REALIZATION OF THE VICTORY—NO SIN IN THE CAMP (6-11).

Israel's basic strategy for victory was to divide and conquer the land of Palestine. As a result, the first campaign was in the central portion of the land (6-9) beginning with Jericho. But defeat followed when sin was found in the camp (cf. ch. 7). Next, they engaged in the southern campaign (10) which brought them against the weaker countries. Finally, they held the more difficult campaigns in the northern section of the land (11). The victory at Jericho and the defeat at Ai because of sin in the camp were vital lessons for spiritual success. These lessons of reliance on God were applied to all their subsequent battles (cf. 7:1; ch. 10).

C. THE RECORD OF THE VICTORY—TRIUMPH IN THE CAMP (12).

With victory in hand Joshua reviewed and recorded Israel's success. He wrote, "Joshua took the whole land, according to all that the Lord had spoken to Moses" (Josh. 11:23). This means that Israel took the land as a whole even though there were many specific areas they had not subdued (see Judg. 1).

III. Possessing the promised land (13-24).

It was not enough for Israel simply to enter and conquer the land of promise. It was also necessary for the people of God to possess the land by faith. As a result, Joshua charged, "There remains yet very much land to be possessed" (Josh. 13:1).

A. DISTRIBUTION OF THE LAND (13-21).

Once the land was taken, each tribe was allotted its portion of it. In accordance with their request two and a half tribes were given their portion on the east side of the Jordan (13). The still vigorous Caleb asked for a possession at Mt. Hebron where he could tackle the difficult sons of Anakim in the hill country (14). This too was granted. Then, the possessions of the remaining nine and a half tribes were allotted on the west of the Jordan (15-19) by the casting of lots (cf. Prov. 16:33). Finally, the Levites were given their portions in and around the cities of refuge scattered throughout the land (20-21).

B. THE DISPUTE ABOUT THE ALTAR (22).

A misunderstanding arose about the altar built by the two and a half tribes who settled on the east side of the Jordan. The dispute was settled when it was understood that the altar would not be used for sacrifice but as a witness to the children that the Lord was their God. Thus, all the tribes of Israel would maintain a central place of worship in the Tabernacle of God. At that time the Tabernacle was located at Shiloh.

C. DISCOURSE AND DEATH OF JOSHUA (23-24).

The Book of Joshua concludes with two discourses. In the first discourse Joshua charged Israel to remember to keep the law of God (23). In the second he reminded them that the land they possessed was a gift from God and that it was, therefore, their responsibility to serve the Lord. As for Joshua's own testimony, it was clear: "But as for me and my house, we will serve the Lord" (24:15).

*   *   *

EXPLAINING SOME PROBLEMS IN THE BOOK OF JOSHUA.

A scientific problem—Joshua's long day (10:10-13).

It has been objected from a scientific point of view that if the planet earth had slowed in its rotation to make a forty-eight-hour day, everything on the earth's surface would have undergone a series of stupendous catastrophes. For the Christian who believes in an all-powerful God who created and who controls the world, there is no problem in believing that God could have supernaturally prevented these catastrophes.

There are three possible interpretations for the phenomenon of Joshua's long day. (1) Prof. Totten of Yale University (*Our Race*) claimed to have found one full day missing in the astronomical calendar. Some attempt to support this view by supposed Egyptian, Chinese, and Hindu reports of a long day. Harry Rimmer (*The Harmony of*

Science and Scripture) advocated this position. (2) Other scholars, such as Robert Dick Wilson of Princeton University, translate the verse, "Sun be silent or cease, leave off." From this they argue that Joshua's prayer held back the burning midday sun so that his troops could press the battle under more favorable conditions. (3) C. F. Keil and F. Delitzsch (*Biblical Commentary on the Old Testament*) argue that it would have been difficult to determine that the time was forty-eight hours rather than twenty-four if the sun could not be used for calculations. Instead, they suggest that the visibility of the sun may have been prolonged by an atmospheric reflection. Rendle Short (*Modern Discovery and the Bible*) points out that because of the krypton in the atmosphere it may at times be possible to see the sun wherever it is.

All of these interpretations are possible. The last one seems to present the fewest scientific difficulties and at the same time remains faithful to the biblical account. In any case, the fact that God performed a miracle on behalf of the Israelites need not be doubted on scientific grounds.

A moral problem—the slaughter of the Canaanites (Josh. 6, 8, 10).

Israel was commanded by God to completely exterminate the Canaanite inhabitants of the land including men, women, and children. This has been called a primitive and barbaric act of murder perpetrated on innocent lives.

Several factors must be kept in mind in viewing this situation. (1) There is a difference between murder and justifiable killing. Murder involves intentional and malicious hatred which leads to life-taking. On the other hand, the Bible speaks of permissible life-taking in capital punishment (Gen. 9:6), in self defense (Exod. 22:2), and in a justifiable war (Gen. 14). (2) The Canaanites were by no means innocent. They were a people cursed of God from their very beginning (Gen. 9:25). They were a vile people who practiced the basest forms of immorality. God described their sin vividly in these words, "I punished its iniquity, and the land vomited out its inhabitants" (Lev. 18:25). (3) Further, the innocent people of the land were not slaughtered. The story of Sodom and Gomorrah clearly demonstrates that God would save a whole city for ten righteous people (Gen. 18:22f.). In that incident, when God could not find ten righteous people, He took the four or five righteous ones out of the place so as not to destroy them with the wicked (Gen. 19:15). On another occasion God saved some thirty-two thousand people who were morally pure (Num. 31:35). Another notable example is Rahab, whom God saved because she believed (cf. Heb. 11:31). (4) God waited patiently for hundreds of years, giving the wicked inhabitants of Canaan time to repent (cf. II Peter 3:9) before He finally decided to destroy them (Gen. 15:16). When their iniquity was "full," divine judgment fell. God's judgment was akin to surgery for cancer or amputation of a leg as the only way to save the rest of a sick body. Just as cancer or gangrene contaminates the physical body, those elements in a society—if their evil is left to fester—will completely contaminate the rest of society. (5) Finally, the battle confronting Israel was not simply a religious war; it was a theocratic war. Israel was directly ruled by God and the extermination was God's direct command (cf. Exod. 23:27-30; Deut. 7:3-6; Josh. 8:24-26). No other nation either before or after Israel has been a theocracy. Thus, those commands were unique. Israel as a theocracy was an instrument of judgment in the hands of God.

STUDY QUESTIONS

1. Who wrote Joshua? Upon what evidence do we base this belief?
2. What is the doctrinal purpose of Joshua?
3. What is the Christological purpose of Joshua?
4. How was the promised land divided among the twelve tribes of Israel?
5. Briefly discuss the alleged scientific problem in the Book of Joshua.
6. Briefly discuss the alleged moral problem in the Book of Joshua.

12

The Oppression of the Nation

JUDGES, RUTH

There is a stark contrast between the moods of the Books of Joshua and Judges. In this shift of moods Israel moves from victory to defeat, from freedom to bondage, and from progress to decline. In Joshua Israel was in possession of the land but in Judges they were oppressed by the people of the land. Their song of joy turned into a sob of sorrow. Their faith had faded into faithlessness. The people who had trusted the Spirit for victory were now living by the flesh.

Ruth, which is appended to Judges in some Hebrew listings of the Old Testament, is a notable exception to the gloomy days of the judges. Hers is a story of loyalty in a day of anarchy, an example of purity in a time of immorality. In Ruth the narrative moves from the battlefield to the harvest field and from the warrior's cry to the gleaner's song. Ruth is a lily in the mud pond of Judges.

Who wrote Judges and Ruth?

Evidence indicates that Samuel the prophet or some of his prophetic students penned Judges and Ruth. (1) The books were composed after the death of Joshua and the elders who outlived him (Judg. 2:7). That means they were written some time after 1381 B.C. (2) They were composed after the days of the judges, since they refer to those days as past by such phrases as "in those days there was no king in Israel" (Judg. 17:6; 18:1; 19:1; 21:25), and "in the days when the judges were judging" (Ruth 1:1). (3) These books were probably written before the seventh year of king David's reign (1004 B.C.), since the Jebusites still held Jerusalem when Judges was written (Judg. 1:21; cf. II Sam. 5:6). Likewise, Judges 1:29 refers to the Canaanites as dwelling in Gezer—had Judges been written in Solomon's time they would probably have been referred to as submitting to Israel's sovereignty (I Kings 9:16f.; cf. I Chron. 6:67). (4) The reference to a "king in Israel" (Judg. 17:6; 18:1, etc.) implies a time of the early monarchy before the unhappy division after Solomon. The fact that the genealogy in Ruth ends with David would further support a time before Solomon. (5) The books were written from a prophetic point of view as is indicated by their moral tone (cf. Judg. 3:7; 4:1). The standard by which Israel is measured is their relation to God's law (see Judg. 3:4). (6) The person who best fits into the time period and who exercised prophetic leadership in the early monarchy was Samuel the prophet.

WHEN WERE THE BOOKS OF JUDGES AND RUTH WRITTEN?

Based on the preceding calculations, Judges and Ruth must have been written after 1043 B.C., when Saul was crowned king, and just before 1004 B.C., when David captured Jerusalem.

One problem with this early dating of Judges and Ruth is found in Judges 18:30, which makes reference to the "tribe of the Danites until the day of the captivity of the land." If this refers to the Assyrian conquest of the area, the date would be 722 B.C. Merrill F. Unger (*Introductory Guide to the Old Testament*) says this verse may be an insertion by a later editor. Gleason Archer (*A Survey of Old Testament Introduction*) translates the Hebrew word *'eres* as "ark" (*ārōn*) instead of "land" (a change of one letter in Hebrew). He identifies this event with I Samuel 4:21, when the ark was captured by the Philistines. There is, however, no manuscript evidence to warrant making this change in the text. Others take this statement simply as a reference to the Philistine captivity of the land during the time of the judges. Both the context (Judg. 18:31) and the reference to this event in Psalm 78:61 as a "captivity" support this last position.

TO WHOM WERE JUDGES AND RUTH WRITTEN?

If the early monarchical period be assumed as the date of composition, Judges and Ruth were written by the prophet Samuel to the nation of Israel which had only recently been established under kings Saul and David. The constant reminder to them that in the days of the judges "there was no king in Israel" (Judg. 17:6; 18:1) supports this view. In effect that statement could read, "See how thankful you can be now that God has given us stability under the Davidic kingdom and that we are not living in those near anarchy conditions of the days of the judges when everyone did what was right in his own eyes" (cf. Judg. 21:25).

WHERE WERE THEY LOCATED?

The map of the land allotted to each tribe changed as a result of the oppression during the time of the judges. Much of the land went into the hands of the Philistines and the Amalekites. The Jebusites still occupied the city of Jerusalem (Judg. 1:21), but most of the rest of the land was occupied by Israel. The Danites had moved from their far southern allotment to the far north (Judg. 18:1f.).

WHY WERE JUDGES AND RUTH WRITTEN?

The historical purpose of Judges.

The Book of Judges records the history of the cycles of Israel's decline, oppression, and deliverance between Joshua and the monarchy under Saul and David. As such it serves as an explanation and defense of the early monarchy of Israel. Israel went through this period of turmoil before being consolidated as a kingdom.

The doctrinal purpose of Judges.

There are a number of teachings that emerge from the Book of Judges. First, there is the obvious truth that disobedience or even incomplete obedience to God brings oppression and bondage. Second, there is evidence in the events of Judges to indicate that a theocratic nation needs a righteous king. Since this is the case, Judges provides an apologetic for the establishment of the monarchy under Saul and David. Third, Judges reveals the truth that God responds in deliverance to the repentance and prayers of His oppressed people. This teaches the long-suffering and love of God for His own.

The Christological purpose of Judges.

Each judge was a statesman-savior. They served as spiritual and political deliverers. As such they represent the role Christ has as the Savior-King of His people. The need for a Righteous King is everywhere apparent in Judges, and Christ is indeed the "Righteous One."

The historical purpose of Ruth.

The Book of Ruth has an important function in Israel's history. It supplies an important link in the ancestry of king David and shows how the birth of David into the messianic and monarchical line was providentially guided by God. As such it indicates the divine origin of the Davidic dynasty.

The doctrinal purpose of Ruth.

One very significant doctrinal emphasis of the Book of Ruth is its demonstration of the function of the law concerning the Kinsman Redeemer (Ruth 4; cf. Deut. 25:5f.). Ruth also presents the doctrine of the divine origin of the kingdom of David and contains one of the finest examples of filial love and piety in literature.

The Christological purpose of Ruth.

The Book of Ruth beautifully portrays several messianic purposes. It shows how Christ, our Kinsman Redeemer, purchases us for Himself. It also illustrates the grace of God as Ruth the Gentile is brought into the line of messianic blessing (see Matt. 1:5).

WHAT ARE THE BOOKS OF JUDGES AND RUTH ABOUT?

The Book of Judges narrates seven cycles of God's people as they moved from sin to servitude to supplication and salvation through a deliverer-judge. Rebellion is followed by retribution from God which leads to repentance and then rest from Israel's enemies. The Book of Judges describes and delineates three kinds of judges:

> the warrior judge—Gideon, Samson
> the priest judge—Eli
> the prophet judge—Samuel

For the Christian, this is a portrayal of Jesus Christ as Prophet, Priest, and Warrior (King) (cf. Rev. 19). The following overview will help demonstrate the overall thrust of the Book of Judges.

I. The reason for judges—apostasy (1-3a).

A. THE BACKWARD LOOK TO ISRAEL'S SIN (1-2a).

The key to Israel's failure is seen in the oft-repeated phrase, they "did not drive out the inhabitants" of the land (Judg. 1:21, 27, 29, 30, etc.). These incomplete victories soon led to Israel's defeat and subjection.

B. THE FORWARD LOOK TO ISRAEL'S SERVITUDE (2b-3a).

This passage provides a microcosm of the rest of the book. First, the people sinned: "the people of Israel did what was evil in the sight of the Lord and served the Baals" (2:11). Next, they found themselves in servitude to a foreign people: "So the anger of the Lord was kindled against Israel, and he gave them over to . . . their enemies round about, so that they could no longer withstand their enemies" (2:14). Then, the people entreated God by earnest supplication. They turned to God, groaning "because of those who afflicted and oppressed them" (2:18). Last, God provided salvation for His afflicted people: "Then the Lord raised up judges, who saved them out of the power of those who plundered them" (2:16).

II. The rule of the judges—loyalty (3b-16).

The reason judges were needed in the first place was the disloyalty of the people to God their king. Their failure to be a true theocracy (ruled by God) led to their defeat. Nevertheless, the rule of the judges did provide a sporadic example of true loyalty whereby God miraculously intervened on behalf of His people.

The seven cycles of sin, servitude, supplication, and salvation in the Book of Judges are as follows:

> The first cycle (3b).
>> Depression by Mesopotamia—8 years.
>> Deliverance by Othniel—40 years.
> The second cycle (3c).
>> Servitude to Moab, Ammon, and Amalek—18 years.
>> Salvation by Ehud (and Shamgar?)—80 years.
> The third cycle (4-5).
>> Retribution through Canaan—20 years.
>> Rest by Deborah—40 years.
> The fourth cycle (6-8a).
>> Vindication by way of Midian—7 years.
>> Victory through Gideon—40 years.
> The fifth cycle (8b-10a).
>> Ruination from Abimelech—3 years.
>> Release by Tola and Jair—45 years.
> The sixth cycle (10b-12).
>> Loss to Ammon—18 years.
>> Liberty through Jephthah, Ibzan, Elon, and Abdon—31 years
> The seventh cycle (13-16).
>> Ensnarement by Philistines—40 years.
>> Emancipation by Samson—20 years.

III. The ruin of the judges—anarchy (Judg. 17-21; Ruth 1-4).

The apostasy (falling away) of Israel from God is the reason that judges were raised up for their deliverance. Even their temporary rule of loyalty, however, gave way to the ruinous conditions of anarchy, for without a king "every man did what was right in his own eyes" (Judg. 21:25). This fact is pathetically obvious in this section of the Book of Judges.

The story of *decline—idolatry* (17-18)—among the Danites (in the north).

The story of *debasement—immorality* (19-21)—at Shiloh (in the central area).

The story of *devotion—fidelity* (Ruth 1-4)—at Bethlehem (in the south).

> Deciding—love's resolve (daughter)—country of Moab (Ruth 1).
> Serving—love's response (gleaner)—field of Bethlehem (2).

Resting—love's request (suppliant)—threshing floor (3).

Rewarding—love's reward (wife and mother)—gate of the city (4).

How to explain the chronology of Judges.

All the years indicated during which both the judges and foreign powers reigned over Israel total 410 years. If the period of Judges began in 1381 B.C. and ended with king Saul in 1043 B.C., it was only 338 years. The most obvious solution to this apparent discrepancy is that there are overlappings of the various judges and foreign rulers. In other words, while some of the land was under oppression, another area might be in a state of deliverance. The picture does seem to indicate that there were several occasions on which judges ruled over portions of Israel and at the same time foreign rulers reigned over other portions of the land. Further, it was common for rulers to claim a whole year when they reigned for only part of it.

Judges also provides some additional important chronological data about the Old Testament. Judges 11:26, for example, indicates that it was 300 years from the time of Joshua to the period just before Jephthah, when the Ammonites oppressed the land (1405-1105 B.C.). This agrees with the reference in I Kings 6:1 that says it was 480 years from the Exodus to the fourth year of Solomon's reign (1445-966 B.C.). It also corresponds with the New Testament reference to 450 years (Acts 13:19) between the end of Israel's conquering of the land and Solomon's death (1381 to 931 B.C.). Taken as a whole, all these data provide strong arguments for what is called the "early" date of the Exodus (1445 B.C.).

STUDY QUESTIONS

1. Compare and contrast the mood of the Book of Judges with the mood of Ruth.
2. What messianic purpose does the Book of Ruth fulfill?
3. In what ways do the judges prefigure Christ?
4. What significant type of Christ is found in the Book of Ruth?
5. What spiritual lesson may be found in the fourfold cycle which the nation of Israel repeatedly experienced?
6. What is the significance of the repeated phrase, "in those days there was no king in Israel and every man did that which was right in his own eyes"?

13

The Stabilization of the Nation

I SAMUEL

The Books of I and II Samuel were placed together as one book in the Hebrew Bible. Basically, I Samuel is about king Saul while II Samuel is about king David. Together they provide the history of the early monarchy in Israel from the moral or prophetic point of view. The authorship, date, destination, and purpose of the two books will be treated together.

WHO WROTE I AND II SAMUEL?

There is no direct claim for the authorship of the Books of Samuel. But the evidence indicates that the books were compiled by someone in the prophetic school using the documents of the prophets Samuel, Nathan, and Gad. The compiler of the book is unknown, but the time he lived and the sources he used can be deduced from the following evidence. (1) The books may have been completed only after Solomon's death (931 B.C.), since there is a reference to the divided monarchy in which Judah is separate from Israel (I Sam. 27:6). (2) Since the narration of Samuel ends with the death of David, it can be assumed that the original written record comes from some time after 971 B.C. (3) The books seem to have been written before the captivity of the northern kingdom by the Assyrians (722 B.C.), since there is no reference to this important event. (4) Samuel the prophet died before David began reigning (1011 B.C.) in I Samuel 25:1. Hence, he could not be the author of the rest of I Samuel or of any part of II Samuel. (5) Samuel founded a school of prophets over which he was head (I Sam. 19:20). Samuel himself wrote a book about the "acts of King David" as did the prophets Nathan and Gad (I Chron. 29:29). No doubt the prophet who compiled I and II Samuel used these prophetic histories in compiling his books.

WHEN WERE I AND II SAMUEL WRITTEN?

The answer to this has already been discussed. The original records were written some time after the death of David and probably compiled as the Books of Samuel some time after the death of Solomon (931 B.C.). At least they were compiled before the Assyrian captivity of Israel (722 B.C.).

TO WHOM WERE I AND II SAMUEL WRITTEN?

The Books of Samuel were directed to the monarchy of Israel originally united under David but later divided after Solomon's death.

WHERE WERE THE PEOPLE LOCATED?

The people lived under David and Solomon in the land of Palestine, and their religious life was centered around Jesusalem, which had been captured by David (II Sam. 5:7), and later around the Temple that Solomon built there (I Kings 6).

WHY WERE I AND II SAMUEL WRITTEN?

Three purposes may be seen in the Books of Samuel.

The historical purpose.

There are two historical purposes revealed in Samuel. First, it is a record of the divine origin of the Davidic dynasty. Secondly, it reveals the significant role of the prophets both in the transition from the judges to the kings and in their moral exhortations to the kings.

The doctrinal purpose.

There are several spiritual lessons in Samuel. First, Saul is a tragic lesson of the truth that "to obey is better than sacrifice" (I Sam. 15:22). Second, Saul is a notorious example of the words of Hosea: "I have given you kings in my anger, and I have taken them away in my wrath" (Hos. 13:11). Third, David is a classic example of the truth that "the Lord sees not as man sees" (I Sam. 16:7). Finally, the choice of David as king reveals the divine origin of the messianic house of David, that is, of the family through whom the Messiah would one day come (II Sam. 7:12f.).

The Christological purpose.

Samuel is the first biblical book to use the word *anointed* (I Sam. 2:10), which is the origin of the word *messiah,* that is, one anointed to be king. The primary messianic theme in Samuel is the coming Messiah, the Son of David (II Sam. 7:12f.; cf. Matt. 21:9; 22:45).

WHAT IS I SAMUEL ABOUT?

Three figures loom large in I Samuel—Samuel the prophet, Saul the king, and David the shepherd. The setting, by contrast with the anarchical instability in Judges, is one of monarchical stability. The people requested a king, albeit from the wrong motives, and God acceded to their demands.

I. The judgeship of Samuel (1-7).

First Samuel begins in the declining and decadent days of the judges when Eli was priest. There is no king and Eli's sons are notoriously immoral. The scene is ripe for the intervention of God. The birth and call of the prophet Samuel are God's answer to the moral plight of Israel in those dark days of the judges.

A. SAMUEL'S CALL (1-3).

Samuel came as an answer to the prayer *request* of a faithful mother, Hannah (1). Having dedicated her son to the Lord, Hannah *rejoiced* in the prospect of God's salvation for His people (2). The young Samuel was reared with Eli in the ministry of the Tabernacle at Shiloh and *responded* to the call of God while only a lad (3).

B. SAMUEL'S COMMISSION (4-7).

"All Israel from Dan to Beer-sheba knew that Samuel was established as a prophet" (3:20). At this time the Israelites were suffering *defeat* at the hands of the Philistines, who had stolen the ark of God from the Tabernacle (4-5). Under Samuel's prophetic encouragement and with divine assistance Israel gained *victory* over the Philistines and recaptured the ark of the covenant (6-7).

II. The kingship of Saul (8-15).

Samuel's sons proved to be unjust and corrupt judges, and the elders of Israel demanded that Samuel make them a king "like all the nations" (8:5). This was obviously the wrong *motive* for establishing a king. Also wrong was the *criterion* by which the people chose their king: he was "a handsome young man . . . taller than any of the people" (9:12). Finally, they chose a man from the wrong *tribe*, Benjamin (9:1)—God had predicted long before through Jacob that "the scepter shall not depart from Judah, nor the ruler's staff from between his feet" (Gen. 49:10). Nonetheless, God acquiesced to the nation's demands and told Samuel to anoint Saul king.

A. THE SELECTION OF SAUL (8-12).

The reasons for choosing Saul were less than spiritual, as has already been pointed out (8-9). He was, nonetheless, anointed by Samuel to *reign* as king over Israel (10). Spirits were high as the Israelites went to Gilgal to *renew* the kingdom with the Lord (11). But Samuel *reviewed* Israel's history and sternly warned them, "If you still do wickedly, you shall be swept away, both you and your king" (12:25).

B. THE REJECTION OF SAUL (13-15).

Despite the clear warning of Samuel, Saul and the people began to act wickedly. First, Saul acted *presumptuously* in that he assumed the role of a priest (an office forbidden to kings by the law—cf. II Chron. 26:18) and offered up sacrifices (13-14). Second, Saul only *partially* obeyed the command of God to utterly destroy the Amalekites (15). God responded to Saul through Samuel, saying, "Behold, to obey is better than sacrifice, and to hearken than the fat of rams. For rebellion is as the sin of divination, and stubbornness is as iniquity and idolatry" (15:22, 23).

III. The kingship of David (16-31).

Saul was the people's choice; David was God's choice. Saul was a man after the people's heart; David was a man after God's own heart. This is a dramatic illustration of the truth that "man looks on the outward appearance, but the Lord looks on the heart" (16:7).

A. DAVID'S KINGSHIP ANNOUNCED BY SAMUEL—DAVID THE SHEPHERD (16-17).

It was not inappropriate that God chose a shepherd to lead His people. Moses too learned valuable lessons of leadership from forty years at the same occupation. David was anointed by Samuel from among the sons of Jesse (16). And when David slew the giant Goliath he was acclaimed by the court of Saul (17).

B. DAVID'S KINGSHIP ACKNOWLEDGED BY JONATHAN—DAVID THE COURTIER (18-19).

One of the most touching stories in Scripture is the unselfish devotion of Jonathan to David despite the fact that he knew David was God's choice to succeed to the throne of his jealous father. Jonathan willingly *sacrificed* the throne for David, giving his very robe and sword to David (18). What is more, Jonathan made earnest *supplication* to his father to save the life of David.

C. THE KINGSHIP OF DAVID ATTACKED BY SAUL—DAVID THE FUGITIVE (20-31).

Saul sought to kill David and almost succeeded. David was forced to flee from the king's presence. With the cooperation of Jonathan and by means of a masterfully conceived escape plot David managed to find *protection* from Saul (20). The king was further enraged and the following chapters record Saul's *pursuit* of David from place to place throughout the land (21-27). The flight of David may be traced on the following map.

During the long pursuit David displayed both his cunning and yet his humility and respect for the king as God's anointed. Saul, by con-

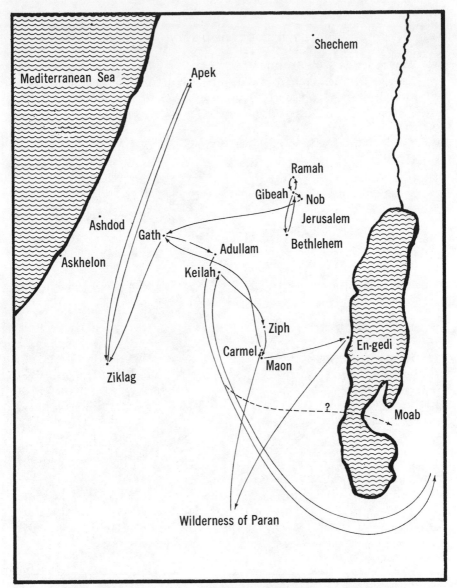

Mediterranean Sea

Shechem

Apek

Ramah

Gibeah · Nob

Jerusalem

Ashdod

Gath

Bethlehem

Askhelon

Adullam

Keilah

En-gedi

Ziph

Carmel

Maon

Ziklag

?

Moab

Wilderness of Paran

DAVID'S FLIGHT FROM SAUL

trast, displayed both the symptoms of insanity and the lack of morality that led to his final downfall. The *plight* of Saul is described in the last chapters (28-31). Despite the fact Saul put the witches out of the land at the command of God, he went to the witch of Endor to contact the dead prophet Samuel. The Lord therefore rebuked Saul and pronounced his doom (28). Meanwhile God led David to victory in battle (29-30), but Saul met his fate in battle with the Philistines and died by his own sword (31). Thus a life of jealousy, disobedience, witchcraft, and murderous intent ended in suicide.

The pools of Ein Gedi form an oasis on the shore of the Dead Sea. David used the oasis as a hiding place when fleeing from the wrath of King Saul. Israel Gov't Tourist Office Photo

STUDY QUESTIONS

1. What evidence is there that Samuel was written by a prophet?
2. What spiritual lessons are to be learned from I and II Samuel (cf. I Cor. 10:11)?
3. What was wrong with the people's choice of Saul for their king?
4. What characteristics did king David possess that qualified him as a spiritual leader of his people?
5. Why did God finally reject king Saul?
6. What was David's attitude toward Saul's kingship?

14

The Expansion of the Nation

II SAMUEL

The authorship, date, and purposes of II Samuel have already been discussed (ch. 13). Here we will treat only the content of II Samuel.

WHAT IS II SAMUEL ABOUT?

Whereas the kingdom was established under Saul it was extended by David. Saul's monarchy provided *stabilization* as compared to the anarchical days of the judges, and David's reign brought *expansion* of the kingdom of Israel.

I. The recognition of David on the throne (1-10): David's fame.

"Saul has slain his thousands and David his ten thousands" became a slogan in Israel that betokened David's fame. His reputation and success as a warrior had secured the monarchy from its surrounding enemies.

A.   DAVID'S KINGSHIP OVER JUDAH IN HEBRON (1-4)—7½ years.

The Book of II Samuel begins with the vain attempt of the Amalekite to gain glory by claiming credit for the *death* of Saul (1). After Saul's death the *dynasty* of David was established over Judah at Hebron (2). Abner, Saul's captain, *defected* to David (3), and this led to the *death* (by assassination) of Ish-bosheth, the son of Saul who was king over Israel in the north (4).

B.   DAVID'S KINGSHIP OVER ALL ISRAEL IN JERUSALEM (5-10) —33 years.

The defection of Abner and death of Ish-bosheth paved the way for the uniting of all Israel. So "they anointed David king over Israel" (5:3).

1. *The establishment of David's kingdom* (5-7). After the *corona-tion* of David (5a) and the capturing of Jerusalem, the stronghold city of the Jebusites (5b), David led his people in bringing the ark into the *center* of Israel to the city of David (Jerusalem) (6). Then David's desire turned to building a temple, a permanent *citadel* for God's presence in the midst of His people (7). God commended David for his desire and promised him a messianic dynasty through his son (7:12f.). But because David was a man of war and bloodshed it was left for his son Solomon, the man of peace, to build the House of God (cf. I Chron. 22:8).

2. *The extension of David's kingdom* (8-10). David was a man of mighty military strength, as is evident in his extending the kingdom by *capturing* some of the surrounding lands of the Philistines, Moabites, Syrians, Ammonites, and Edomites, among others (8). David was also a man of great spiritual character as is indicated by his *compassion* on the house of Saul in the person of Mephibosheth (9). He was also a man of great *conquering* ability—witness the story of how he conquered the Syrians when they joined with the Ammonites to fight against him (10). So great was David's victory that all the kings subservient to Syria came and "made peace with Israel, and became subject to them" (10:19).

II. The rejection of David from the throne (11-18): David's shame.

The Bible does not glorify the heroes of the faith to the neglect of their sin. In fact one of the marks of the truthfulness of Scripture is its balanced presentation of both the bright and dark sides of the lives of men of God.

A. DAVID'S SIN (11).

There is no question that David yielded to the temptation which Bathsheba presented and was guilty both of coveting another man's wife and of planning the death of Uriah to get her. David's sins were two: gross lust which led to adultery and premeditated murder, albeit of a very subtle variety (he sent Uriah to die in battle).

B. DAVID'S SORROW (12a).

Moses had long ago warned God's people, "Be sure your sin will find you out" (Num. 32:23). After Nathan the prophet had trapped David with a parable to which the king responded by unwittingly pronouncing his own sentence in advance, "Nathan said to David, Thou art the man" (12:7, ASV). David, who despite his sin was a genuine man of God, responded in true sorrow, saying, "I have sinned against the

Lord" (12:13). For David's full confession Psalm 51 should be read at this point. David's sins were forgiven but he suffered the consequences nonetheless. "For whatever a man sows, that he will also reap" (Gal. 6:7).

C. DAVID'S SUFFERING (12b-18).

David had unwittingly pronounced a fourfold judgment on himself in his responses to Nathan's parable (12:6). God took David at his word and there followed in David's life four tragic events by which he suffered the consequences of his sin. First, the baby born of his lust for Bathsheba died (12b). Second, David's daughter Tamar was defiled (13a). Third, David's son Amon was killed in revenge for his defilement of Tamar (13b). Finally, the kingdom of David was divided and Absalom his son was killed (14-18). Absalom was a handsome prince who "stole the hearts of the men of Israel" (15:6). By prearrangement the trumpet was sounded throughout Israel and it was pronounced, "Absalom is king at Hebron" (15:10). David fled from his throne, crying, "Behold, my own son seeks my life" (16:11). Absalom, however, was trapped by his own plot and beauty. He was caught in a tree by his curly hair, and Joab's armorbearers "surrounded Absalom and struck him, and killed him" (18:15). The consequences of David's sins brought greater sorrow on him than had he died himself. David's wailing at the news of Absalom's death manifests his anguished spirit, "O my son Absalom, O Absalom, my son, my son!" (19:4).

III. The restoration of David to his throne (19-24): David's name.

God was gracious to David and restored him to his throne. Things, however, were never quite the same as they were before. The glory had faded with the sin. David's fame was shadowed by his shame. God did, nevertheless, preserve the name of David as He had promised.

A. DAVID'S ASCENSION TO THE THRONE (19-21).

Upon the death of Absalom David realized that he was again king in the land (19). He asked, "For do I not know that I am this day king over Israel?" (v. 22). The people too *recognized* that David was king (20). But David was immediately faced with a famine because of Saul's *revenge* on the Gibeonites (21a). The famine did not stop until seven of Saul's descendants had been hanged by the Gibeonites. After this David secured the *respect* of a proper burial for the bones of Saul and Jonathan (21b).

B. DAVID'S ASPIRATIONS ON THE THRONE (22-24).

As David mounted again the throne of Israel his psalmist heart uttered these words, "The Lord is my rock, and my fortress, and my deliverer." This psalm is also preserved in the Book of Psalms (Ps. 18).

This poem expresses David's feelings just after he *ascended again his earthly throne* (22). It is entitled "the last words ... of David, the son of Jesse" (23:1). In these words David gave testimony to the inspiration or divine origin of his writings, which include over seventy Psalms (see the introduction to Psalms, ch. 26). He said, "The Spirit of the Lord speaks by me, his word is upon my tongue" (v. 2). II Samuel ends with an *acknowledgment of those who stood with him as he sat on his earthly throne* (23b). The final chapter deals with the *anger of God against David's throne,* because he numbered and took stock of his own military might, a gesture of self-confidence rather than reliance on the power of God. Taking a census as such was not evil. Moses did this at God's command several times. But the pride that prompts a display of one's own human power can be a sign of rebellion against God. Rudyard Kipling said this very well in his "Recessional," written when England was at the zenith of her power (the Diamond Jubilee of Queen Victoria).

> God of our fathers, known of old,
>   Lord of our far-flung battle-line,
> Beneath whose awful hand we hold
>   Dominion over palm and pine—
> Lord God of Hosts, be with us yet,
>   Lest we forget—lest we forget!
>
> The tumult and the shouting dies;
>   The Captains and the Kings depart;
> Still stands Thine ancient sacrifice,
>   An humble and a contrite heart.
> Lord God of Hosts, be with us yet,
>   Lest we forget—lest we forget!
>
> * * *
>
> If drunk with sight of power, we loose
>   Wild tongues that hold not Thee in awe,
> Such boastings as the Gentiles use
>   Or lesser breeds without the Law—
> Lord God of Hosts, be with us yet,
>   Lest we forget—lest we forget!
>
> For heathen heart that puts her trust
>   In reeking tube and iron shard—
> All valiant dust that builds on dust,
>   And guarding calls not Thee to guard,
> For frantic boast and foolish word—
>   Thy mercy on Thy people, Lord!

HOW TO EXPLAIN SEVERAL PROBLEMS IN THE BOOKS OF SAMUEL.

The witch of Endor and the raising of Samuel.

The Old Testament explicitly forbids witchcraft and communication with the dead (see Exod. 22:18; Lev. 20:6, 27; Deut. 18:9-12; Isa. 8:19).

Saul himself knew this and at the command of God had put all the witches out of the land (I Sam. 28:3). Nevertheless, in disobedience to God he went to the witch at Endor, who appeared to make contact with the dead prophet Samuel (I Sam. 28:8f.). The problem here is that the Bible appears to lend validity to the powers of witchcraft to contact the dead.

Several possible solutions have been given to this episode at Endor. (1) It is possible that the witch worked a miracle by demonic power and actually brought Samuel back from the dead. In support of this may be cited a number of biblical passages indicating that demons have the power to perform amazing things (Matt. 7:22; II Cor. 11:14; II Thess. 2:9, 10; Rev. 16:14). The objections to this view are that death is final (Heb. 9:27) and that Scripture indicates that the dead cannot return (Luke 16:24-27). (2) A second view seems even less plausible. In this view the witch by demonic or magical powers merely faked a miracle and did not really get in touch with Samuel. This seems unlikely since the passage both represents Samuel as really appearing and provides a message from Samuel that actually came to pass as though it were the word of God. Although there are "familiar spirits" or demons who monitor the lives of individuals so that they can imitate them when men try to contact them after death (cf. Lev. 19:31; Deut. 18:11; I Chron. 10:13) and although demons sometimes utter what is true (cf. Acts 16:17), the context does not seem to indicate that such was the case here. (3) A more likely interpretation is that God intervened and performed a miracle in the house of the witch and actually brought Samuel back from the dead in order to rebuke Saul for his sin and to prophesy his doom. Several facts support this view: (a) the witch herself is startled at the appearance of Samuel (v. 12); (b) there is an implicit condemnation of witchcraft in this passage (vv. 9, 12); (c) God sometimes speaks in unsuspected places through unusual means (cf. Baalam's ass); (d) the miracle is not performed through the witch but *in spite of* her witchcraft; (e) Samuel really appears, rebukes Saul, and pronounces his death (vv. 15f.). The fact that God once intervened to bring back a departed spirit does not sanction human efforts of this type. As a matter of fact, God explicitly condemns necromancy and consulting mediums with "familiar spirits."

The two reports of the death of Saul.

I Samuel 31 reports that the wounded Saul died by falling on his own sword, but II Samuel 1 records that as he was about to lean on his spear, he was killed by an Amalekite. Some have taken the story of the Amalekite as true but supplementary. They claim that Saul attempted suicide but was not dead when the Amalekite arrived to finish the job. The fact that the Amalekite had Saul's crown and bracelet is used to support the truth of his story. However, it seems more likely that the Amalekite's story is a fabrication to gain glory for himself. He no doubt came upon the crown after Saul had died. He does seem to know that Saul died by a sword and not a spear. David killed the Amalekite on the basis of his self-confessed guilt (1:16). Instead of the fabrication of the Amalekite recorded in II Samuel 1, I Chronicles 10 repeats the story of I Samuel that Saul committed suicide.

The slaying of Goliath.

II Samuel 21:19 reads that "Elhanan . . . slew Goliath the Gittite," whereas it was David who killed him according to I Samuel 17. This apparent contradiction is probably the result of a scribal error in copying the manuscript and should read "Elhanan . . . slew Lahmi the brother of Goliath the Gittite" (cf. I Chron. 20:5).

The twofold introduction of David to Saul.

In I Samuel 16 David is hired to play his harp to comfort the king. But in the next chapter, after David has killed Goliath, Saul inquires, "Whose son are you, young man?" (17:58). Although it is possible Saul did not recognize him as the same young man who played the harp for him, it seems more likely that he was inquiring not who David was but who David's father was. Saul was accustomed to placing the most valiant men available in his personal bodyguard (14:52). He may have wondered if there were any more such brave men in David's family. Or he may have simply wished for a more complete identification of this brave young man in view of his extraordinary accomplishment of killing the giant. In either case there is no contradiction here.

STUDY QUESTIONS

1. Why is Jerusalem called the city of David (II Sam. 5)? Why is Bethlehem also called the same (cf. Ruth 4)?
2. What characteristics did David possess that qualified him to be a leader?
3. Why was David not allowed to build the Temple (cf. I Chron. 17)?
4. In what ways did David pay for his sin with Bathsheba?

15

The Glorification of the Nation
I KINGS 1-11

The Books of Kings are so named because their chief subject is the kings of Israel and Judah. These books are a history of the kingdom from the time of Solomon to the time of the Babylonian exile and were written from a prophetic point of view.

WHO WROTE I AND II KINGS?

Evidence points to the prophet Jeremiah as the author of the Books of Kings. The following summary will suffice. (1) The author lived before the Babylonian exile or captivity, as is indicated by the repeated phrase "to this day" (I Kings 8:8; 12:19, etc.). (2) The book is clearly written from the prophetic point of view, stressing the idolatry and immorality that brought down the judgment of God (cf. I Kings 11:1f.). (3) The style of writing is similar to that of the Book of Jeremiah, and II Kings 24:18—25:30 is the same as Jeremiah 52. (4) Jewish Talmudic tradition attributes the Books of Kings to Jeremiah (*Baba Bathra* 15a). (5) The last chapter may have been written by someone else, since it appears to come from Babylon and Jeremiah was exiled into Egypt (Jer. 43:1-8). (6) The author of Kings used several sources in writing his books: (a) the Acts of Solomon (I Kings 11:41); (b) the Chronicles of the Kings of Judah (I Kings 15:7), (c) the Chronicles of the Kings of Israel (I Kings 14:19) (these were probably the notations of the official court recorder [II Sam. 8:16]); (d) a possible fourth source is Isaiah 36-39, large sections of which appear in II Kings 18-20. Jeremiah incorporated material from these sources, together with his own observations, into the Books of Kings.

WHEN WERE I AND II KINGS WRITTEN?

The bulk of the books was written before the Babylonian captivity (586 B.C.). This is evidenced by two main facts. First, throughout the books the phrase "to this day" (e.g., II Kings 17:34, 41) is used in describing the iniquity of the people before the captivity. Second, the last chapters of the Book of II Kings record the captivity itself (24-25). The last chapter goes thirty-seven years into Jehoiakim's captivity (605 B.C.), which would be 568 B.C.

TO WHOM WERE THE BOOKS WRITTEN?

The bulk of the books was written to the divided and declining monarchies of Israel and Judah. The final chapters record the captivity and relate to the Babylonian captives. From Solomon's death (931 B.C.) the divided nations of Israel (northern kingdom) and Judah (southern kingdom) found themselves not only in a state of political disunity but also in a condition of gross immorality and idolatry, sins against which the prophets had often warned. It was to this divided, declining, and ultimately deported nation that Jeremiah wrote the Book of Kings.

WHERE WERE THEY LOCATED?

After the division (I Kings 12) the kingdoms were separated politically as well as geographically. The northern ten tribes made Samaria their capital, although they had idol centers in Dan and Bethel. The southern kingdom was centered both politically and religiously in Jerusalem (see map of the divided kingdoms).

WHY WERE THE BOOKS OF KINGS WRITTEN?

There were three purposes for writing these books: historical, doctrinal, and Christological.

The historical purpose.

One aim of Kings is clearly to provide a historical record of the main acts of the kings of Israel and Judah from the glory of Solomon's united kingdom to the shame and judgment of the divided and then captive kingdoms.

The doctrinal purpose.

While the record of these books is primarily historical, another purpose is obviously moral teaching. The central doctrinal teaching is that conformity to the law of God brings prosperity while apostasy leads to captivity.

The Christological purpose.

The messianic implication of Kings is clear: despite human sin and failure God is faithful to the Davidic covenant (II Sam. 7). The Messiah will come through the tribe of Judah and will be a son of David; the

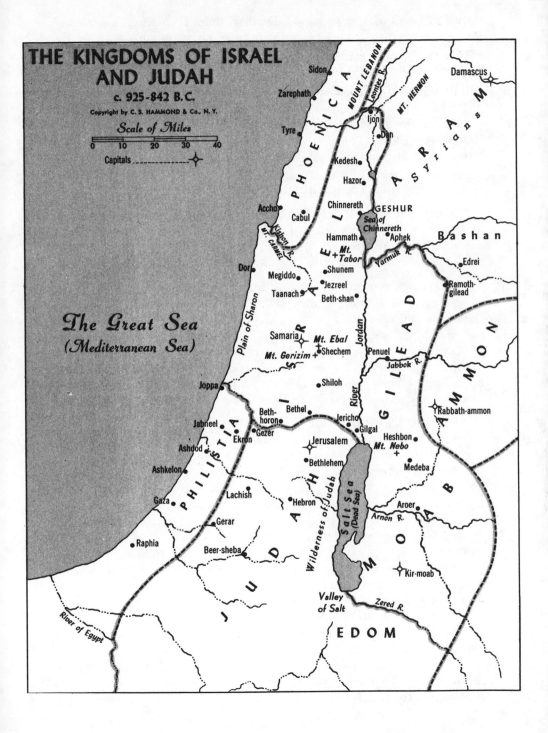

THE KINGDOMS OF ISRAEL
AND JUDAH
c. 925-842 B.C.
Copyright by C. S. HAMMOND & Co., N. Y.

Scale of Miles

0   10   20   30   40

Capitals ----------------

The Great Sea
(Mediterranean Sea)

throne of Israel will be preserved. Further, there is in Kings a beautiful illustration of the splendor of the coming kingdom of Christ in the person of Solomon. Indeed, with the coming of Christ it was truly said, someone "greater than Solomon is here" (Matt. 12:42).

WHAT IS I KINGS 1-11 ABOUT?

I Kings divides into two parts: the united monarchy under Solomon (1-11) and the divided monarchies which began under Jeroboam and Rehoboam (12-22). The first section is a story of great glory while the latter is one of great shame. We will discuss here the first part.

I. The glorification of the nation (1-11).

There are several elements in the glory of Solomon's reign. The writer of I Kings singles out two main areas: Solomon's wisdom and his wealth. But his wickedness is not neglected. For, as is often the case in the Bible, what begins with divine glory ends in human shame.

A. SOLOMON'S WISDOM (1-3).

Solomon was *anointed* king (1), *appointed* king after the death of David (2), and *acknowledged* to be God's chosen one (3). It was wisdom, not wealth, for which Solomon prayed and God granted him his request, as is evidenced by the king's decision regarding the two women and the baby. It was Solomon himself who wrote, "The fear of the LORD is the beginning of knowledge . . . wisdom and instruction" (Prov. 1:7). Thus God-fearing wisdom became the foundation of Solomon's kingdom.

B. SOLOMON'S WEALTH (4-10).

Solomon's wealth was as great as his wisdom. This wealth was reflected in three aspects of his kingdom: the domestic prosperity, the religious achievements, and the political stability.

1. *Domestic prosperity* (4). Solomon reigned over a region stretching from Babylon to Egypt. All brought tribute to him. "Judah and Israel were as many as the sand by the sea; they ate and drank and were happy" (v. 20). Not only were there prosperity and plenty but there was also domestic tranquility, for "he had peace on all sides round about him" (v. 24). There was also a great increase in knowledge and music, for Solomon "uttered three thousand proverbs; and his songs were a thousand and five" (v. 32).

2. *Religious achievements* (5-8). Solomon's crowning religious achievement was the magnificent Temple he built in Jerusalem. David desired to build the Temple, but God would not allow him to build it because he was a man of bloodshed. It was more fitting that Solomon, the man of peace, be commissioned to erect the Temple of God. The preparation for the Temple was made (5), the building was erected (6),

The pillars of Solomon rise from the desert hills near Eilat. Not far from the pillars are the ancient copper mines worked by King Solomon and the new mines being worked by present-day Israelis. Israel Gov't Tourist Office Photo

the vessels were dedicated (7), and then Solomon dedicated the whole building (8). He prayed, "But will God indeed dwell on the earth? Behold, heaven and the highest heaven cannot contain thee; how much less this house which I have built!" (8:27). Solomon bound his people with an oath to remain faithful to God, and the ceremony was completed with the offering of thousands of sacrifices.

3. *Political stability* (9-10). By a series of treaties, marriages and international diplomacy, Solomon built an unsurpassed network of relationships with surrounding countries. His marriage to the daughter of Pharaoh (9) and the visit of the Queen of Sheba (10) illustrate the political glory of Solomon's kingdom. When the queen saw all that Solomon had, she declared "the half was not told me" (10:7). When she saw Solomon's servants and silver, his nation and his navy, his gold and his glory, there was scarcely breath left in her.

C. SOLOMON'S WICKEDNESS (11).

The fame of Solomon reached great heights but was in the end outweighed by his shame. The ominous words, "Now King Solomon loved many foreign women" (v. 1), tell the story. Solomon proved the validity of God's warning that foreign women would turn the hearts of His people after foreign gods (v. 2). Solomon had one thousand wives and concubines (v. 3). As might be expected, this moral wickedness is what spelled the final doom of Solomon's kingdom. It was *immorality* and *idolatry* that corrupted his kingdom from within. The subsequent political *disunity* was really a result of spiritual shortcomings.

HOW TO EXPLAIN POLYGAMY IN THE BIBLE.

Polygamy presents a problem for the student of the Bible. On the one hand, the Bible teaches monogamy: one man married to one wife. As Paul said, "Each man should have his own wife and each woman her own husband" (I Cor. 7:2). He also wrote of church leaders that they should be "the husband of one wife" (I Tim. 3:2, 12, KJV). Jesus taught that God intended that marriage be between one male and one female (Matt. 19:8). Yet on the other hand, God apparently blessed the polygamy practiced by some of the great saints of the Old Testament—Abraham, David, and Solomon. The problem is this: if God designed and commanded monogamy, then why did He bless polygamy and allow some of His choice servants to go uncondemned as polygamists?

In answering this problem several facts must be kept in mind. First, polygamy is not *taught* as God's ideal anywhere in the Bible; polygamy was merely *permitted* or tolerated as an accommodation to the realistic circumstances of human sin. Like divorce, polygamy was merely allowed "for your hardness of heart" but "from the beginning it was not so" (Matt. 19:8).

Second, monogamy was taught in the Old Testament as well as the New Testament as God's standard for marriage. The New Testament passages have already been cited. The Old Testament taught monogamy in several ways: (1) it was taught by *precedent* in the case of Adam and Eve. That is, God made only one man and one woman as the prime and perfect example of what marriage should be. (2) Monogamy was also taught by the *proportion* of the population. (About half of the people born are male and half female). If polygamy had been intended then the proportion of females to males would have been much greater. (3) Monogamy was taught by *practice* in the Old Testament. Those who perverted God's ideal of one man and one woman paid bitterly for their polygamy. Polygamy arose amid a sinful society in rebellion against God (Gen. 4:23). Abraham, David, and especially Solomon all suffered the consequences of their polygamous sins. Solomon's heart was turned from God to idolatry and his glorious kingdom came to eventual shame because of his polygamy (I Kings 11:3, 4). (4) Finally, monogamy was taught by *precept* in the Old Testament. The law of Moses clearly commands, "You shall not multiply wives" (Deut. 17:17). In the same spirit the children of Israel were forbidden to add foreign wives, as Solomon was reminded when God's judgment came on him (I Kings 11:2).

In brief, God neither intended nor blessed polygamy. In fact, He both commanded against it and condemned the practice of it. Like other sins, God permitted polygamy because of the sinful hardness of the human heart. God hates polgyamy as much as He hates divorce (Mal. 2:16), for both spoil the ideal relationship of a husband and wife that is so perfectly illustrative of the relation of Christ and his bride, the Church (Eph. 5:32).

STUDY QUESTIONS

1. What is the evidence that Jeremiah wrote I and II Kings?
2. Give three purposes for which the Books of Kings were written.
3. What did Solomon request of God? What did God give Solomon in addition to what he requested?
4. Name three kinds of wealth which Solomon had.
5. What two things brought about the corruption of Solomon's kingdom?
6. What is God's attitude toward polygamy?

16

The Division of the Nation

I KINGS 12-22

In the previous chapter we studied the *united* monarchy under Solomon. In this chapter we will summarize what occurred in the *divided* monarchies of Israel and Judah after Solomon's death.

I. The divided monarchies of Israel and Judah (12-22).

As was previously noted, Solomon's kingdom was really eroded from within. Idolatry and immorality paved the way for disunity. The first overt manifestation of division in the kingdom came in the revolt of Jeroboam and the northern ten tribes.

A. THE REVOLT OF THE TEN TRIBES OF ISRAEL (12).

At Solomon's death, Rehoboam, his son, was crowned king. He unwisely took counsel of the younger men and placed an even heavier yoke of taxation on the people than had his father Solomon. This prompted Jeroboam, the captain of Solomon's army, to lead the northern tribes in revolt. Upon concluding that they had no portion left in the inheritance of David, the northern tribes set up their own centers of idolatrous religion at Dan and Bethel. They made calves of gold and proclaimed, "Behold your gods, O Israel, who brought you up out of the land of Egypt" (12:28).

B. THE REIGN OF THE EARLY KINGS OF ISRAEL AND JUDAH (13-16).

Two themes are carried throughout the narrative in the Books of Kings: the *morality* of the kings and the *ministry* of the prophets. The kings of Israel (the northern ten tribes) were all wicked. Among the kings of Judah in the south there were notable exceptions who instituted reforms under the influence of some of the great prophets. Here is a list of the kings and the prophets of this early period (see the chart of the kings for a complete chronology):

Kings of Israel (13-16)	Prophets	Kings of Judah (13-16)
1) *Jeroboam I* 931-910		1) Rehoboam 931-913
2) Nadab 910-909		2) Abijam 913-911
3) *Baasha* 909-886	Jehu	3) *Asa 911-870
4) Elah 886-885		4) *Jehoshaphat 872-848
5) *Zimri* 885		
6) Tibni 885-880		
7) *Omri* 885-874	Elijah	
8) Ahab 874-853		

Several things should be noted about the kings of this early period. The throne of Israel was occupied by four different dynasties, those of Jeroboam, Baasha, Zimri, and Omri (founders of new dynasties are italicized in the list). The kings of Judah were of course one dynasty, the Davidic dynasty as God had promised (II Sam. 7). Again, all of the kings of Israel were evil in that they practiced idolatry; and only the last two kings of Judah in this early period, Asa and Jehoshaphat, were morally upright (good kings are denoted by asterisk). God blessed the faithfulness of these two with long reigns (a total of sixty-six years). Amid all the evil and idolatry it is refreshing to read, "And Asa did what was right in the eyes of the Lord, as David his father had done" (15:11). He removed idols and presented offerings to the Lord. Of Jehoshaphat it was said, "He walked in all the way of Asa his father... doing what was right in the sight of the Lord" (22:43). Note, too, that the dates of some reigns overlap due to co-regencies in which two monarchs reigned together.

C.   THE REFORMS OF ELIJAH (17-19).

That there is a marked prophetic emphasis in the Books of Kings is obvious from the large amount of space devoted to the great prophets. Jehu ministered to Baasha (ch. 16) but the most dominant prophetic figure in I Kings is clearly Elijah.

1. *Elijah and the famine* (17). Wicked king Ahab and his infamous wife, Jezebel, provoked the Lord with their aggressive idolatry. Elijah responded by calling down a famine on the land. Elijah himself fled to the brook Cherith where God miraculously had ravens bring him food. In the same vein, Elijah performed miracles for the widow of Zarephath —supplying food and raising up her dead son.

2. *Elijah and the fight on Mt. Carmel* (18). King Ahab and Israel were worshiping the god Baal. Elijah boldly challenged the pagan prophets of Ahab to a test in order to prove that Jehovah and not Baal (whom they were worshiping) was the true God. On the top of Mt. Car-

mel God miraculously vindicated Himself and His prophet Elijah by consuming the sacrifices on the altar with fire. Then Elijah called to God for rain and the famine stopped when God sent abundant showers. Again God had spoken against idolatry through His prophet.

3. *Elijah and the flight from Jezebel* (19). Ahab told the wicked queen Jezebel what Elijah had done. She immediately informed the prophet that she was out to get him. Elijah responded by running for his life! It is an ironical picture to see the fearless man of God who called down both famine and fire from heaven now fleeing like a coward before human threats. While the prophet pouted and wished to die, God spoke to him gently by "a still small voice" and assured him that there were thousands besides himself in Israel who had not "bowed the knee to Baal." Elijah picked himself up and at God's command returned to anoint a young man named Jehu (not to be confused with the prophet) as the next king of Israel, for Ahab and Jezebel were soon to meet their doom.

D.   THE REIGN OF AHAB (20-22).

1. *Ben-hadad, his enemy* (20). Ahab reigned from Samaria, the capital city of Israel. Ben-hadad, the king of Syria, along with thirty-two other kings, besieged Samaria. But by the word of an unnamed prophet God spared Ahab from his enemies.

2. *Naboth, his envy* (21). Ahab coveted the vineyard of Naboth the Jezreelite, who would not relinquish his family inheritance at the king's demand. But Ahab's evil wife Jezebel plotted against Naboth to deprive him of his land. False witnesses testified that Naboth had cursed God; the people of the city then stoned him for his alleged sin. But God commanded Elijah to confront Ahab with his murderous deed and to pronounce the king's doom: "Thus says the Lord, 'Have you killed, and also taken possession? . . . In the place where dogs licked up the blood of Naboth shall dogs lick your own blood'" (v. 19). And of Jezebel, the prophet also predicted, "The dogs shall eat Jezebel by the wall of Jezreel" (v. 23, KJV). God's final epitaph on this wicked couple would read: "There was none who sold himself to do what was evil in the sight of the Lord like Ahab, whom Jezebel his wife incited" (v. 25).

3. *Jehoshaphat, his end* (22). After three years of war with Syria, Ahab convinced Jehoshaphat the king of Judah to join forces with him. But in what proved to be a fatal move, Ahab disguised himself as a common soldier and went into battle with his men. He was mortally wounded by a chance shot, and was returned to Samaria for burial. Ahab had been unwilling to heed the true prophet of the Lord, Micaiah, but listened rather to the lying prophets who told him only the good things he wanted to hear. Jehoshaphat, on the other hand, inquired of the true prophet

of God before joining Ahab in the battle in which the wicked king met his doom. The prophetic implication of the Books of Kings is clearly set forth here: the kingdom would prosper only if the king hearkened to the voice of God through His prophets.

How to explain some problem texts in Kings and Chronicles.

There are several apparent problems and contradictions in Kings and Chronicles that should be discussed.

The problem of the "lying spirits" from God (I Kings 22:22).

The Bible teaches that God is truth (Deut. 32:4) and that He cannot lie (Heb. 6:18). Further, God commands us not to lie (Exod. 20:16) and condemns those who do lie (Rev. 21:8). And yet the Lord is pictured in I Kings 22 as enlisting a lying spirit to entice Ahab to go to his doom. The record says, "Now therefore behold, the Lord has put a lying spirit in the mouth of all these your prophets" (v. 23).

In response to this problem several factors should be considered. First, this is a vision, that is, a divine and dramatic picture of God's authority spelled out in regal imagery. Second, the picture presents God in final authority over all things, good and evil. Even the evil spirits submit to His sovereign control. Third, in the Bible (cf. Job 1) God alone is in ultimate control over all creatures, whereas in a pagan dualism there is an ultimate evil force controlling the realm of evil. Fourth, the Bible often speaks of God "hardening" men's hearts (cf. Rom. 9:18) or sending men "strong delusion" (II Thess. 2:11). However, on closer examination of the text one discovers that it is the rebellious man who first hardens his heart (e.g., Pharaoh) and only those who "did not believe the truth but had pleasure in unrighteousness" are sent strong delusion (II Thess. 2:12). In brief, God is neither *commanding* nor *commending* lying in I Kings 22. Rather God is *permitting* and *using* lying to accomplish His own sovereign purposes of judgment. There is an important difference between God's perfect will and His permissive will; the first includes only good, whereas the latter includes evil. For God and God alone can use evil to bring about a greater good. Even the wrath of man shall praise God. The truth being conveyed in this passage may be summarized this way: "God for judicial purposes suffered Ahab to be fatally deceived" (John W. Haley, *Alleged Discrepancies of the Bible,* p. 98).

Some chronological problems.

If one were to add up the reigns of all the kings from the death of Solomon (931 B.C.) to the Babylonian captivity (586 B.C.), he would discover that they equal considerably more than 345 years (931 minus 586 = 345). Two reasons for this have been demonstrated by recent chronologists (see E. R. Thiele, *The Mysterious Numbers of the Hebrew Kings*, 1951, and D. J. Wiseman, *Chronicles of the Chaldean Kings in the British Museum*, 1956). The first reason can be readily observed on the chart of the kings (p. 134): many of the kings had co-regencies with their predecessors. This overlapping accounts for many of the "extra" years. The second reason for the apparent discrepancies is more complex. Simply put, it has to do with whether a king counted a fraction of a year at the beginning of his reign as a full year or waited until the first full year of his reign to begin counting. This practice varied from time to time in both kingdoms. For example, if a king began to reign on New Year's Eve and reigned a year and two days, his reign could have been counted as three years. If we take these two factors into consideration, the major problems of chronology can be explained away.

STUDY QUESTIONS

1. Why did Jeroboam lead a revolt against Rehoboam?
2. How did the morality of Israel's early kings compare with that of Judah's early kings?
3. What were the evils of king Ahab and his wife Jezebel, and what steps did God take to deal with them?
4. How can you explain the fact that God enlisted a lying spirit to entice Ahab to his doom?
5. Why do we get more than 345 years when we add the years of each king that reigned from 931 B.C. to 586 B.C.?

THE KINGS OF ISRAEL AND JUDAH

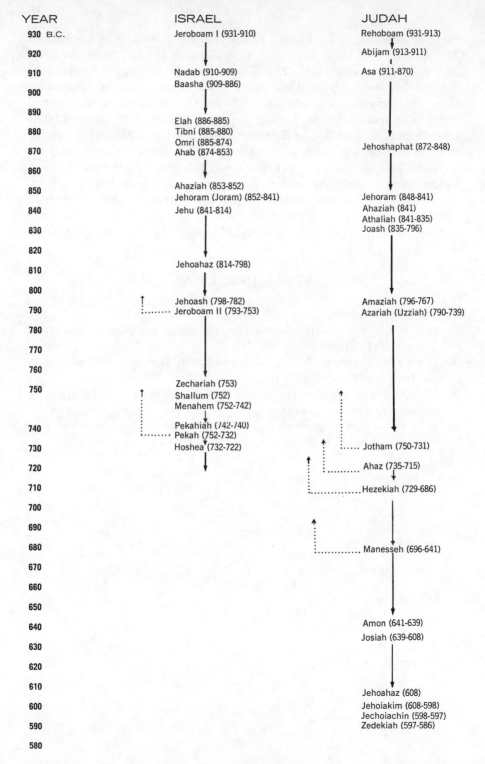

YEAR	ISRAEL	JUDAH
930 B.C.	Jeroboam I (931-910)	Rehoboam (931-913)
920		Abijam (913-911)
910	Nadab (910-909)	Asa (911-870)
900	Baasha (909-886)	
890		
880	Elah (886-885)	
	Tibni (885-880)	
870	Omri (885-874)	Jehoshaphat (872-848)
	Ahab (874-853)	
860		
850	Ahaziah (853-852)	
	Jehoram (Joram) (852-841)	Jehoram (848-841)
840	Jehu (841-814)	Ahaziah (841)
		Athaliah (841-835)
830		Joash (835-796)
820		
810	Jehoahaz (814-798)	
800		
	Jehoash (798-782)	Amaziah (796-767)
790	Jeroboam II (793-753)	Azariah (Uzziah) (790-739)
780		
770		
760		
750	Zechariah (753)	
	Shallum (752)	
	Menahem (752-742)	
740	Pekahiah (742-740)	
	Pekah (752-732)	Jotham (750-731)
730	Hoshea (732-722)	
720		Ahaz (735-715)
710		Hezekiah (729-686)
700		
690		
680		Manesseh (696-641)
670		
660		
650		
640		Amon (641-639)
630		Josiah (639-608)
620		
610		
600		Jehoahaz (608)
		Jehoiakim (608-598)
590		Jechoiachin (598-597)
		Zedekiah (597-586)
580		

17

The Deterioration of the Northern Tribes

II KINGS 1-17

The moral *decadence* that began with Solomon led to the *division* of the kingdom between Jeroboam and Rehoboam which in turn led to the continued *deterioration* of the monarchies of Israel and Judah and eventually to their final *deportation*. The prophets were raised up by God to warn of final doom but their voices went unheeded.

The dominant prophetic figure of I Kings was *Elijah*. In the first part of II Kings the central prophetic personage is Elijah's successor, *Elisha*.

I. The deterioration of Israel and Judah (1-17).

There were two phases in the deterioration of the monarchies: the *decline* of the monarchies and their *deportation* to a foreign land. The first half of II Kings treats the initial decline of both Israel and Judah (1-16) and the final deportation of the northern tribes of Israel (17).

A. THE DECLINE OF ISRAEL AND JUDAH (1-16).

Israel's Kings	Prophets	Judah's Kings
9) Ahaziah 853-852	Elijah	5) Jehoram 848 841
10) Jehoram (Joram) 852-841	Obadiah	6) Ahaziah 841
11) *Jehu* 841-814	Elisha	7) Athaliah 841-835
12) Jehoahaz 814-798	Joel	8) *Joash 835-796
13) Jehoash 798-782		9) *Amaziah 796-767
14) Jeroboam II 793-753	Jonah	10) *Azariah (Uzziah)
15) Zechariah 753	Amos	790-739
16) *Shallum* 752		
17) Menahem 752-742	Hosea	
(captivity of 2½ Tribes)		
18) *Pekahiah* 742-740		
19) *Pekah* 752-732		11) *Jotham 750-731
20) *Hoshea* 732-722	Isaiah and	12) Ahaz 735-715
	Micah	

This list of the later kings of Israel contains five more dynasties, those of Jehu, Shallum, Pekahiah, Pekah, and Hoshea. This makes a total of twenty kings and nine dynasties in the northern tribes of Israel. The south (Judah) also had twenty kings but all were of one dynasty, the house of David. Again, all of Israel's kings were wicked in God's eyes, while Judah produced several more good kings during this period including Joash, Amaziah, Azariah (Uzziah), and Jotham. Note also that the earliest of the writing prophets (Obadiah and Joel) begin this period and the greatest writing prophet (Isaiah) ends it.

Ahaziah's reign was short-lived. He was unsuccessful in regaining Moab and failed in a joint naval expedition with Jehoshaphat. Elijah warned the king of his death (1) because Ahaziah sought information and aid from Baalzebub, the god of Ekron. By way of contrast, Elijah himself did not taste death but was translated into heaven, passing on the mantle of his ministry with double blessing to Elisha (2).

Jehoram's (or, Joram's) reign was longer but no more successful than his brother's. He attacked Moab in a joint venture with Jehoshaphat, king of Judah, but returned without victory and was later fatally wounded. He died without an heir to his throne. During his reign the miraculous ministry of Elisha, with its double divine blessing, came into prominence. Elisha predicted Moab's defeat at Israel's hands (3), miraculously filled the vessels of a poor prophet's wife (4a), raised up the Shunammite woman's dead son (4b), and rendered the poisoned pottage harmless (4c). The leper Naaman was miraculously cured at Elisha's command to dip seven times in the Jordan River (5). The prophet made the axe-head swim in the water (6), predicted the fate of Samaria that made possible the deliverance of four lepers (7), and pronounced the recovery of Ben-hadad, king of Syria (8).

Jehoram, king of Judah, was the contemporary of Ahaziah, Jehoram (Joram), and Jehu. He was an evil king, for "he walked in the way of the kings of Israel, as the house of Ahab had done, for the daughter of Ahab was his wife" (8:18).

Ahaziah, Jehoram's son, had a short but wicked reign in Jerusalem. He too had made the fatal mistake of walking in the ways of the house of Ahab (8:27). (See the end of this chapter for a chronological problem regarding his age when he began to reign.)

Jehu reigned twenty-eight years (9-10). He gained fame both as the slayer of the evil Jezebel and as the king of Israel mentioned in the famous Black Obelisk as a vassal of the Syrian king Hazael, the son of Ben-hadad. "But Jehu was not careful to walk in the law of the Lord . . . ; he did not turn from the sins of Jeroboam, which made Israel to sin" (10:31).

Athaliah, the only woman in the regal list, was the "Bloody Mary" of the Old Testament. Her reign of terror was relatively short (six years) but she almost succeeded in eliminating the bloodline of the Messiah. She killed all the heirs to the Davidic throne except baby Joash, whom Jehosheba, sister of Ahaziah, nursed and hid from the wicked queen (11).

Joash was crowned king at the tender age of seven after Athaliah was "slain with the sword at the king's house." Joash reigned forty long and righteous years during the time of the ministry of Joel the prophet. Joash is responsible for repairing the Temple of God and restoring the worship of the Lord in Jerusalem (12).

Jehoahaz and *Jehoash,* kings of Israel, were contemporaries of Joash. But, like their father Jehu, "they did that which was evil in the sight of the Lord" and "the anger of the Lord was kindled against them." God "gave them continually into the hands of Hazael and Ben-hadad, kings of Syria" (13).

Amaziah reigned over Judah for twenty-nine years. In general he was a good king but the altars erected to idols in the high places were not destroyed during his reign. Amaziah's venturesome attitude toward king Jehoash of Israel led to a shameful defeat in which the Temple was ransacked and the vessels of the Lord were carried away to Samaria (14a).

Jeroboam II was the most prosperous of all the northern kings (14b). His borders were enlarged during the ministries of Jonah the prophet and Amos the prophetic herdsman from the Judean hills of the south. But his forty-one-year reign was far from righteous. For "he departed not from all the sins of Jeroboam the son of Nebat" (14:24, KJV). Already in his day the growing Assyrian power of the north was encroaching on its surrounding neighbors, including Israel. The reluctance of Jonah to go to Nineveh (Jon. 4) is understandable in view of the bitter animosity with which the violent Assyrians were viewed by their fearful neighbors.

Azariah (Uzziah) of Judah behaved much like his father Amaziah, doing that which was right in the eyes of the Lord. However, he also failed to tear down the high places and the people still offered burned incense to idols there (15a). According to II Chronicles 26, because of his presumptuous attempt to act as a priest, he contracted leprosy.

Zechariah and *Shallum* of the north had very short reigns of six months and one month respectively. The latter ascended the throne in a bloody coup and began a new dynasty which ended with his son ten years later. Shallum is an example of the truth that those who live by the sword die by the sword, for he was himself the victim of assassination at the hands of his own son, Menahem (15b).

Menahem was king of Israel when the aggression of the Assyrian Tiglath-Pileser (or Pul) reached its apex. Not only was Israel forced to pay tribute to Assyria but the tribes east of the Jordan (Reuben, Gad, and half of the tribe of Manasseh) were taken captive during his reign (c. 745 B.C.; cf. I Chron. 5:26) (15c).

Pekahiah and *Pekah* were the next kings of Israel. The former had a short two-year reign cut off by assassination at the hands of his captain, Pekah, who then reigned for twenty years. However, Tiglath-Pileser of Assyria made further inroads into Israel by carrying off into captivity all the tribe of Naphtali (15:29). It goes without saying that both Pekahiah and Pekah were wicked kings in God's eyes (15d). It was during this whole tumultuous time from Zechariah to Pekah that the prophet Hosea was dramatically depicting God's love for His people Israel.

Jotham ascended the throne of Judah at the death of Uzziah (the year Isaiah had his famous vision of the "Lord high and lifted up" as recorded in Isaiah 6). Jotham continued the anti-Assyrian policy of his father for some twenty years (15e).

Ahaz, king of Judah, is famous for erecting the sundial which God later used to indicate to Hezekiah that He was granting him fifteen more years of life. Ahaz was an idol worshiper, burning his son as a sacrifice. His pro-Assyrian policy resulted in the removal to Assyria of some of the treasured adornments of the Temple of God (16).

B. THE DEPORTATION OF ISRAEL TO ASSYRIA (17).

Hoshea, the last king of the northern tribes, was taken into captivity by the Assyrians in 722 B.C. during the reign of Ahaz in the south. In the ninth year of Hoshea, Shalmaneser took Samaria and carried the remaining tribes into Assyrian captivity. By leaving some Israelites behind and transplanting some other captives from foreign lands, the Assyrians set the stage for the development, through intermarriage, of a people known as Samaritans, who were later despised by the Jews (cf. Jon. 4:9). The final pronouncement on Israel by the prophetic writer of Kings reads: "And they served idols, of which the Lord had said to them, 'You shall not do this.' Yet the LORD warned Israel and Judah by every prophet and every seer, saying, 'Turn from your evil ways! . . . But they would not listen, but were stubborn, as their fathers had been, who did not believe in the LORD their God. . . . Therefore the LORD was very angry with Israel, and removed them out of his sight; none was left but the tribe of Judah only" (17:12-18).

Thus ends the record of the deterioration of the northern tribes of Israel. Under twenty kings and nine dynasties her history was characterized by idolatry and immorality. Moses had warned of this over seven hundred years before (Deut. 28). All the prophets after Moses had exhorted the kings to turn from their sins, and finally the judgment of God fell. Israel was taken into captivity and only Judah remained. The strong prophetic ministry of men like Isaiah and Jeremiah saved the south from a similar fate for nearly one hundred and fifty years.

How to explain some numerical discrepancies in Kings and Chronicles.

There are several numerical contradictions in Kings and Chronicles. For example, II Kings 8:26 reads that Ahaziah was *twenty-two* years old when he began to reign, whereas II Chronicles 22:2 says he was forty-two years old when he began to reign. This is an obvious contradiction, for both passages clearly intend the same man (mentioning the same father and the same son) and there is no co-regency involved.

This contradiction can be explained as an error made by an early scribe in copying the numbers. Hebrew numbers are distinguished from each other by small notation marks, some of which were undoubtedly blurred or missing in older manuscripts. The reading in Chronicles ("forty-two") must be in error, since Ahaziah's father died at about forty years of age (v. 17). Hence, Ahaziah could not have begun reigning at age forty-two, for he would then have been two years older than his father. It is noteworthy that the Jewish scribes who copied this error down through the centuries were undoubtedly aware it was wrong. Nevertheless, out of reverence for the text before them and in faithfulness to their task to copy accurately what was in the manuscript, they did not tamper with the text. Hence, this scribal error is in itself a rather amazing testimony to the extraordinary faithfulness with which the text of Scripture was transmitted.

In this connection, we should be reminded that it is not the *copies* of Scripture that are without error. Only of the *originals* is it claimed that they are inspired of God and without error. Furthermore, in the case of this error and many others like it, no major or even minor doctrinal teaching of the Bible is adversely affected. And in this particular case we are assured by the context and the parallel passage that the correct reading is "twenty-two years old."

Another example of contradiction in the copies of Scripture is found in I Kings 4:26, which states that Solomon had "forty thousand stalls of horses," whereas II Chronicles 9:25 gives the number as "four thousand stalls." Here again the context would indicate that "forty thousand" is the correct reading (II Chron. 9:26). Dropping a zero is an easy error to make in copying a series of numbers.

STUDY QUESTIONS

1. What were the results of the moral decadence of the Jewish nation that began with Solomon?
2. What were some of the miracles performed by the successor of Elijah?
3. What is the origin of the people known as Samaritans?
4. Why should not the numerical discrepancies between Kings and Chronicles destroy the belief that the Bible is without error?
5. How do numerical discrepancies show that our copies of Scripture were very faithfully copied?

18

The Deportation of the Southern Tribes

II KINGS 18-25

The last half of II Kings treats only the southern kingdom, Judah, which remained behind after the captivity of the northern tribes. It is divided into two sections: the *decline* of the Davidic dynasty (18-23b) and the *deportation* of the Davidic dynasty (23c-25). The following outline lists the kings who reigned and the prophets who ministered before the Babylonian exile.

I. The deportation of Judah (18-25).

A. THE DECLINE OF THE DAVIDIC DYNASTY (18-23b).

Prophets	Kings of Judah
Isaiah and Micah	13) *Hezekiah 715-686
	14) Manasseh 695-642
Nahum	15) Amon 642-640
Zephaniah and Habakkuk	16) *Josiah 640-609
Jeremiah	17) Jehoahaz, 609
	18) Jehoiakim 609-597
	19) Jehoiachin 597
	20) Zedekiah 597-586

Judah like Israel had twenty kings in all. Israel, however, had nine dynasties compared to the one dynasty of David in Judah. And whereas all the kings of Israel were wicked, some eight kings of Judah "did that which was right in the eyes of the Lord." The two good kings of this later period are Hezekiah and Josiah.

Hezekiah (18-20) began his twenty-nine-year reign by destroying the brazen serpent which Moses had made in the wilderness because Judah had misused it as an object of worship (18:4). His reforms were

The inscriptions on this clay hexagonal prism tell of the conquests of Sennacherib, king of Assyria. Sennacherib boasts of defeating forty-six strong cities of Judah and beseiging Jerusalem. The Oriental Institute

A section of the inscription reads as follows (courtesy, Inter-Varsity Fellowship):

ḫa - za - qi - a - ú	mat ia - ú - da - a - a
Hezekiah	the Judaean

kima iṣṣuri	qu - up - ḫi	ki - rib	al	ur - sa - li - im - mu
like a	caged bird	within	the city of	Jerusalem

al	sami - ti - šú	e - sir - šú
his	capital city	I shut up

comprehensive; they included breaking down idols and destroying the high places. His reformation was followed by the celebration of the Passover (II Chron. 30), to which even the remnant of the northern tribes was invited.

Early in his reign Hezekiah engaged in a successful aggressive war against the Philistines. Hezekiah's greatest task, however, was to throw off the yoke of tribute with which the Assyrians had saddled Judah during the time of his predecessors. He fortified the nation, building up the military defense, and expanded trade. Hezekiah also built the famous Siloam Tunnel discovered by archaeologists. This tunnel provided fresh water within the wall of Jerusalem, an essential service when a city is under siege. Through these preparations and by divine intervention (19:35), Judah was able to ward off the attack of the Assyrian kings which culminated in Sennacherib's massive but unsuccessful attempt to take Jerusalem. The famous Taylor Prism of the British Museum (a polygonal clay cylinder on which Assyrian kings recorded their campaigns) vividly depicts the story of the siege of Jerusalem. It quotes Sennacherib as saying, "As for Hezekiah, the Jew, who did not submit to me. . . I shut up Jerusalem, his royal city." The Scriptures tell us that God spared Hezekiah because of his spiritual preparation.

But Hezekiah was not without flaw. He manifested foolish pride in showing the Babylonian embassy all his many treasures. For this he was sternly rebuked by the prophet Isaiah (Isa. 39). All in all, however, Hezekiah's spiritual and political leadership preserved the nation against a formidable foe who only a few years before had taken the northern kingdom of Israel into captivity.

Manasseh reigned longer than any other king of Israel or Judah— some fifty-five years. He ascended the throne at the early age of twelve and yielded to the idolatrous influence of the party of Ahaz. He became in his day a fanatical idolater, restoring the high places and the worship of Baal. Paganism was rife, wizards filled the land, and even a statue of Moloch, an idol on which parents offered their children as burnt offerings, was erected. Manasseh's wickedness did not go unrebuked by the prophets, but he retaliated against them with fierce persecution. According to Josephus, the Jewish historian, daily executions of prophets occurred (*Antiquities* X.3.1).

But divine retribution was not far behind Manasseh's sins. Foreign powers such as Moab and Ammon began to revolt (cf. Jer. 47-49; Zeph. 2) and the Assyrians inflicted a severe blow by taking Manasseh captive to Babylon (II Chron. 33:11). The Assyrian inscription of Esarhaddon states proudly, "I commanded the kings of Syria and those across the sea— Ballu, king of Tyre; Manasseh, king of Judah. . . . I gave them their orders." Manasseh was eventually brought to repentance before God and restored to his throne. He removed the altars and statues erected to idols and restored the worship of the LORD. However, the people continued to worship in the high places. Manasseh died and was buried in the garden of Uzzah (21a).

Amon, the son of Manasseh, ascended the throne when he was twenty-two years old and reigned for two short but sinful years. He followed his father's earlier idolatrous practices, but Amon never made repentance. He fell victim to a court conspiracy. The people avenged his death on the conspirators, buried him with Manasseh in the garden tomb of Uzzah, and installed Amon's eight-year-old son, Josiah, on the throne (21b).

Josiah had a long and godly reign of thirty-one years. He clearly possessed the faith of his great-grandfather, Hezekiah. At age sixteen Josiah initiated a great revival. He overthrew idolatrous worship, purged Judah and Jerusalem of the high places, executed the pagan prophets of Bethel and cleansed and restored the Temple of God.

In the course of his temple duties a pious priest, Hilkiah, discovered the Law of Moses. After consulting with a prophet of God, Josiah held a public reading of the Word of God and concluded with a solemn vow to the Lord. And in the steps of his great-grandfather, Josiah's spiritual renewal was followed by the celebration of the Passover. Young Josiah is a vivid example of the positive results that can be generated by a dedicated young man who places himself and his people under the powerful influence of the Word of God. Not long afterward, Josiah was mortally wounded in a battle with Egypt. Josiah is mentioned in the prophecies of both Jeremiah and Zephaniah. He was the last of the godly kings of Judah. He died only four years before the captivity of Daniel and the other young noblemen of Judah (22-23a).

Jehoahaz was the third son of Josiah. He reigned for only three months after the death of his father. At the age of twenty-three he was raised to the throne in preference to his elder brothers. He found the land full of trouble and idolatry and is himself described as an evildoer and oppressor. He was removed from the throne by Pharaoh-Neco, who put Jehoiakim in his place. Jehoahaz was taken first to Syria and then to Egypt where he died (23b).

B. THE DEPORTATION OF THE DAVIDIC DYNASTY TO BABYLON (23c-25).

Jehoiakim reigned for eleven years. He was the brother of Jehoahaz and second son of Josiah. He was taken captive along with Daniel in the fourth year of his reign (605 B.C.) by Nebuchadnezzar. For some reason he was apparently not taken to Babylon but made a vassal and allowed to stay on his throne (II Kings 24:1; Jer. 25:1). In the fifth year of his reign he cut up a written prophecy of Jeremiah and burned it in fire. God therefore commanded Jeremiah to rewrite the prophecy and to add a dreadful denunciation of the king (Jer. 36). Under the influence of the Egyptian party, Jehoiakim was convinced to withdraw his tribute to Babylon. Subsequently, sweeping bands of Chaldeans, Syrians and Moabites cruelly harassed his country. Eventually Jehoiakim, as predicted, came to a violent end. He was an idolatrous, vicious, and cruel man whose impious belligerence to the Word of God sealed his doom. He received a dishonorable burial. Jehoiakim's character was an appropriate symbol of the final deterioration of the nation of Judah when the Babylonian captivity came as a divine judgment for its many years of immorality and idolatry (23c).

Jehoiachin, the son of Jehoiakim, was also called Coniah (Jer. 22). He reigned only three months and ten days. He undoubtedly opposed the Babylonian interest, for Nebuchadnezzar besieged Jerusalem only three months after he was crowned, as Jeremiah had predicted (Jer. 22:18-20). Jehoiachin was carried captive to Babylon along with ten thousand others. Mattaniah, the only surviving son of Josiah, was placed on the throne by Nebuchadnezzar. He changed his name to Zedekiah. Jehoiachin was placed in prison in Babylon until the death of Nebuchadnezzar. The next king, Evil-merodach, released Jehoiachin, gave him a seat at his dinner table, and provided him an allowance. Modern archaeology in the area of Babylon has given remarkable corroboration of Jehoiachin's captivity (see *Biblical Archaeology* V, 4, Dec., 1942) (24).

Zedekiah (Mattaniah), the remaining son of Josiah, was only a puppet of Babylon (25). In the early part of his eleven-year reign, Zedekiah took the lead in building affinity with surrounding nations. This culminated in a political alliance with Egypt which Babylon interpreted as a declaration of enmity. The eastern power was prompted to invade the land of Judah. The besieger's fire was aided by a severe famine. Jerusalem was leveled, the Temple was burned (see Lamentations), and Zedekiah was blinded and carried off to Babylon. Thus, precisely as it was predicted, Zedekiah *saw* the invading king (Jer. 34:3), his eyes were put out (II Kings 25:7), and then he was taken to Babylon, a land he would *"not see"* (Ezek. 12:13). This fateful date is 586 B.C.

Jeremiah the prophet had predicted a seventy-year period of captivity in Babylon. This was fulfilled in two senses. First, there was a *political captivity* in which the city of Jerusalem lay in ruins for seventy years as a result of the political domination of Babylon. This lasted from 605 B.C. to 536 B.C., when a remnant returned to Judah under Zerubbabel (Ezra 1). Second, there was the *religious captivity* which dates from the destruction of the Temple in 586 B.C. to the completion of its rebuilding in 516 B.C. It has been observed that Israel and Judah had forsaken the command of God to give one year in seven to God by allowing the land to rest from agricultural use (Lev. 25). Now approximately 490 years after the establishment of the kingdom God took His seventy years of sabbatical all at once in the seventy years of the Babylonian captivity (see II Chron. 36:21).

STUDY QUESTIONS

1. How was Hezekiah able to ward off the attack of the Assyrian kings?
2. Compare and contrast the reigns of Hezekiah and Manasseh.
3. Which of the later kings of Judah suppressed idolatry?
4. Describe the revival under Josiah.
5. In what two senses was Jeremiah's prediction of a seventy-year captivity fulfilled?

19

The Preparation for the Temple

I CHRONICLES

I and II Samuel and I and II Kings provide the *political* history of Israel and Judah; Chronicles presents the *religious* history of Judah. The former books were written from a moral and prophetic point of view; the latter were penned from a spiritual and priestly point of view. Samuel and Kings center around the history of the people and their kings, but Chronicles revolves around the history of the Temple. I Chronicles covers roughly the same ground as I and II Samuel while II Chronicles treats the same period as I and II Kings.

WHO WROTE CHRONICLES?

Tradition points to Ezra the priest as the author of Chronicles and the external evidence is not incompatible with this ancient attribution.

(1) First of all the books appear to have been written between 450 and 425 B.C. The historical narration ends with Cyrus' proclamation that the Jews could return to their land (539 B.C.). I Chronicles 3:17-24 lists six names after Zerubbabel. It is possible that these names could represent six successive generations after Zerubbabel covering about a hundred years (i.e., from 525 B.C. to 425 B.C.). It has also been suggested that these names do not represent successive generations, but are merely the sons of Zerubbabel (Young, *Introduction to the Old Testament,* p. 383). It is not an uncommon practice in Chronicles to list all the sons born to one set of parents.

(2) Chronicles is definitely written from a priestly point of view. It is a history of the Temple, stressing the priests and the theocratic line of David in Judah. There are only tangential references to Israel in the north, and there is a general absence of references to prophetic figures (in contrast to Kings).

(3) The Books of Chronicles bear continuity in substance, viewpoint, and style with the Books of Ezra-Nehemiah, which were probably written by Ezra (see ch. 21). Notice that II Chronicles ends with the same verse that begins Ezra and that both books speak from the same priestly vantage point in their Temple-centered history.

(4) The Jewish Talmud ascribes the Books of Chronicles to Ezra (*Baba Bathra* 15a). This tradition is plausible in view of the fact that Ezra, as the great leader of the repatriated remnant, was a likely chronicler of the history of these returned peoples.

(5) According to II Maccabees 2:13 governor Nehemiah "founded a library and collected books about the kings and prophets and the writings of David. . . ." If this is true, then it is reasonable to assume that his close associate Ezra would have had access to this collection in compiling Chronicles. Note that the author of Chronicles refers to many written sources of his work: (a) the Chronicles of Samuel the Seer, (b) the Chronicles of Nathan the Seer, (c) the Chronicles of Gad the Seer (I Chron. 29:29), (d) the History of Nathan the Prophet (II Chron. 9:29), (e) the Chronicles of Shemaiah the Prophet and Iddo (II Chron. 12:15), (f) the Story of the Prophet Iddo (II Chron. 13:22), (g) the Book of the Kings of Judah and Israel (II Chron. 16:11), (h) the Chronicles of Jehu, recorded in the Book of the Kings of Israel (II Chron. 20:34), (i) the Chronicles of the Kings of Israel (II Chron. 33:18).

WHEN WAS CHRONICLES WRITTEN?

In line with the above analysis Chronicles was probably completed by 450-425 B.C. This would be contemporaneous with Nehemiah the governor, Malachi the prophet, and Artaxerxes I of Persia. In terms of Jewish history, Chronicles was completed in the post-exilic period after the return from the Babylonian captivity.

TO WHOM WERE THE BOOKS OF CHRONICLES WRITTEN?

The Books of Chronicles were composed for the returned remnant who, after the seventy-year captivity, were rebuilding Jerusalem under the spiritual leadership of Ezra, the architectural guidance of Nehemiah, and the moral exhortations of Malachi. Zerubbabel had led the first remnant back some years before, but the completion of the repatriation process was left to Ezra, Nehemiah, and Malachi. It was to this returned remnant of Judah who were rebuilding Jerusalem that Chronicles was written.

WHERE WERE THEY LOCATED?

The action centers in and around Jerusalem in the southern kingdom of Judah. Only citizens of the southern kingdom returned from Babylonian captivity. The northern tribes of Israel had gone into Assyrian captivity never to return. I and II Chronicles record the history of the Temple at Jerusalem for the remnant who returned there to restore their religious and national heritage.

WHY WERE THE BOOKS OF CHRONICLES WRITTEN?

The purposes of Chronicles are divided, like the other Old Testament books, into three groups.

The historical purpose.

The chief historical theme in Chronicles is the record of priestly worship from Saul to Cyrus. It is a priestly religious history of Judah.

The doctrinal purpose.

Three teachings stand out in the record of Chronicles: (1) the faithfulness of God in keeping His promises to His people, (2) the powerfulness of the Word of God, and (3) the essential and central role of worship in the life of God's people.

The Christological purpose.

There are two dominant Christological themes in Chronicles, one more explicit than the other: first, there is the obvious recording of the Davidic kings and their descendants through whom the Messiah was to come (cf. Matt. 1 and Luke 3).

Second, there is the less explicit but highly important testimony concerning the typological significance of the Temple as it points to Jesus Christ, who said, "I tell you, something greater than the temple is here" (Matt. 12:6). John added of the New Jerusalem, "And I saw no temple in the city, for its temple is the Lord God the Almighty and the Lamb" (Rev. 21:22).

WHAT IS CHRONICLES ABOUT?

In Hebrew, the title of these books is "words of days" or "journals." In the Greek Old Testament (Septuagint or LXX) the word is "paralipomenon," meaning "omission." They are so named because they contain material not included in Kings. The English word *Chronicles* was derived from Jerome's translation of the Hebrew title.

Although I Chronicles begins with a brief genealogy of the primitive and patriarchal periods (1-10), the primary concern is obviously with the Davidic dynasty and the origin of the Temple (11-29).

I. The predecessors of the Temple (1-10).

The primeval period (1a).
The patriarchal period (1b-2a).
The national period (2b-10).

The primary purpose of these ten chapters is to provide the genealogy of David, whose spiritual desire and preparation made possible
the later construction of the Temple. It is the record of men from Adam
to David who preceded the construction of the Temple in Jerusalem.

II. The preparations for the Temple (11-29).

Two areas of preparation for the Temple are described in this
section of the book: David's preparations for the construction and the
operation of the Temple.

A. DAVID'S PREPARATIONS FOR THE CONSTRUCTION OF THE TEMPLE (11-22).

First David captured from the Jebusites the *city* (Jerusalem) in
which the Temple was to be built (11). Then the citizens of all Israel
were united around David so that there would be *centrality* and unity
of worship in one Temple (12). Following this David brought up the ark
of the *covenant* for the Temple from Kiriath-jearim to Jerusalem (13-15).
David further prepared for the worship of Israel by setting up the temple
choir and by composing psalms for the occasion (16; cf. Ps. 105). Eventually God laid on David's heart a *concern* to build the Temple (17) and
even allowed David to *conquer* lands which had the materials needed to
build the Temple (18). As a result of David's spiritual concerns for the
Temple of God, the Lord *consolidated* and strengthened the kingdom
of David over foreign powers (19-20). But in consequence of David's
sin, God commanded him to *construct* an altar on the future site of the
Temple, the threshing floor of Ornan the Jebusite (21; cf. II Chron.
3:2). Finally, before David's death, he *charged* Solomon his son with
the responsibility of building the Temple. David had received the plans
and had gathered the materials for the Temple, but being a man of
bloodshed (21:8), he was not allowed to build the Temple. Solomon,
the man of peace, was commissioned to construct the Temple (22).

B. DAVID'S PREPARATIONS FOR THE OPERATION OF THE TEMPLE (23-29).

David's preparations for the Temple were complete and comprehensive. He not only prepared for the physical construction of the Temple
(11-22) but also for the ongoing operation of the Temple (23-29). The
Levites were commissioned for the *menial* tasks of the Temple, in order
to keep it in continual service (23). The *priests* were given the *ministerial*
functions such as offering the sacrifices (24). *Singers* were appointed for
the *musical* functions in God's house (25) and *porters* or gatekeepers were
assigned the *material* tasks (26). *Soldiers* were commissioned with a
military function, course by course throughout the year (27a). David
also set up *stewards* to serve the municipal needs (27b) and *counselors*
to handle the *mental* problems of the kingdom (27c). Finally, David

gathered *princes* of the people, charging them with the *managerial* responsibilities (28) and the *people* with the *monetary* or financial obligations of providing the wherewithall for building God's house (29).

I Chronicles ends with the death of David and the extension and glorification of the kingdom under Solomon by the hand of God. II Chronicles will describe how God through Solomon fulfilled David's desire and completed his preparations to build the Temple in Jerusalem. The preparation for the Temple was the work of David, but it did not come to fruition until his son Solomon constructed this magnificent building.

STUDY QUESTIONS

1. Compare and contrast the main thrust of Samuel and Kings with that of Chronicles.
2. What evidence can be given to show that Ezra wrote Chronicles?
3. What are the historical, doctrinal, and Christological purposes of Chronicles?
4. How did David prepare for the construction of the Temple?
5. Why was David not allowed to build the Temple himself?
6. What preparation did David make for the operation of the Temple?

20

The Destruction of the Temple

II CHRONICLES

Although the first part of this book deals with the construction of Solomon's Temple (1-9), the bulk of II Chronicles treats the deterioration and final destruction of this glorious religious edifice (10-36). The narration parallels that of I and II Kings, except that it deals almost exclusively with the southern kings of Judah and is penned from a priestly rather than a prophetic perspective. II Chronicles divides naturally into two parts: the *majesty* of the Temple under Solomon and the *history* of the Temple after Solomon. In the first section we have the *construction* of the Temple and in the second part the *deterioration, renewal,* and finally *destruction* of the Temple.

I. The majesty of the Temple under Solomon (1-9).

The period of Solomon was the golden age of Israel. The kingdom was not only united but it was extended to its furthest boundaries. The Queen of Sheba had come "from the end of the earth" to see its glory and then exclaimed that "the half had not been told." The first nine chapters treat the construction of Solomon's magnificent Temple in Jerusalem, as David his father had made elaborate preparations for it. They begin with the *confirmation* of the covenant of David by an appearance of God to Solomon (1). Then Solomon *commissioned* the workmen to begin working on the timber, precious metals, and jewels to be used in the Temple (2). The temple was *constructed* on Mt. Moriah, built after the pattern of the Tabernacle of Moses (3-4). The work was *completed* in the eleventh year of Solomon's reign (960 B.C.) (5), and was immediately *consecrated* to God in one of the great prayers of Scripture: "But will God dwell indeed with man on the earth? Behold, heaven and the highest heaven cannot contain thee; how much less this house which I have built!" (6). When Solomon was finished with his dedicatory prayer, God revealed His acceptance of the Temple and proclaimed that He had *chosen* this Temple as the place of sacrifice, the center of religion for His people (7). Solomon's kingdom, like his father's, was consolidated and strengthened over foreign countries as a result of his building the House of God (8). This section of II Chronicles ends with the *commendation* of the Queen of Sheba. We read that "when the queen of Sheba had seen . . . his burnt offerings which he offered at the house of the Lord, there was no more spirit in her" (9).

II. The history of the Temple after Solomon (10-36).

The history of the Temple after Solomon is not so glorious. In fact, it is a most inglorious record of deprivation, renewal, and final destruction.

A. THE APOSTASY OF THE NORTHERN KINGDOM FROM THE TEMPLE (10-11).

The rebellion of Jeroboam and the northern ten tribes from the divinely chosen Davidic kingdom divided Solomon's once glorious kingdom after his death. Not only did the northern tribes of Israel bring about a *political* separation of the nation (10), but they also instituted a *religious* apostasy by setting up their own worship centers in Dan and Bethel (11). Nothing more of significance is recorded of the apostate northern tribes in II Chronicles.

B. THE LOYALTY OF THE SOUTHERN KINGDOM TO THE TEMPLE (12-36).

Here in the later part of II Chronicles the history of the kings of Judah is recorded insofar as it relates to the Temple that Solomon had built for God. God had chosen Jerusalem and the Temple there as a place of worship, and it was the center of spiritual strength for the nation. Not all the southern kings were loyal to the Temple, but all were related to it in one way or another.

Rehoboam was not a righteous king in general but he did find *refuge* in the Temple: "And when he humbled himself the wrath of the LORD turned from him, so as not to make a complete destruction" (12). *Abijam* had a short and generally evil reign but is credited with withstanding a *rebellion* against the Temple-centered kingdom of Judah by Jeroboam and the northern tribes of Israel (13).

King *Asa* sponsored a vast Temple-*renewal* program. He destroyed the foreign altars and idols in Judah (14). He renewed the altar of the LORD and offered sacrifices to the LORD in the Temple (15). Asa, however, was rebuked by the LORD for using treasures out of the Temple to make a political alliance with Ben-hadad, king of Syria, rather than trusting in the LORD for guidance in foreign policy (16).

Jehoshaphat gained *rest* from his enemies because he honored the worship of God in the Temple and taught the Word of God to the people. Jehoshaphat destroyed the high places of idolatry in Judah and sent his princes out to teach the Law of Moses in the cities of Judah (17). He also sought the Lord through the prophet of God before going into battle (18) and instituted a system of judges and justice in Jerusalem (19). When the men of Judah were in the midst of battle with the Ammonites, "Jehoshaphat stood in the assembly of Judah and Jerusalem, in the house of the LORD" and committed the cause to God (20).

Jehoram brought the *retribution* of God on his head by walking in the ways of the wicked northern king, Ahab, even to the point of marrying his daughter. Under Jehoram the people of Judah were led astray into both harlotry and idolatry in the high places of the land. God smote Jehoram with an incurable and fatal disease of the intestine (21).

Ahaziah was no less evil than his father. Both he and his mother, queen Athaliah, *rejected* the worship of God and walked in the idolatrous ways of king Ahab. The chronicler wrote: "But it was ordained by God that the downfall of Ahaziah should come about" (22).

Under *Joash* both the Temple and the worship of the Lord were *restored*. He reinstituted the offerings to the Lord (23) and engaged in extensive *repairs* on the Temple, for it had been broken up by the wicked sons of Athaliah. The restoration was financed by reinstituting the tithe as described in the law of Moses (24).

Amaziah's loyalty was not complete. He worshiped the gods of Edom and was unsuccessful in defending the *riches* of the Temple against the attack of Jehoash, king of Israel. Amaziah was slain in a conspiracy against him (25).

Uzziah (Azariah) was a good and strong king. "But when he was strong he grew proud, to his destruction. For he was false to the LORD his God, and entered the temple of the LORD to burn incense." The law forbade anyone but a priest to do this. And the Lord smote Uzziah with leprosy until the day of his death. Thus Uzziah received *recompense* from God for his sin in the Temple (26).

Jotham had *respect* for the Temple. He rebuilt the gate of the Temple and "became mighty, because he ordered his ways before the LORD his God" (27).

Ahaz was a wicked king. He made molten images and *rifled* the Temple of God. "Ahaz gathered together the vessels of the house of God and cut in pieces the vessels of the house of God . . . ; and he made himself altars in every corner of Jerusalem" (28).

Hezekiah effected the *reopening* of the Temple. In the first year of his reign he reopened the doors of the Temple and repaired them. The sanctuary was cleansed and sacrifices were offered once again on the altars. "Thus the service of the house of the LORD was restored" (29). The Passover was celebrated once again by both Judah and representatives from Israel in the north (30). Moreover, the tithes and offerings of Moses' law were reinstituted and observed by the people. In fact, "every work that he undertook in the service of the house of God and in accordance with the law and the commandments, seeking his God, he did with all his heart, and prospered" (31). Despite the fact that the northern tribes fell to the Assyrian invasion, "the LORD saved Hezekiah and the inhabitants of Jerusalem from the hand of Sennacherib king of Assyria and from the hand of all his enemies" (32).

Manasseh and his son *Amon* brought foreign *religions* into the Temple of God. Manasseh built again the high places of Baal which Hezekiah had broken down. "And he built altars in the house of the LORD, of which the LORD had said, 'In Jerusalem shall my name be for ever.' " Amon "did what was evil in the sight of the LORD, as Manasseh his father had done"; his servants conspired against him and killed him in his house (33).

Josiah began early in his reign to seek God. His earnest spiritual concern resulted in a great *revival* of Temple-centered worship. His iconoclastic activity was extensive. In the process of repairing the Temple, the Law of Moses was discovered and read, producing a revival (34). Like Hezekiah, Josiah observed the Passover with full Levitical ritual. "No passover like it had been kept in Israel since the days of Samuel the prophet." Thousands of sacrifices were offered in accordance with the law of Moses (35).

Jehoahaz, Jehoiakim, and *Jehoiachin* were successive witnesses to the final *ravaging* of Solomon's magnificent Temple. During Jehoahaz' reign, Neco, king of Egypt, took some of the Temple treasures by taxation (36a). Later, during Jehoiakim's reign, Nebuchadnezzar carried off the vessels from the House of God to Babylon (36b). On a return trip, during Jehoiachin's reign, Nebuchadnezzar carried away to Babylon the "goodly vessels" from the Temple in Jerusalem (36c).

Zedekiah, the last king of Judah, witnessed the final blow, the *ruination* of the Temple (36d). Everything remaining in the Temple was pilfered and the Temple was burned. Thus began the seventy years of religious captivity during which time the Temple lay in ruins (586-516 B.C.).

How can some differences between Kings and Chronicles be explained?

It has already been pointed out that Chronicles was written by Ezra the priest from a religious point of view, while Kings was compiled by Jeremiah from a prophetic perspective. The following comparison illustrates the differences of emphasis. Chronicles stresses more strongly the divine activity in national events as well as their religious implications.

SAMUEL-KINGS: HISTORICAL EVENT	CHRONICLES: THEOLOGICAL EXPLANATION OR IMPLICATION
1. I Samuel 12—Isaac's son called Jacob ("supplanter").	I Chronicles 1—Isaac's son called Israel ("prince with God").
2. I Samuel 31—Philistines killed Saul.	I Chronicles 10—God killed Saul.
3. II Samuel 2:8—Saul's son called Ish-bosheth ("man of shame").	I Chronicles 8:33—He is called Esh-baal ("man of Baal").
4. II Samuel 6—One chapter on the recovery of the ark.	I Chronicles 13, 15, 16—Three chapters.
5. II Samuel 6—Uzziah was smitten.	I Chronicles 15—*Why* he was smitten.
6. II Samuel 7—David told he cannot build the Temple.	I Chronicles—*Why* David could not build the Temple.
7. II Samuel 11-12—David's great sin.	Chronicles—No reference to it. God forgives and forgets.
8. II Samuel 24—David sinned in numbering Israel.	I Chronicles 21—Satan instigated David to number Israel.
9. I Kings 11:1—Solomon's sin.	II Chronicles 9—No reference to it.

STUDY QUESTIONS

1. Into what main sections does II Chronicles divide? What is the main point of each?
2. In what way was the Temple the House of God? Could a house made by man really contain God?
3. Divide the kings of Judah into two lists, one list showing those who were basically good, the second those who were basically evil.

21

The Reconstruction of the Temple

EZRA

No historical book offers a running narrative of the seventy-year captivity though Jeremiah, Ezekiel, and Daniel do write of the exile and only of the exile. At the completion of the seventy years in Babylon, God faithfully fulfilled His promise to bring His people back into their land as Jeremiah had predicted (Jer. 25). Ezra records the return of the remnant to their homeland and their struggles to rebuild the Temple and re-establish the nation's religion.

WHO WROTE THE BOOK OF EZRA-NEHEMIAH?

The Books of Ezra and Nehemiah were one book in the original Hebrew Old Testament (see ch. 3). They are really Ezra-Nehemiah. Hence, the authorship and purpose of these books will be considered together. The evidence would indicate that Ezra the priest, leader of the second group of the remnant returning from Babylon, is the author of Ezra-Nehemiah.

(1) First of all much of the Book of Ezra (7:28–9:15) is written in the first person (from the "I" point of view). Nehemiah 1:1–7:5 represents itself as quoting "the words of Nehemiah" in the first person. This no doubt was compiled by Ezra from Nehemiah's firsthand account.

(2) Ezra 1:1 connects the book with the last verse of II Chronicles, which was also written by Ezra (see ch. 19).

(3) Both Chronicles and Ezra-Nehemiah are the work of a priestly chronicler, manifesting a priestly interest, emphasis, and point of view.

(4) The vividness and continuity of the accounts favor an eyewitness author like Ezra.

(5) Ezra had access to the library of Nehemiah (cf. II Macc. 2:13) from which he could have compiled material for the events of which he was not an eyewitness.

(6) The Jewish Babylonian Talmud (*Baba Bathra* 15a) attributes this book to Ezra.

WHEN WAS EZRA-NEHEMIAH WRITTEN?

The book is post-exilic, written during the days of Ezra and Nehemiah his contemporary (Neh. 8:2) and during the reigns of Artaxerxes I (Longimanus) (464-423 B.C.) and Darius II (the Persian) (Neh. 12:22).* Since Ezra arrived in Jerusalem after 458 B.C. in "the

The Tripylon Stairway to Darius' palace at Persepolis. The Oriental Institute

seventh year of the king" (Ezra 7:8) and Nehemiah in 445 B.C. in "the twentieth year" of Artaxerxes (Neh. 1:1) and Nehemiah returned to Babylon "in the thirty-second year" (Neh. 13:6), which would be 433 B.C., the book must have been finally compiled after 433 B.C.

Some have objected to this date on the basis that Nehemiah 12:11 mentions Jaddua, whom Josephus (*Antiquities* XI. viii. 4) says was priest during the time of Alexander the Great (c. 330 B.C.). There are two possible solutions. (1) Jaddua's name in Nehemiah 12:11 may be a later addition included in order to complete the genealogical listing. (2) If Jaddua was young, say twenty, in 400 B.C., then he would have been ninety in 330 B.C. This is not an impossible age span.

---

*Darius II, the Persian (423-404 B.C.) is not to be confused with Darius the Mede (Dan. 6) (539-525 B.C.) or with Darius I (Hytaspes) (521-486 B.C.).

Note also that the "Darius" mentioned in Nehemiah 12:22 was not the Darius of Alexander's day (c. 330 B.C.), but Darius II (423-404 B.C.). Likewise, the phrase "the days of Nehemiah" (Neh. 12:26) is not a reference to a long past event but an allusion by Ezra to the chief contemporaries of his day (the references to Joiakim, Ezra, and Zerubbabel in Neh. 12:26, 47 are of the same manner). We conclude, therefore, that there is no substantial reason to doubt the evidence that Ezra wrote the Books of Ezra and Nehemiah before 400 B.C.

To whom was Ezra-Nehemiah written?

Ezra-Nehemiah was composed for the remnant returning from the Babylonian captivity. Zerubbabel had returned with the original remnant of nearly fifty thousand who rebuilt the Temple by 516 B.C. Later (458 B.C.) Ezra returned with another two thousand people. It was to this latter group as they struggled to rebuild the city of Jerusalem and defend themselves against surrounding enemies that Ezra wrote these books.

Why was Ezra-Nehemiah written?

The purposes of these books fall into three categories.

The historical purpose.

The apparent historical aim of Ezra-Nehemiah is recording the rebuilding of the Temple and city of Jerusalem by the returned remnant of Babylonian exiles.

The doctrinal purpose.

One of the main teachings of these books is the faithfulness of God to His covenantal promises to Judah. God had promised them a land and religious center in Jerusalem as well as a return after seventy years of captivity (Jer. 25), and He kept His promises. Further, as in Chronicles, Ezra the priest reflects here the centrality of the Temple worship to the whole life of the Jewish nation. Another obvious lesson in these books is the power of prayer (Ezra 9; Neh. 9) and of the Word of God (Neh. 8).

The Christological purpose.

God had promised David to keep his line of descendants alive, for one of them, the Messiah, the Son of David, would one day reign on his throne in Jerusalem. Ezra-Nehemiah shows how God kept this hope alive by repatriating His people.

What is the Book of Ezra about?

Ezra's overall theme is the return of the Jews and the rebuilding of the Temple. The book divides into two sections: the earlier return under Zerubbabel (1-6) and the later return under Ezra (7-10). The first return resulted in the rebuilding of the Temple and the second return under Ezra initiated a reformation of the people.

I. The restoration of the nation's religious center (1-6).

At least the returned remnant wanted to put first things first. Building the House of God was their primary goal and duty. The hope of doing this was aroused by the proclamation of Cyrus.

A. THE REMNANT'S EMANCIPATION FROM BABYLON (1-2).

In the first year of his reign (539 B.C.) Cyrus king of Persia made a proclamation that allowed the Jews of the Babylonian captivity to return to their homeland. The tribes of Judah and Benjamin along with priests from the tribe of Levi began to make preparations to return to Jerusalem in accordance with the *decree of Cyrus* (1). Under the leadership of Zerubbabel the people packed to leave Babylon. With a detailed enumeration (49,690), Ezra records the *departure of the captives* for Jerusalem (2).

B. THE REMNANT'S OCCUPATION OF JERUSALEM (3-4).

Upon reaching Jerusalem the remnant manifested their *observation of the law* by building an altar, offering sacrifices, and keeping the feast of tabernacles (538 B.C.). The foundation for the Temple was laid soon after they became established in the land (535 B.C.). (3). *Opposition from their enemies* hampered their work, for these enemies convinced the king of Persia to stop the reconstruction (4).

C. THE REMNANT'S COMPLETION OF THE TEMPLE (5-6).

Under the powerful ministries of Haggai and Zechariah the prophets, the remnants were exhorted to overcome their opposition and complete the Temple. An *investigation into the work* by the king of Persia proved to be favorable to the Jewish cause and the work on the Temple commenced again (5). The decree for the building of the Temple was reissued and the *consummation of the work* occurred in 516 B.C. (6).

(There is an interval of some one hundred years between Ezra 6 and 7. It is during this period that the events recorded in the Book of Esther occur [486-464 B.C.].)

II. The reformation of the nation's religious life (7-10).

It is now some generations later and the spiritual tide in Israel is low. The return of Ezra the priest with a faithful remnant to revive the nation was God's answer to this lapse in faith.

A. THE DECLARATION OF ARTAXERXES (7).

Ezra, the scribe of the law, and some two thousand others whose hearts God had touched carried both written authority and gifts from the king to Jerusalem for the House of the Lord there. Ezra records the scene firsthand: "I took courage, for the hand of the LORD my God was upon me, and I gathered leading men from Israel to go with me" (v. 28).

B. THE REPATRIATION OF THE REMNANT (8).

More than 1750 men are numbered among those who returned with Ezra. Prayer and the providential protection of God brought them safely to the House of God in Jerusalem. There they offered their sacrifices to God in thanksgiving for His gracious hand upon them.

C. THE INTERCESSION OF EZRA (9).

Like Daniel 9 and Nehemiah 9 this chapter is one of the great intercessory prayers of the Bible. Ezra identifies with the sins of his people as he prays: "From the days of our fathers to this day we have been in great guilt. . . . O LORD the God of Israel, thou art just, for we are left a remnant that has escaped, as at this day. Behold, we are before thee in our guilt, for none can stand before thee because of this" (vv. 7, 15).

D. THE REFORMATION OF THE JEWS (10).

Following this great prayer of confession and intercession, a great revival took place. For "while Ezra prayed and made confession, weeping and casting himself down before the house of God, a very great assembly of men, women, and children, gathered to him out of Israel; for the people wept bitterly" (v. 1). The people made a covenant with God, reordered their lives to conform to God's law, and offered sacrifices for their sin.

A reading of the Book of Malachi reveals the nature of the social and moral abuses that were prevalent during this period (ch. 39). Cheating, stealing, foreign marriages, divorce, and violence were among the more notable sins. But when the people were exposed to the Word of God and when the resultant spirit of conviction of sin led to confession and intercession, there was a mighty revival. And this spiritual revival led, as others have down through history, to appropriate social reforms. Indeed, the Word of God and fervent prayer are the wellspring of effective social change.

STUDY QUESTIONS

1. What evidence is there that Ezra the priest is the author of Ezra-Nehemiah?

2. What difficulties are there in positing a late fifth century B.C. date for the compiling of Ezra-Nehemiah?

3. What were the three returns from captivity, their respective leaders and dates, and how many came in each return?
4. How did the remnant which returned under the leadership of Zerubbabel show their willingness to obey the law? How about the remnant which returned under Ezra?
5. How would you characterize the revival under Ezra?

22

The Reconstruction of the City

NEHEMIAH

Ezra and Nehemiah were contemporaries (Neh. 8:2, 9). Both were men of God but from different professional backgrounds. Ezra was a priest; Nehemiah was a layman, cupbearer to king Artaxerxes. Hence, Ezra's prime duty was religious and Nehemiah's occupation was civil or domestic. Each man was particularly prepared for the task to which he was called. Ezra, as priest and scribe of God's law, was an ideal man to lead the people back to a spiritual renewal based on God's law and centered around His Temple. Nehemiah's expertise in the king's court equipped him adequately for the political and physical reconstruction necessary for the remnant to survive. As a team of leaders, one spiritual and one social, these two men made a lasting impact on the post-exilic remnant. Indeed, throughout the Old Testament God was pleased to work powerfully through similar combinations of men who joined their separate vocations in a God-directed effort to bring about lasting social change. One need only think of such teams as Moses and Aaron, Hezekiah and Isaiah, and Zerubbabel and Zechariah to illustrate this point.

Nehemiah stresses the importance of dedicated laymen in the work of God. Several characteristics of Nehemiah are exemplary for laymen who desire to do God's work in a wholehearted and effective way.

Nehemiah had his heart in his work. When he heard of the deteriorated conditions of the city he said, "I sat down and wept, and mourned for days" (1:4).

Nehemiah was a man of prayer. Upon hearing of the situation of his people he immediately turned to God and "continued fasting and praying before the God of heaven" (1:4). And like Ezra, he offered one of the great prayers of confession and intercession in the Bible (ch. 9).

A section of Nehemiah's Wall excavated by Kathleen Kenyon. Levant Photo Service

Nehemiah sought firsthand information about the needs at hand. He was not content with secondhand information about the situation; rather, he requested leave and for several days made a personal survey on the scene (2:11f.).

Nehemiah engaged in self-denying labor. Without reward or fanfare he left his comfortable and secure job in the royal palace for a difficult sacrificial life in a ruined city (cf. 1:3 and 2:5).

Nehemiah was able to inspire others to work. Seeing the broken walls of the city he said to the people, "Come, let us build the walls of Jerusalem. . . . And they said, 'Let us rise up and build' " (2:17, 18). By personal involvement and inspiration he got the job done.

Nehemiah was not easily sidetracked from his work. Despite persistent attempts to lure him from the work, he replied firmly and resolutely, "I am doing a great work and I cannot come down. Why should the work stop while I leave it and come down to you?" (6:3).

Nehemiah was undismayed and undisturbed by opposition. His enemies mocked him from outside the walls and controversy arose within the walls (5), but Nehemiah committed the problems to God, took immediate action to rectify the situation, and the work continued uninterrupted (4:6, 9 and 5:6, 7).

Nehemiah was ready and willing to give the credit to God. Nehemiah engaged in no vain attempt to steal the glory. From the very beginning he confessed, "God had put into my heart" to restore Jerusalem. And when the job was complete Nehemiah still gave the credit to God for what was accomplished (7:5).

WHAT IS NEHEMIAH ABOUT?

Ezra relates the *restoration* of the nation's *Temple* and Nehemiah records the *reconstruction* of the nation's capital *city*. Together they provide an account of the religious and political activities of the remnant which had recently returned from the Babylonian captivity.

I. The rebuilding of the city (1-7).

Nehemiah was the cupbearer of King Artaxerxes of Persia (464-423 B.C.). When word came to him that the walls of Jerusalem were broken and the gates of the city burned he began to take action on behalf of the remnant. He began both prayer and preparation for personal involvement.

A. INTERCESSION FOR THE CITY (1).

As a man of God, the first expression of Nehemiah's concern was prayer. He cried out, "O LORD God . . . I now pray before thee day and night for the people of Israel thy servants, confessing the sins of the people of Israel, which we have sinned against thee" (vv. 5, 6). He pleaded that God remember His covenant with Israel to bless them if they repented of their sins (Deut. 30) and that God grant him favor in the sight of the king (1:11).

B. INVESTIGATION OF THE CITY (2).

Once God granted Nehemiah the permission of Artaxerxes to visit Jerusalem, Nehemiah immediately began his firsthand investigation of the situation. Having observed the broken-down and defenseless state of affairs in the city he proposed to the nobles and rulers that the walls and gates be rebuilt.

C. RECONSTRUCTION OF THE CITY (3).

Under the inspiration of Nehemiah, various groups rose up to repair the broken gates. Eliashib the high priest and his brethren led the way with the restoration of the "sheep" gate. Others followed until Jerusalem was completely restored and made secure.

D. OPPOSITION TO RESTORING THE CITY (4-5).

The work of God never lacks either external or internal opposition. The external opposition came from Sanballat, ruler of Samaria (4). First he mocked Nehemiah's work, saying, "If a fox goes up on it he will break down their stone wall" (v. 3). But Nehemiah absorbed the criticism and "built the wall; and all the wall was joined together to the half its height. For the people had a mind to work" (v. 6). Sanballat was angry at the progress and gathered other enemies of the surrounding territories against Jerusalem. But God brought to naught their evil intentions as Nehemiah set half of the people to work on construction and half on military watch (v. 6).

The internal opposition was no less difficult; it took the form of complaints about the need to mortgage property in order to meet the Persian tax burden (5). But once again employing prayer and decisive action Nehemiah, now appointed governor, relieved the burden and continued the work. Nehemiah led by example, refusing to draw even a governor's salary, thus demonstrating his sacrificial leadership (v. 18).

E. COMPLETION OF REBUILDING THE CITY (6-7).

Despite the devious intentions evident in his enemies' diversion tactics, Nehemiah was not detoured from his task. He refused four invitations from other rulers in the land with the reply, "I am doing a great work and I cannot come down. Why should the work stop while I leave it and come down to you?" (6:3). It was such resolute determina-tion that made possible this amazing achievement: "So the wall was finished . . . in fifty-two days" (6:15).

Not only did Nehemiah complete the physical rebuilding but, hav· ing discovered a genealogical record, he restored the people of Israel to the cities that had been their family inheritance. "So the priests, the Levites, the gatekeepers, the singers, some of the people, the temple servants, and all Israel, lived in their towns" (7:73).

II. The revival of the citizens (8-13).

Once the physical work was complete and the cities were repossessed in accordance with the genealogical record, the people requested of Ezra the priest that the Law of Moses be read to them. The ancient "Biblethon" that followed precipitated a great revival, which instigated renewed dedication and social reforms.

A. THE COMMANDMENTS READ TO THE PEOPLE (8).

For many days the people listened to the Scripture all morning long. The Levites made sure the people understood it, for it was read clearly and its sense or meaning was explained to them. The people wept when they heard God's Word, but Ezra and Nehemiah exhorted them to return to their homes and rejoice that they had heard and understood the Word of God. And in accordance with the law (Lev. 23), the people made booths to celebrate the feast of booths (tabernacles), a sort of autumn "camp meeting" that had not been properly celebrated since the days of Joshua. The Scripture reading continued for the whole week of the feast (8:18).

B. THE CONFESSION RENDERED BY THE PEOPLE (9).

The result of sincere and prolonged exposure to the Word of God was predictable—a revival swept the nation. The people assembled in sackcloth, and fasted. The Bible was read for one quarter of the day and the people confessed their sins and worshiped for a quarter of the day (v. 3). The Levites led in a prayer of confession which spanned Israel's history from the time of Abraham to their own day and which acknowledged the greatness and mercy of God in sparing His people. As a pattern for true worship this chapter should be seriously studied and earnestly followed. Several important elements of worship should be noted. First, it springs from the reading and teaching of the Word of God. Second, it is centered in a knowledge of the greatness, holiness, and mercifulness of God. Third, both confession and adoration of God are the natural consequences of reading the Word of God and meditating on His person and precepts.

C. THE COVENANT RENEWED WITH THE PEOPLE (10).

Another result of true revival is a renewal of one's obligations and vows to God. All the people made a firm written covenant with God to separate themselves from the evil people of the land and to walk in His commandments (vv. 28, 29). They promised, too, that their first fruits and tithes would be brought to God—this is another by-product of a proper relationship with God. The commitment of one's purse follows closely upon the commitment of one's person to God.

D. THE CITIES REPOSSESSED BY THE PEOPLE (11-12a).

As Joshua had done almost a millennium earlier, the people cast lots to see who (a tenth of the total population) would dwell in Jerusalem. The rest of the people then returned to their inheritance elsewhere in the land. The people blessed those who willingly responded to the allotment of God by staying in Jerusalem. Thus once again the chosen nation had resettled the Holy Land, awaiting the final fulfillment of messianic prophecy.

E. THE CITY OF JERUSALEM REDEDICATED BY THE PEOPLE (12b).

At the dedication ceremony for the walls of Jerusalem the Levites were assigned to lead the festivity with joy and thanksgiving. Complete with band and choir they fulfilled their task with gladness, and the people responded with tithes and offerings for the priests and Levites.

F. THE CIVIL REFORMS AMONG THE PEOPLE (13).

It was Ezra's Biblethon which had precipitated the revival and the covenant renewal. But the work of spiritual revival is never complete until it has social or civil consequences. The reforms that took place upon Nehemiah's return from his trip to Persia were sweeping social changes. The Temple was cleansed, the sabbath was enforced, and all foreign wives were put away as Moses had commanded.

STUDY QUESTIONS

1. In what ways were Ezra and Nehemiah especially equipped for their respective roles as leaders of God's people?
2. In what ways is Nehemiah an example of how to do God's work?
3. What were the various obstacles to building the city wall and how were they overcome?
4. Describe the causes and characteristics of the revival which followed the completion of the city.
5. Name the civil reforms brought about by the revival.

23

The Protection of the People

ESTHER

The Book of Esther fits chronologically between Ezra 6 and 7. It is an amazing story of God's providential protection of the Jews who did not return from the captivity. The *name* of God does not occur in the book but the *hand* of God is clearly manifested.

WHO WROTE THE BOOK OF ESTHER?

The Book of Esther appears to have been written by an unknown Persian Jew. The following factors must be considered in discussing the authorship of Esther.

Some have suggested Ezra or Nehemiah as the author. But the vocabulary and style of Esther do not bear a close resemblance to the vocabulary and style of Ezra-Nehemiah.

Others have suggested Mordecai since he is said to have kept records (9:20). But it has been pointed out that Esther 10:2, 3 seems to refer to his career as already finished (see Archer, *A Survey of Old Testament Introduction,* p. 403).

Whoever the author was, it may be reasonably concluded that (1) he was a Jew—note his pro-Jewish attitude and detailed knowledge of Jewish customs; and (2) he was a Persian Jew—he seems to be an on-the-scene witness of the events and apparently had access to Persian records (9:20).

In view of the scant evidence, it seems best to leave the author unnamed. The best guesses available seem to be Mordecai or, better, a younger contemporary of Mordecai who used Mordecai's records. The fact that Mordecai is referred to in the third person and is very highly regarded would support the position that someone else compiled the book.

WHEN WAS THE BOOK OF ESTHER WRITTEN?

The indications point to a date somewhere between 450 and 400 B.C. It must have been composed after the death of Xerxes (Ahasuerus) in 464 B.C., for his reign is referred to as having ended (10:2). Moreover, there are no indications from the linguistic style or historical references that the book comes from the Greek period (330 B.C. and after). Indeed, there is every indication that the book was written shortly after the events recorded. This points to a date between 450 and 400 B.C.

TO WHOM WAS THE BOOK OF ESTHER WRITTEN?

Unlike the other post-exilic books, Esther is addressed to the Jews who did not return. The book indicates that one should not impugn the piety of those who did not return, nor assume that God did not exercise His providential care for Jews who were not part of the remnant that returned. There were apparently many godly Jews, descendants of those of the captivity, who for legitimate reasons (domestic, social, economic, etc.) elected not to return to the land. It is these exiles about whom and for whom Esther was written.

WHY WAS THE BOOK OF ESTHER WRITTEN?

The aim of the author of Esther can be categorized into three areas.

The historical purpose.

The manifest intention of the Book of Esther is to give the historical foundation for the origin and celebration of the feast of Purim (see Esther 7).

The doctrinal purpose.

The primary doctrinal lesson concerns the providential care of God for His own. A subsidiary but important theme is the truth stated later in Luke 14:11: "Every one who exalts himself will be humbled, and he who humbles himself will be exalted."

The Christological purpose.

Esther shows that God has not forgotten the Jews who did not return. Predictions of a second return (e.g., Isa. 11:11), which has in fact been in the process of fulfillment since before 1947 (when the modern state of Israel was re-established), indicated that indeed the nation was to be reborn some day in the future. According to Revelation 7 and 14 there will be in Palestine in the end time thousands from every tribe.

Esther, whose name means "star," is a beautiful picture of Christ. Both put themselves in the place of death for their people but received the scepter of the King's approval (5:1f.).

WHAT IS THE BOOK OF ESTHER ABOUT?

The main theme is the providential protection of God for His people, even those who did not return from exile. The grave danger that faced them at the hands of evil Haman (1-4) was triumphantly overcome by the great deliverance wrought through Esther (5-10). The result was the institution of the feast of Purim.

I. The grave danger to the Jews (1-4).

Haman was the Adolf Eichmann of the Old Testament. His master plot to annihilate the Persian Jews was conceived in envy and executed with evil ingenuity. But the prayerful and providential activity of some pious Jews thwarted their enemy and delivered their people.

A. THE VICES OF AHASUERUS (1).

The Persian king Ahasuerus (Xerxes) was scarcely a paragon of virtue. One night with drinks flowing freely he demanded that queen Vashti sacrifice her modesty and dignity before his court. The flat refusal of the queen threw the king and his court into consternation. Fearing that the queen's action might lead to insubordination by women throughout the kingdom, Ahasuerus deposed Vashti and sought another to replace her.

B. THE VIRTUES OF ESTHER (2).

Mordecai, a gatekeeper for the king, viewed this as an opportunity to recommend his cousin Esther for the beauty pageant at which the king would pick the new queen. Esther was not only physically beautiful, she was also morally pure. Esther found favor in the eyes of the king above all the other women. This favor enabled Esther to inform the king about how Mordecai had successfully warded off an assassination plot against him.

C. THE VILIFICATION OF THE JEWS (3).

Haman, the captain of the king's princes, hated the Jews and sought to destroy all of them. By alleging that the Jews did not keep the laws of the king, he managed to acquire the king's agreement to a plan to destroy them. Men, women, and children were to be slain simultaneously on the same day (December 13) throughout the whole kingdom.

D. THE VISION OF MORDECAI (4).

But when Esther's cousin Mordecai heard of the proclamation, he immediately consulted with Esther and her maidens. They made the situation a matter of urgent fasting and prayer. The plan was proposed for Esther to make an unscheduled visit before the king to make an appeal for her people. At the suggestion of Mordecai, Esther bravely concluded that she had been called by God to her high position in the kingdom for such an hour as this. In an act of unparalleled courage she volunteered to go before the king without an invitation, even if it meant she would perish (v. 16).

II. The great deliverance of the Jews (5-10).

It becomes obvious at this point in the story that God has not forsaken His people. His merciful hand is in evident operation, for Esther's plea to the king is received with favor. His plot foiled, Haman is hanged on his own gallows and the Persian Jews are spared from annihilation.

A. THE VENTURE OF ESTHER (5).

Employing great tact and caution, Esther did not blurt out her request to the king. Apparently working on the premise that the quickest way to a man's heart is through his stomach, she invited him to a banquet. During the banquet the king volunteered to grant her anything up to half of the kingdom, but her only request was that he attend another banquet.

B. THE VENGEANCE OF HAMAN (6-7).

Haman, bristling with vengeance, constructed gallows seventy-five feet high on which to hang Mordecai. Meanwhile the king happened to read in the royal records how Mordecai had saved him from an assassination plot. To show his appreciation to Mordecai, the king honored him by following the unwitting advice of Haman: he dressed Mordecai in rich apparel and paraded him through the streets on a royal horse (6).

Meanwhile Esther prepared her final banquet. The king again offered her any request up to half of his kingdom. Esther petitioned that her people be spared and that their adversary be judged. At the king's command, Haman was hanged on the very gallows which he had prepared for Mordecai (7).

C. THE VINDICATION OF THE JEWS (8).

The king issued a proclamation against killing the Jews and sealed it with his own ring. On March 23 the king's scribes wrote up the new proclamation. Out of the palace at Shushan the king's emissaries carried the message on swift horses to all corners of the empire. And as a result of the obvious hand of God upon the Jews many non-Jews became Jewish proselytes (v. 17).

D. THE VICTORY OF THE JEWS (9-10).

On December 13, the very day the Jews were originally supposed to be destroyed, their enemies were destroyed. Haman and his sons were hanged and the next two days, December 14 and 15, were set aside as national Jewish holidays. This was called the feast of Purim (from the word *Pur,* meaning "lots"—Haman had cast lots to determine the day on which to destroy the Jews) (9).

Mordecai the Jew, Esther's cousin, was exalted next to the king and he acquired great favor for his people. Esther's mission had succeeded: the Jews' enemies were squelched and the Jewish seed was preserved. God had protected His people.

HOW CAN WE EXPLAIN THE ABSENCE OF THE NAME OF GOD IN ESTHER?

It has always been a bit embarrassing to the claim of divine inspiration for the Book of Esther to acknowledge that a book God inspired does not have the name of God in it. This embarrassment no doubt had something to do with the creation of the apocryphal "Additions to the Book of Esther," which mentions the name of God in the very first verse and in many verses thereafter.

Several suggestions have been offered in an effort to explain the absence of God's name in Esther.

(1) Some have suggested that because the Persian Jews were not directly associated with the theocracy, God's name was not associated with them. But this seems unlikely; God's name was associated with the exiles in Daniel and it is promised even to Gentiles who trust Him (Isa. 60-61).

(2) There is no doubt some basis for the fear of using God's name in a document written in a foreign country—the name might be profaned or the story changed by the simple substitution of a pagan god's name.

(3) It is also plausible that the book was compiled from the Persian royal records (9:20; 10:2); surely the name of the Jewish God would not be found in the Persian records.

(4) It should be pointed out, however, that although the *name* of God is absent, yet God Himself is everywhere present in the book. (a) The providence of God is clearly evident (4:14). (b) Prayer is offered to God (4:16). (c) A religious festival is instituted (9:31). (d) Many people of the land become proselytes to the Jewish religion (8:17).

(5) Finally, it seems more than accidental that at four crucial junctures in the book (1:20; 5:4; 5:13; 7:7) the name of God is found in acrostic form in Hebrew (see William Scroggie, *Unfolding Drama of Redemption,* Vol. 1, p. 470).

With or without the name of God, the Book of Esther is a prime example of the power and protection of God in keeping His people. One of the great miracles of history has been the preservation of the Jewish people despite worldwide anti-Semitic activity. God said to Abraham, "I will bless them that bless thee, and him that curseth thee will I curse: and in thee shall all the families of the earth be blessed" (Gen. 12:3, ASV).

STUDY QUESTIONS

1. What is the main theme of the Book of Esther?
2. Why was Mordecai honored and how did the king choose the particular honor with which to honor him (see Esther 6)?
3. How does the feast of Purim relate to the Book of Esther?
4. What explanations can be given for the fact that God's name does not appear in the Book of Esther?
5. In what events of the Book of Esther is the activity of God evident?

PART FOUR

The Books of Poetry:

The Aspiration for Christ

24

Introduction to the Books of Poetry

The books from Genesis to Nehemiah span the whole history of the Old Testament. All of the Poetical and Prophetical books fit somewhere into the history represented in the record from Genesis to Nehemiah. The following chart illustrates this point.

The place of poetry in the Old Testament.

The Old Testament is divided into four sections. These four sections relate to God's chosen people as follows:

Legal literature—moral life of the people.

Historical literature—national life of the people.

Poetical literature—spiritual life of the people.

Prophetical literature—future messianic life of the people.

In the first five books of the Old Testament Moses laid down the *ethical* code which governed the conduct of the theocratic nation. The historical books from Joshua to Nehemiah depict the *political* life in view of these moral norms. Meanwhile, the poetical books reflect the *spiritual* experiences of the people. These religious experiences comprise some of the greatest treasures of the Old Testament and even of world literature. The New Testament, our Lord, and the Christian church down through the ages are fundamentally indebted to this spiritual literature of the Hebrews for its expression of worship as well as for its wisdom.

The periods of poetry in the Old Testament.

Hebrew poets expressed their experiences throughout the whole of the history of their nation. There were, however, three primary periods of poetic literature:

BIBLICAL
BOOKSHELF

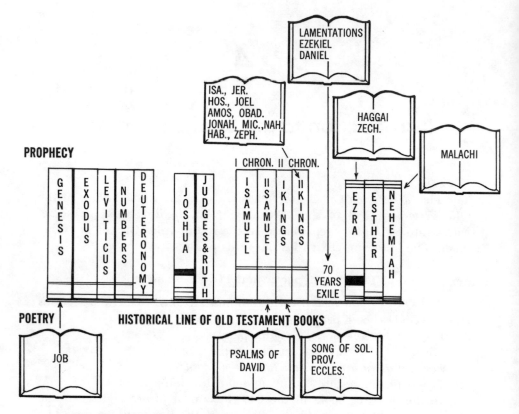

Patriarchal period—Job (c. 2000 B.C.)
Davidic period—Psalms (c. 1000 B.C.)
Solomonic period—Song of Solomon—a young man's love
                   Proverbs—a middle-aged man's wisdom
                   Ecclesiastes—an old man's sorrow (c. 950 B.C.)

Job is one of the great religious epics from antiquity. The story emanates from the patriarchal period, somewhere around the time of Abraham. Job, Proverbs, and Ecclesiastes are generally called Wisdom Literature because of their stress on principles of prudent living. The Song of Solomon is an ode to love, filled with beautiful and picturesque images of oriental romance. Psalms, of course, is the hymnal of the Hebrews. The psalms of praise are the backbone of Christian worship to this day. It is noteworthy that three of the great saints in the Old Testament are responsible for the majority of these poetical books: Moses (see ch. 25), David, and Solomon.

The presentation of Christ in poetry.

At this point it is well to stand back and view the overall Christocentric structure of the Old Testament once more (see ch. 2). The following fourfold outline has already been given:

Law—the foundation for Christ.

History—the preparation for Christ.

Poetry—the aspiration for Christ.

Prophecy—the expectation of Christ.

The books of the Law, it will be remembered, laid the foundation for Christ by choosing (Gen.), redeeming (Exod.), sanctifying (Lev.), guiding (Num.), and instructing (Deut.) the theocratic nation through whom Christ would come.

The books of History show the preparation made for Christ: the conquest of the Holy Land (Josh.), the overcoming of oppression (Judg.), stabilization under a king (I Sam.), an expansion (II Sam.) and development (I Kings) of the nation. And despite the fact that the nation was deported (II Kings) and its Temple destroyed (Chron.) the Temple was reconstructed (Ezra) and the nation rebuilt (Neh.) and even its exiled people were protected from annihilaton (Esther). In brief, the holy nation was returned to the Holy Land so that they could prepare for the Holy One (Christ), the Son of the Highest, who was to be born (cf. Luke 1:32, 35).

Whereas the *foundation* was laid for Christ in the Law and *preparation* was made for Christ in the books of History, the books of Poetry reveal the *aspiration* for Christ in the hearts of the people. They aspired to a life fulfilled in Christ in both an explicit and an implicit way, both consciously and unconsciously. The following list will serve as an overall guide to the Christ-centered aspirations of the poetical books:

Job—aspiration for *mediation* by Christ.

Psalms—aspiration for *communion* with Christ.

Proverbs—aspiration for *wisdom* in Christ.

Ecclesiastes—aspiration for ultimate *satisfaction.*

Song of Solomon—aspiration for *union* in love with Christ.

As the contents of each of these books are examined these key Christocentric themes will become more explicit. A brief description will suffice for the moment. *Job,* working out of the practical context of everyday suffering, cried out for a mediator, someone who could plead his cause with God and unfold the mystery of his calamities (cf. 9:33). At times Job seems to acknowledge outwardly that a coming Redeemer will provide this help for him (19:25, 26). At other times his aspiration for Christ seems more inward—his perplexity at his pain and his plea for both understanding and deliverance. The *Psalms* have many obvious messianic themes (e.g., 16, 22). But overall there is a desire for communion with God in the discouragements, despair, and triumphs of life. This intimate fellowship with God was provided by Christ (cf. I John 1:5-7), for whom the psalmists aspired. *Proverbs* manifests a desire for wisdom which the New Testament informs us is found in Christ alone (Col. 2:3). Solomon personified wisdom as the Creator of the world (Prov. 8; cf. John 1:2) and thus as the most valuable of all the treasures a man can seek. *Ecclesiastes* depicts a search for the *summum bonum* ("greatest good"), for ultimate satisfaction. The sage tried everything under the sun—including wine, worldliness, and women— but found that all is vanity. His diligent quest reveals a desire to find the happiness found only in the waters of life which Christ offers in order to satisfy completely and eternally (John 4). The *Song of Solomon* is a beautiful portrayal of the longing for marital union which so perfectly depicts the mystery of the union of believers with Christ (Eph. 5:31, 32). In sum, each poetical book is aspiring for what is only, ultimately, and fully provided in Jesus Christ.

Parallelism of poetry in the Old Testament.

The chief characteristic of Hebrew poetry is its parallel lines. Old Testament poetry has no rhyme; it is distinguished by its parallelisms. It is debatable whether there is even a strict meter in Hebrew poetry (see Archer, *A Survey of Old Testament Introduction,* p. 420), but there does seem to be a kind of cadence which moves in a series of accents. Some see in the Song of Solomon a lyrical meter with a 2 + 2 accent. Lamentations is supposed to have a dirge meter of 3 + 2 and Job and Proverbs an epic or didactic rhythm of 3 + 3. These differing accents, however, are not strictly observed and it is a mistake to use them as a mathematical formula to "correct" the Hebrew text as some critical scholars do.

Several kinds of parallelism exist in Hebrew poetry. Only the more important ones will be mentioned here.

A. *Synonymous parallelism*—both lines say substantially the same thing only in different words.

Job 38:7: "When the morning stars sang together,
        and all the sons of God shouted for joy."

Here the phrases "morning stars" and "sons of God"
phrases referring to angels (see Job 1:6; 2:1), and "sang" and
are parallel descriptions of their rejoicing when the creatio
world occurred.

B. *Antithetical parallelism*—the second line provides a contra
parallel to the truth of the first line.

Proverbs 14:34: "Righteousness exalts a nation,
　　　　　　　　but sin is a reproach to any people."

In this parallelism "sin" is contrasted to "righteousness" as the negative facet of the positive truth stated in the first line.

C. *Synthetical parallelism*—one line builds on the previous line.

Psalm 1:3: "He is like a tree planted by streams of water,
　　　　　　that yields its fruit in its season,
　　　　　　and its leaf does not wither.
　　　　　　In all that he does, he prospers."

In this verse the righteous man is one whose life is first "planted"
so that it "yields" and "does not wither" until it finally "prospers." The
progress from one line to the next is obvious.

D. *Exemplar parallelism*—one line metaphorically illustrates the
literal truth of the other.

Proverbs 27:17: "Iron sharpens iron,
　　　　　　　　and one man sharpens another."

The first line is a metaphorical illustration of the literal truth that
one man's wit (or personality) is sharpened by another's. An even more
vivid example is Proverbs 27:15:

"A continual dripping on a rainy day
and a contentious woman are alike."

The parallels may be in *couplets* (Distichs)—Psalm 36:5
　　　　　　　　　　　triplets (Tristichs)—Job 3:9
　　　　　　　　　　　quatrains (Tetrastichs)—Psalm 1:3.

The value of parallelism lies in its simplicity and translatability.
Biblical poetry can be translated into almost any language without con-
cern for rhyme or meter. The unsurpassed beauty of the Psalms in the
King James Version is proof of this.

STUDY QUESTIONS

1. How does each of the poetical books show man's aspiration for Christ?
2. Name four types of parallelism in Hebrew poetry and the characteristic of each.
3. Into what three primary time periods does the poetic literature fall?

25

The Aspiration for Mediation by Christ

JOB

The Book of Job is one of the most fascinating in the Bible. Its primary theme concerns the suffering of the righteous. The period from which the story comes is probably patriarchal, and the author is not known for sure.

WHO WROTE THE BOOK OF JOB?

The author of the Book of Job is unknown, but the time, nature, and theme of the book fit with the tradition that Moses compiled the book, possibly from records of the conversations made by Elihu (cf. 32:10-18). This conclusion can be drawn from the following:

(1) The story of Job comes from before Moses' day (see "When was Job written?" below).

(2) Some of the words and phrases of the book are characteristically Mosaic, such as "sons of God" (1:6; 21; cf. Gen. 6:2), "fire from God" (1:16; cf. Gen. 19:24), "but" (*ulam*), "hawk" (*netz*), "judge" (*pelil*), and "Almighty."

(3) An early talmudic tradition ascribes Job to Moses (*Baba Bathra* 14b).

(4) The theme of suffering fits with Moses' concern for the suffering Israelites in Egypt.

(5) The land of Uz where Job lived is adjacent to Midian where Moses spent forty years contemplating the sufferings of his people in Egypt.

(6) Moses possessed the authority and interest to commend this non-Hebrew story to Israel.

WHEN WAS JOB WRITTEN?

In a discussion of the time of Job a distinction must be made between two periods:

A. *When the events happened—Patriarchial period* (c. 2000 B.C.).

1. There is no reference to the Exodus or the law of Moses; the events of Job seem to have occurred in an earlier period.

2. The characteristic patriarchal name for God, "the Almighty," occurs more than thirty times (Job 5:17; 6:4, etc.; cf. Gen. 17:1; 28:3, etc.).

3. The family-clan type of social unit is pre-Mosaic (cf. Job 1).

4. The word for "money" (*Quesitah*) suggests a date at least as old as Joshua (Josh. 24:32), if not patriarchal (Gen. 33:19).

5. The comparative rarity of the name "Lord" (*Jehovah* or *Yahweh*, *JHVH*) and the common usage of "God" (*Elohim*) suggest a pre-Mosaic date (cf. Exod. 6:3).

6. The longevity of life seems to be patriarchal. Job lived 140 years after his family was already grown (42:16)—compare Abraham who lived 175 years (Gen. 25:7).

B. *When the record was composed—Mosaic period* (c. 1500 B.C.).

It has been suggested that while living in Midian, Moses compiled Job from records taken of the conversations in Uz by Elihu. If this is true, then Job was composed by Moses between 1485 and 1445 B.C.

There are others who argue for a date of composition during Solomon's time. The evidence adduced includes (1) the apparent leisure of the period to pursue philosophical matters; (2) the similarity of the praise of wisdom in Proverbs 8 and Job 28; (3) the devotion of the age of Solomon to the pondering of wisdom; (4) the wide knowledge of foreign countries (such as could be obtained in Solomon's day) demonstrated in the Book of Job. The difficulty with this view is the large time lag between the patriarchal events (c. 2000 B.C.) and the supposed time of composition in Solomon's day (950 B.C.).

Some even argue for a date as late as the seventh century on the basis of a similarity between the conditions of Job's and Manasseh's day or the book's linguistic similarities to Jeremiah's writings. However, there is no definitive evidence to support this view. A Mosaic date seems to be a better supposition.

TO WHOM WAS JOB WRITTEN?

If we adopt the suggestion that Moses wrote Job, it would seem natural to assume that Moses, while living for forty years in Midian, compiled the book for the suffering Israelites who were being oppressed by Pharaoh.

WHERE WERE THEY LOCATED?

Job lived in Uz (northern Arabia) and his friends came from nearby countries. At the time, the children of Israel were living in Egypt and Moses was exiled to Midian, just adjacent to Uz.

WHY WAS JOB WRITTEN?

There are three reasons for the Book of Job:

The historical purpose.

Originally Job may have been composed as part of an ancient "court" proceeding or perhaps of a dialogue of the wise men of the land. Possibly Moses saw in God's dealing with Job a parallel as to why God allowed His people Israel to suffer. In any event, Job was composed in the face of the suffering of God's people to provide them consolation: Job reminds God's people of His providential purposes in allowing their pain.

The doctrinal purpose.

The central teaching of Job appears to be that the presence of pain is allowed by the providence of God for the purifying and perfecting of His people.

The Christological purpose.

Christ is presented or anticipated in several ways in Job. Job cries out for a Mediator (9:33; 33:23); he acknowledges a Redeemer (19:25); and he knows he needs someone who can explain the mystery of "suffering by suffering, the just for the unjust" (I Peter 3:18) and thus bring victory over the plague of evil and pain (Rev. 21:4).

WHAT IS JOB ABOUT?

The Book of Job is about the suffering of the righteous. It asks: What is the significance of suffering? What is the purpose of pain? Why calamities? There are several answers suggested in the book:

1) Author—suffering is *pernicious* (Satan is behind it)—Chs. 1-2.

2) Job—suffering is a *puzzle* (Sadistic attitude)—Ch. 3, etc.

3) Friends—suffering is *penal* (Sin must be punished)—Chs. 4-31.

4) Elihu—suffering *purifies* (Shortcomings occasion pain)—Chs. 32-37.

5) God—suffering is *providentially* allowed (Sovereignty of God is the source)—Chs. 38-42.

There is some truth in all these views of suffering. But as applied specifically to Job's situation, the friends were wrong: Job was not suffering because of his sins. God allows Satan to inflict suffering, even on those who have not brought it on themselves by sinful living, so that in His providential purposes He can purify and perfect His people.

The Book of Job is divided into three sections: the *affliction* of Job (1-2), the *discussion* with Job (3-41), and the *restoration* of Job (42). Respectively, the three sections deal behind the scene, on the scene, and beyond the scene of Job's suffering. Without the first and the last sections, the middle section would be an insoluble mystery. As it is, when one understands the movement of Satan *behind* the scene in instigating suffering and the activity of God *beyond* the scene in rewarding the sufferer, then the suffering *on* the scene becomes both understandable and tolerable.

I.   The affliction of Job (1-2) behind the scene.

A.   THE AFFLICTED—JOB (1a).

Job was both rich and respected. He was righteous and religious. In brief, he was the candidate least likely to be inflicted with calamity brought on neither by himself or by a good God. Therein lay the apparent inscrutability of his situation.

B.   THE AFFLICTER—SATAN (1b).

The author of Job depicts the ultimate source of evil in the world as personal—Satan. The pernicious plans of this perverse plotter are the ultimate source of both sin and suffering. Satan is the accuser of God's people (cf. Rev. 12:10) and his sneering attack on Job prompted God's providential permission of Job's suffering.

C.   THE AFFLICTION (1c-2).

In three unheralded and lightning-like strokes Job lost his sons and daughters, his sheep and herds, and his servants. Finally he lost his health. Sitting on a pile of ashes, scraping the bleeding boils on his blistered body, Job managed to retain his faith and declare: "The Lord gave, and the Lord has taken away; blessed be the name of the Lord" (1:21). While Job later (ch. 3) curses the day he was born, it is important to remember that he never curses God.

II.   The discussion with Job (3-41) on the scene.

Job's comforters sat in silence for seven days in the face of his suffering before opening their mouths to offer suggestions regarding his somber situation. Job's first extended expression was a severe and understandable lamentation.

A.   THE LAMENTATION OF JOB (3).

Job broke the silence with a lamentation on his pathetic condition. He wished he had never been born or that he had died immediately after birth. He regretted that he had not been carried from the womb to the tomb in order that he might have been spared all his suffering.

B. THE ACCUSATION OF THE FRIENDS (4-31).

The friends had but one explanation (though with many variations) of Job's suffering—it was because of sin. Their logic was very simple:

> All suffering is the result of sin;
> Job is suffering;
> Therefore, Job has sinned.

Perhaps Job had sinned privately or even by proxy through his children, but surely he had committed some great sin or he would not be subject to this great calamity. Their accusation continued through a three-round debate in which each friend spoke with Job replying to each speech. The participants spoke in order of age. Their approach may be characterized as follows:

Eliphaz the *theologian* based his arguments on a vision of God's *greatness*.

Bildad the *traditionalist* based his view on time-honored concepts of *justice*.

Zophar the *moralist* based his opinions on a consensus of human *wisdom*.

Each round of debate gains in emotional intensity (more heat and less light!). Job takes almost twice as long to answer as they do to accuse. In each case, Job stoutly defends his innocence. In fact, it is in the process of defending his own righteousness that Job becomes self-righteous and deserving of the condemnation God gives him in the last chapter.

Round one (4-14).
Round two (15-21).
Round three (22-26).
Job's closing monologue (27-31).

In each round except the last, all participants speak. The friends each accuse, and Job replies to each. In the last round, the frustrated Zophar fails to speak, apparently because he sees no hope of convincing the stubborn Job. The indefatigable Job spins out five more chapters after his accusers have run out of steam.

C. THE INTERVENTION OF ELIHU (32-37).

A young observer (and possibly stenographer) of the debates intervened when the others had given up in their attempt to convince Job of his sin. His view was a bit more moderate than that of the friends and he serves as a herald for the voice of God in the last chapters. Elihu suggests that Job's pain is more for the purification of his life than for the punishment of his sins (33:19). Job's suffering is directed at the self-centered pride of life into which he has now clearly fallen in the process of defending himself (v. 17).

D. THE REVELATION OF THE LORD (38-41).

Elihu served as a kind of John the Baptist preparing the way of the Lord. Out of the whirlwind God spoke in sovereign majesty and power, asking Job questions that revealed his finitude and ignorance. "Where were you when I laid the foundation of the earth? Tell me, if you have understanding" (38:4). There follows a series of scientific questions which even modern science has not mastered. Job was left almost speechless.

III. The restoration of Job (42) beyond the scene.

A. THE REPENTANCE OF JOB (42a).

When Job did reply to God it was in repentance and in recognition of God's sovereignty. "I know that thou canst do all things. . . . therefore I despise myself, and repent in dust and ashes" (vv. 2, 6). One of the lessons of Job's life is that even the righteous man needs to repent. Even the "perfect" man has pride and needs to be purified and perfected.

B. THE REWARD OF GOD (42b).

In the end Job was lavishly rewarded: God gave Job twice as many worldly goods as he had had in the beginning. And God gave Job the same number of children as he had to begin with. Note also that he never really lost the ones who died, since they would be his in the resurrection (cf. 19:25, 26). So "the Lord blessed the latter days of Job more than his beginning. . ." (42:12). More precious than any other reward given to Job, however, was the reward of a crown of life, that is, the life crowned with the perfection that comes only through patient suffering (James 1:12). James wrote a most fitting conclusion for the Book of Job: "Behold, we call those happy [blessed] who are steadfast. You have heard of the steadfastness of Job, and you have seen the purpose [end] of the Lord, how the Lord is compassionate and merciful" (James 5:11).

STUDY QUESTIONS

1. What is the main theme of the Book of Job?
2. Briefly give evidence that the events of Job took place in the patriarchal period.
3. List the various answers to the problem of suffering suggested throughout the book. Which answers do not apply in Job's case?

4. How do the opening and closing sections of the book provide the key to understanding the book as a whole?
5. Which of Job's four friends gives the best answer to the problem of Job's suffering?

26

The Aspiration for Communion with Christ

PSALMS

Psalms is the largest book in the Old Testament and the one most often quoted in the New Testament. It was both the hymnal and the devotional guide for Jewish believers. Psalms is divided into five topical sections that correspond to the Torah or Five Books of Moses. Psalms was written by many men spanning all the periods of Old Testament history. But since David wrote more than anyone else, it is his name that is characteristically and rightly associated with the Book of Psalms. They are in a real sense the Psalms of David.

WHO WROTE THE PSALMS?

According to very ancient (but not part of the original inspired text) inscriptions at the beginning of many psalms, there were psalms written by Moses (90), Solomon (72, 127), Asaph, David's levitical choir director (50, 73-83), the sons of Korah (42-49, 85, 87), Heman the Ezrahite (88), and Ethan the Ezrahite (89). Both Heman and Ethan were renowned for their wisdom (I Kings 4:31). Some seventy-three psalms are ascribed to David.

The authorship of the five sections of Psalms can be roughly designated as follows:

Section 1:   1-41 ⎫
Section 2:   42-72 ⎬ Mostly David's

Section 3:   73-89 Various authors

Section 4:   90-106 ⎫
Section 5:   107-150 ⎬ Mostly anonymous

The evidence for the Davidic authorship of the Psalms at the beginning of the collection is substantial:

(1) David was a true poet as II Samuel 1:17f. indicates.

193

(2) David possessed the rich imagination needed for poetry (II Sam. 1:19f.).

(3) David was also a good musician (cf. I Sam. 16:18f.).

(4) David composed music used in the Temple that Solomon later built (I Chron. 6:31, 32).

(5) David was endued with the spirit of God (I Sam. 16:13).

(6) David was deeply religious in character and heart (II Sam. 7).

(7) Psalm 18 is also recorded in II Samuel 22, where it is directly attributed to David.

(8) David testified on his deathbed that God spoke through his mouth as the "sweet psalmist" of Israel (II Sam. 23:1, 2).

(9) Both our Lord and the New Testament writers verify that David wrote some psalms. The following psalms are quoted as written by David:
Psalm 2—in Acts 4:25
Psalm 32—in Romans 4:7
Psalm 95—in Hebrews 4:7
Psalm 110—in Matthew 22:44

WHEN WERE THE PSALMS WRITTEN?

The psalms written by Moses, David, and Solomon (among others) were obviously composed when these men lived. There are many other psalms written by unknown authors (many of whom were no doubt Levites) that cover the whole span of Israel's history. The following examples can be studied to give insight into the historical period from which they come or about which they were written.

Patriarchal period —Psalm 110—a psalm of David about this period
Theocratic period —Psalm 90 (see also 42, 87 by the sons of Korah)
Monarchical period—David as shepherd (23)
                        as fugitive (7, 11, 18, 34, 54)
                        as king (24)
                        as sinner (32, 51)
                        as dethroned (3, 4)
                      —Solomon (72, 127)
Exilic period   —after destruction of Temple (74, 79)
                        after arrival in Babylon (137)
Post-exilic period —upon return to the land (126)
                        at the dedication of the rebuilt Temple (147)

David no doubt collected the psalms written before his time (cf. I Chron. 15:16). Hezekiah probably added to David's collection (cf. Prov. 25:1), and Ezra completed the collection in his day (Neh. 8).

To whom were the Psalms written?

The Psalms in one sense are the most universal of all the Hebrew literature. They speak to all men in all conditions for all time. The original destination of the psalms, however, is determined by the period in which each was written. Some psalms are written to the Israelites wandering in the wilderness (90), some to a monarch in regal rejoicing (24), some to sad exiles (137), and still others to the jubilant repatriated remnant (126, 147).

Where were they located?

The children of Israel were located in many different places throughout their history. Some psalms were written while they were yet in the wilderness (90), most of them after they were in the promised land, still others while they were in Babylonian exile (137). But in a general sense, all of the psalms are designed for all people everywhere who can identify with the experiences expressed in these inspired hymns.

Why were the Psalms written?

The psalms, like the other Old Testament books, may be viewed as having three divine purposes in mind.

The historical purpose.

The psalms served a national function for they comprised the worship and service hymnal which was the medium of prayer and praise for the Temple-centered religion of the Jewish people.

The doctrinal purpose.

All the great doctrines of the Old Testament are taught in the Psalms, especially the doctrine of God. Perhaps the easiest way to summarize the great teachings of the Psalms is to refer to the topics of the five sections into which they are divided (see below).

The Christological purpose.

Psalms is perhaps the most messianic book in the Old Testament. Practically the whole of Christ's life and ministry can be found there.

What are the Psalms about?

Outline of Psalms.

Psalms is a book of prayer and praise. Each of the five sections ends with a doxology of praise (41, 72, 89, 106) and the last section has six chapters of doxology (145-150): "Let everything that breathes praise the Lord!"

1. Psalms about man and creation (1-41)—corresponds to Genesis.
2. Psalms about Israel and redemption (42-72)—Exodus.
3. Psalms about worship and the Temple (73-89)—Leviticus.

4. Psalms about our sojourn on the earth (90-106)—Numbers.
5. Psalms about praise and the Word of God (107-150)—Deuteron-
    omy.

MUSICAL TERMINOLOGY IN PSALMS.

In order to understand the Psalms more fully a brief definition of
some of the musical terms is necessary.

1. Alamoth (Ps. 46)—female voices or a stringed instrument.
2. Gittith (Ps. 8, 81, 84)—wine press or vintage song; musical instru-
    ment from Gath.
3. Jeduthun (Ps. 39, 77)—a choir leader in David's day.
4. Maschil—a meditative, didactic or skillful psalm.
5. Michtam—a golden psalm? or atonement psalm?
6. Mismor—to pluck an instrument, pizzicato.
7. Neginoth (Ps. 4, 5, 54, 55, 61, 67, 76)—a stringed instrument.
8. Nehiloth (Ps. 5)—a wind instrument.
9. Selah—a musical interlude which some take as a pause for
    meditation.
10. Sheminith (Ps. 6)—an eighth or octave; male voices.
11. Shiggayon (Ps. 7)—wandering or irregular music.
12. Shir—a song in general (sacred or secular).
13. Tehillah (Ps. 145)—praise (Tehillim = praises, psalter).
14. Tephillah—prayer.

CHRIST'S USE OF THE PSALMS.

The use of the Psalms by our Lord is a most instructive commendation of this great book. The following summary indicates how influential
the Psalms were in the life of Christ.

1. During His childhood Jesus revealed knowledge of Ps. 26:8; 27:4
    (cf. Luke 2:49).
2. In the Sermon on the Mount He quoted Ps. 48:2 and 6:8 (Matt.
    5:35; 7:23).
3. In teaching the multitude He cited Ps. 78:2 (Matt. 13:35).
4. In cleansing the Temple He quoted from Ps. 8:2 (Matt. 21:16).
5. In His reply to the priests Jesus cited Ps. 118:22, 23 (Matt. 21:42).
6. In weeping over Jerusalem Jesus borrowed language from Ps. 91:4
    (Matt. 23:37).
7. In answering the Jews He quoted Ps. 82:6 (John 10:34).
8. At the Last Supper Jesus probably sang the Hallel found in
    Ps. 136 (Matt. 26:30).
9. On the cross Jesus quoted the Psalms twice:
    —Ps. 22:1: "My God, why hast thou forsaken me?" (Matt. 27:46).
    —Ps. 31:5: "Into thy hand I commit my spirit" (Luke 23:46).

10. After the resurrection Jesus referred to the whole Book of Psalms with its messianic contents (Luke 24:44).

It is not an exaggeration to say that both the language and content of the Psalms were a pervasive influence on the entire life and ministry of our Lord.

THE LIFE OF CHRIST PREDICTED (OR DEPICTED) IN THE PSALMS.

The New Testament applies many citations from the Psalms to its teachings about the person and life of Christ.

Teaching	Psalm	New Testament Reference
1. Birth	104:4	Heb. 1:7
2. Humiliation	8:4	Heb. 2:6
3. Deity	45:6	Heb. 1:8
4. Ministry	69:9	John 2:17
5. Rejection	118:22	Matt. 21:42
6. Betrayal	41:9	John 13:18
7. Crucifixion	22	Matt. 27:46
8. Resurrection	2 and 16	Acts 2:27
9. Ascension	68:18	Eph. 4:8
10. Reign	102:26	Heb. 1:11

Many other examples could be given, including the piercing of His hands and feet (Ps. 22:16), the fact that His bones were not broken on the cross (Ps. 34:20), His being mocked while on the cross (Ps. 22:7, 8), the offer of vinegar (Ps. 69:21), and His being the object of the hatred of both Jew and Gentile (Ps. 2:1, 2). Each of these verses should be read and studied in order to see the extensive Christological emphasis of the Psalms.

STUDY QUESTIONS

1. Give evidence that David wrote some of the Psalms.
2. During what time period were the Psalms written?
3. Give the divisions of the Psalms which correspond to the books of the Pentateuch.
4. Give examples of Christ's use of the Psalms in His ministry.

27

The Aspiration for Communion
with Christ (cont.)

PSALMS

No poetical book has more to say about Christ than Psalms. But not all the psalms are prophetic or messianic; there are other kinds as well. Since the Book of Psalms is far too large for a chapter by chapter analysis here, a topical survey will be made, using selected psalms as examples.

A TOPICAL CLASSIFICATION OF THE PSALMS.

1. *Prophetic psalms.* These are psalms in which the life of Christ is either depicted or predicted. That is, they are psalms cited by the New Testament in reference to the life and ministry of our Lord.

2. *Praise psalms.* Praise is characteristic of the Psalms. Each of the five divisions ends with a psalm of praise (41, 72, 89, 106, 150). And the last section ends with five psalms of praise (145-149) and then a final doxology for the whole Book of Psalms (150). "Great is the Lord, and greatly to be praised. . ." (145:3) resounds throughout the Psalms. "Praise the Lord! For it is good to sing praises to our God" (147:1). The crescendo of praise comes to a climax in the last psalm: "Praise the Lord! Praise God in his sanctuary; praise him in his mighty firmament! Praise him for his mighty deeds; praise him according to his excellent greatness. . . . Let everything that breathes praise the Lord! Praise the Lord!" Indeed, praise is the very language of the soul. Shakespeare once noted that a thankless son makes a hapless father. The apostle Paul wrote, "Give thanks in all circumstances; for this is the will of God in Christ Jesus for you" (I Thess. 5:18). God dwells in the praises of His people. The special psalms of praise only accent what is a general characteristic of the Book of Psalms —it is a book of poems praising God.

3. *Petition psalms.* Of course, not all psalms are poems of praise; some are petitions or pleas to God for help. Many of these psalms are

requests for deliverance from one's enemies, from sickness or despair, or from death. "Turn, O Lord, save my life; deliver me for the sake of thy steadfast love" (6:4). "Preserve me, O God, for in thee I take refuge" (16:1). Out of desperation the psalmist cried, "Hear my prayer, O Lord, and give ear to my cry; hold not thy peace at my tears! For I am thy passing guest, a sojourner, like all my fathers" (39:12). In sickness the psalmist pleaded with God, "O Lord, be gracious to me; heal me, for I have sinned against thee!" (41:4).

4. *Penitence psalms.* Many psalms contain confessions of sin. The most famous is Psalm 51, a prayer of David's confession after he had sinned with Bathsheba and Nathan the prophet had confronted him (II Sam. 12). "Have mercy on me, O God, according to thy steadfast love," David cries out to God. "For I know my transgressions, and my sin is ever before me. Against thee, thee only, have I sinned, and done that which is evil in thy sight . . . . Create in me a clean heart, O God, and put a new and right spirit within me" (51:1, 3, 10). And God answers David's penitence, as David acknowledges in Psalm 32, "Blessed is he whose transgression is forgiven, whose sin is covered" (v. 1).

Psalm 130 is another great psalm of repentance. "Out of the depths I cry to thee, O Lord! Lord, hear my voice! Let thy ears be attentive to the voice of my supplications!" For "if thou, O Lord, shouldst mark iniquities, Lord, who could stand?" (vv. 1-3). But, continues the psalmist, "there is forgiveness with thee, that thou mayest be feared" (v. 4).

5. *Pastoral psalms.* Perhaps the most famous of all the psalms is a pastoral psalm, that is, a psalm of God's care for His people as a shepherd cares for his flock. "The Lord is my shepherd, I shall not want; he makes me lie down in green pastures. He leads me beside still waters; he restores my soul." Who can count the thousands who have received comfort from these immortal words, "Even though I walk through the valley of the shadow of death, I fear no evil; for thou art with me; thy rod and thy staff, they comfort me" (23:1-3a, 4)? God's care extends far beyond the grave, for "surely goodness and mercy shall follow me all the days of my life; and I shall dwell in the house of the Lord for ever" (v. 6). It is in the context of this psalm's aspiration that the words of Christ in John 10:11 find fulfilling significance: "I am the good shepherd. The good shepherd lays down his life for the sheep."

6. *Precept psalms.* Besides being the hymnal of the Hebrews, the psalms were also a handbook of doctrine and ethics. Many psalms lay down precepts for man's spiritual and moral life. Psalm 37 is a great precept psalm: "Trust in the Lord, and do good; so you will dwell in the land, and enjoy security" (v. 3). "Refrain from anger, and forsake wrath! Fret not yourself; it tends only to evil" (v. 8). "Better is the

little that the righteous has than the abundance of many wicked" (v. 16). This ethical advice sounds much like the precepts found in the Book of Proverbs.

Psalm 119, the longest psalm, is also a precept psalm. Each verse is a prayer containing some precept about the believer's relation to the Word of God. "How can a young man keep his way pure? By guarding it according to thy word" (v. 9). "Thy word is a lamp to my feet and a light to my path" (v. 105).

Another famous precept psalm is Psalm 19. "The law of the Lord is perfect, reviving the soul; the testimony of the Lord is sure, making wise the simple" (v. 7). Again, "the commandment of the Lord is pure, enlightening the eyes . . . . The ordinances of the Lord are true, and righteous altogether. More to be desired are they than gold, even much fine gold; sweeter also than honey and drippings of the honeycomb" (vv. 8-10). The psalmist's conclusion here is fitting for all precept psalms: "Moreover by them is thy servant warned; in keeping them there is great reward" (v. 11).

7. *Prayer psalms.* Many psalms take the form of general prayers. That is, they are not specifically penitential or petitionary but are simply the soul in communion with God. Psalm 17 begins, "Hear a just cause, O Lord; attend to my cry!" (v. 1). Another example is Psalm 86: "Give ear, O Lord, to my prayer; hearken to my cry of supplication" (v. 6). Moses' psalm is a prayer that begins, "Lord, thou hast been our dwelling place in all generations" (90:1). Often the psalmists would cry to God in distress: "Hear my prayer, O Lord; let my cry come to thee! Do not hide thy face from me in the day of my distress!" (102:1).

The Book of Psalms, more than any other portion of Scripture, has influenced the language of prayer of the Christian church. The phrases, style, and even the requests of the psalmists are the very heart-cry of the Christian. As was noted in the last chapter, even our Lord, in His very hour of agony, expressed the depth of His emotion in the words of the psalmist (cf. Ps. 22:1 and Matt. 27:46). Some of the most meaningful and beautiful expressions in any language are found in the King James translation of the psalms. Psalm 19:14 is a good example of this point: "Let the words of my mouth, and the meditation of my heart, be acceptable in thy sight, O Lord, my strength, and my redeemer."

8. *Profession (of faith) psalms.* Not all psalms are addressed to God. Some are about God but addressed to other men. Psalms that confess or profess faith fit in this category. Some begin, "Rejoice in the Lord, O you righteous!" (33:1). Others exhort the believer, saying, "Let the redeemed of the Lord say so..." (107:2). Some are addressed to one's self or even to all the saints. "Bless the Lord, O my soul; and

all that is within me, bless his holy name! Bless the Lord, O my soul, and forget not all his benefits..." (103:1, 2). The psalmist continues, "Bless the Lord, O you his angels, you mighty ones who do his word.... Bless the Lord, all his hosts, his ministers that do his will . . . in all places of his dominion" (vv. 20, 21). These psalms profess to others the gracious and mighty works of God on behalf of the believer.

9. *Patriotic psalms.* There are several kinds of psalms that deal specially with God's covenant people, the children of Israel. These kinds of psalms reflect a theocratic patriotism. "Thou art my King and my God, who ordainest victories for Jacob" (44:4) is a sample. Likewise, "the Lord of hosts is with us; the God of Jacob is our refuge" (46:7) is definitely national in tone. The words of Psalm 108 are unmistakably patriotic: "Gilead is mine; Manasseh is mine; Ephraim is my helmet; Judah my scepter. Moab is my washbasin; upon Edom I cast my shoe; over Philistia I shout in triumph" (108:8, 9).

Psalm 126 is patriotic. "When the Lord restored the fortunes of Zion, we were like those who dream," the post-exilic prophet proclaimed (126:1). "The Lord bless you from Zion! May you see the prosperity of Jerusalem all the days of your life" (128:5) is decidedly the expression of a loyal Israeli. And Psalm 129 is not atypical of the fervor with which Jewish nationalism is expressed in these patriotic psalms: "May all who hate Zion be put to shame and turned backward!" (v. 5).

10. *Pilgrimage psalms.* The children of Israel would sing psalms on their way to festal holy days in Jerusalem. These are commonly called songs of degrees or ascent, so named from the climb toward Jerusalem. There is a whole series of these in Psalms 120-134. Each psalm, no doubt, had national significance, but overall they served to pass the time in joyful praise and to build a feeling of *esprit de corps* as the people journeyed along.

How can imprecatory psalms be explained?

One particular kind of psalm is problematic; these are called imprecatory psalms (meaning, "to call down a curse"). Sometimes David or others would call down the most vivid kinds of judgment on their enemies: "May his children be fatherless, and his wife a widow. . . . May his posterity be cut off; may his name be blotted out in the second generation!" (109:9, 13).

Other imprecatory psalms are 35, 69, and 137. The problem these psalms pose is ethical: how can one love his enemies yet engage in calling down curses upon them? Jesus said, "Love your enemies and pray for those who persecute you" (Matt. 5:44).

Several factors should be kept in mind in interpreting these psalms:

(1) First, the judgment called for is based on *divine justice* and not on human grudges. David clearly affirmed in an imprecatory psalm that he did not have personal ill feelings. He wrote in Psalm 109: "even as I make prayer for them. So they reward me evil for good, and hatred for my love" (vv. 4, 5). David did not hate his enemies but loved them and prayed for them. He did, however, in the imprecatory prayer, commit them to the justice of God for their due reward. The actions of David in relation to Saul are vivid proof that revenge was not a motivation behind his imprecatory prayers. David forgave Saul and even on occasion spared his life (cf. I Sam. 24 and 26).

(2) Judgment is expressed in the thought patterns of the day. For the Hebrews there was no sharp distinction made between the sinner and his sin; both were conceived personally. Further, a man and his family were considered a unit. They stood or fell together (cf. Noah, Achan).

(3) The New Testament emphasis on judgment after death and ultimate justice helps minimize the need to anticipate or explain judgment in more immediate and earthly terms.

(4) The phenomenon of imprecation is not unique to the Old Testament. Jesus urged His disciples to curse cities that did not receive the gospel (Matt. 10:14). Jesus Himself called down judgment on Tyre and Sidon (Matt. 11:22). Paul declared anathema any who did not love the Lord Jesus (I Cor. 16:22). Even the saints in heaven are pictured as beseeching God for vengeance on those who killed the martyrs (Rev. 6:9, 10). Imprecations are obviously not a primitive or purely Old Testament phenomenon. They are the reverse side of love, that is, prayers based on the holiness and justice of God — attributes which imply judgment on sin.

Even in these imprecations one can see an aspiration for Christ. All judgment has been given to the Son (John 5:22). Those who long for justice are really aspiring for Christ and His righteous kingdom (cf. Rev. 20).

STUDY QUESTIONS

1. What are the ten types of psalms? What is the particular emphasis of each?
2. What factors help to explain the imprecatory psalms, which at first may seem rather unmerciful?

28

The Aspiration for Wisdom in Christ

PROVERBS

As Psalms is the worship and hymn book of the Old Testament, Proverbs is its teachers' manual. Proverbs are maxims which can easily be memorized, and thus used as advice for daily living.

WHO WROTE THE BOOK OF PROVERBS?

The Book of Proverbs was largely composed and compiled by king Solomon. The first twenty-four chapters were apparently put together by Solomon himself, while king Hezekiah's scribes copied the material in chapters twenty-five to twenty-nine out of Solomon's repertory of proverbs. The last two chapters were composed by Agur and Lemuel, about whom we know little besides their names (30–31). The following evidence may be given in support of the Solomonic origin of the bulk of Proverbs:

(1) There are three claims in the book that Solomon wrote these proverbs. The first two claims seem to cover basically the first twenty-four chapters (1:1; 10:1; cf. 22:20). The third claim for Solomonic authorship reads, "These also are proverbs of Solomon which the men of Hezekiah king of Judah copied" (25:1).

(2) The Book of I Kings records that Solomon wrote some three thousand proverbs (I Kings 4:32). Since there are only about eight hundred in the Book of Proverbs, there were more than enough in Solomon's other collections for Hezekiah's scribes to choose from.

(3) Solomon no doubt collected and edited many proverbs which he did not create himself. Ecclesiastes says Solomon studied, weighed, and arranged proverbs (12:9). It is known that proverbs did exist before Solomon (Num. 21:27; I Sam. 24:13). Similar proverbs have been discovered in the literature of surrounding countries.

(4) King Hezekiah, with his keen interest in the Word of God and spiritual reform, set his men to the task of editing more of Solomon's proverbs for the benefit of the people (Prov. 25:1).

The authors of the last two chapters of Proverbs are relatively unknown. All that is known of Agur is that he was a prophet or oracle of God (30:1). Lemuel likewise was a prophet (31:1), apparently from some Arabian country where the worship of the true God was preserved.

WHEN WAS PROVERBS WRITTEN?

The proverbs of Solomon were composed before his death in 931 B.C. Hezekiah's scribes probably completed their editing by around 700 B.C.

TO WHOM WAS PROVERBS WRITTEN?

Solomon addressed his proverbs to the "wise man" (1:5), to his "son" (1:8; 2:1). Kings tells us that Solomon's "servants" listened to his wisdom (I Kings 10:8). Solomon was apparently a kind of headmaster of a school of wise men (Eccles. 1:1, 12:9), as Samuel was head of a school of prophets (I Sam. 19:20). Elijah was teacher or mentor to Elisha and referred to his pupil as his "son." Hence, the "son" to whom Proverbs is addressed may have been a learner in the school of Solomonic wisdom.

WHERE WERE THEY LOCATED?

Solomon's kingdom, as well as Hezekiah's after him, was centered in Jerusalem. This was not only the political but also the spiritual and educational capital of Israel.

WHY WAS PROVERBS WRITTEN?

Three intentions may be distinguished in the Book of Proverbs.

The historical purpose.

The Book of Proverbs may have served as a kind of teacher's manual for the wise men of Israel. Easily memorized, the proverbs themselves were maxims of wisdom meant to give all the people guidance for life.

The doctrinal purpose.

The primary teaching of the wisdom literature is that true wisdom is based in the fear (reverential trust) of God. That is, prudence is based in piety (1:7). Teachings on other matters, including sex, friends, and money, are both invaluable and numerous.

The Christological purpose.

Christ is presented in Proverbs as the Wisdom for which the wise man aspires (cf. Prov. 8). The New Testament declares that Christ was "made our wisdom" (I Cor. 1:30) and that in Christ "are hid all the treasures of wisdom and knowledge" (Col. 2:3).

WHAT IS PROVERBS ABOUT?

The meaning of a "proverb."

The Hebrew word for "proverb" means "parallel," "similar," or "a comparison." It is a description by way of a comparison or figure of speech. In the context of this book it means a moral maxim, a prudent precept, or a sagacious saying. Proverbs are the holy "horse sense" of the Old Testament.

The term "wisdom," as most often used in Proverbs, means something more practical than pure theory. Someone has said, *knowledge* is the apprehension of truth in one's mind, but *wisdom* is the application of truth to one's life. In the Bible the basis of this wisdom is threefold:

It is based on the authority and majesty of God — reverence for God (1:7).

It recognizes the authority and sanctity of the home — respect for parents (1:8).

It acknowledges the authority and moral standards of society — regard for law (1:10f.).

A verse by verse analysis of Proverbs is not possible here. The book, however, does lend itself to an overall analysis of its structure.

I. Words to the wise
— wisdom is valuable; seek it (1-9).

In this section wisdom is characterized as the chief or principal thing in life. The thesis is that the primary value of an education is the acquisition of wisdom. Wisdom has the following characteristics:

A. IT RESPECTS GOD AND PARENTS (1:1-9).

"The fear of the Lord is the beginning of knowledge. . . . Hear, my son, your father's instruction, and reject not your mother's teaching" (vv. 7, 8). These are fundamental words to those who would be wise.

B. IT REBUKES SIN AND EVIL (1:10-33).

"My son, if sinners entice you, do not consent. . . . My son, do not walk in the way with them, hold back your foot from their paths. . . . For the simple are killed by their turning away . . . but he who listens to me will dwell secure and will be at ease, without dread of evil" (vv. 10, 15, 32, 33).

C. IT REWARDS ITS SEEKERS MORALLY (2).

Wisdom is a virtue that is its own reward. "My son," wrote Solomon, "if you receive my words and treasure up my commandments with you . . . if you seek it like silver and search for it as for hidden treasures; then you will understand the fear of the Lord and find the knowledge of

God . . . . Then you will understand righteousness and justice and equity, every good path" (vv. 1, 4, 5, 9).

D. It rewards its seekers physically (3).

Those who trust in the Lord and do not rely on their own insight but acknowledge Him in all their ways find health, prosperity, and happiness. "It will be healing to your flesh and refreshment to your bones. Honor the Lord with your substance and with the first fruits of all your produce; then your barns will be filled with plenty, and your vats will be bursting with wine" (vv. 8-10).

E. It reroutes one's life from evil (4).

Wisdom leads one in paths he would not otherwise have taken. Solomon wrote, "I have taught you the way of wisdom; I have led you in the paths of uprightness. When you walk, your step will not be hampered" (vv. 11, 12). "The path of the righteous is like the light of dawn, which shines brighter and brighter until full day" (v. 18).

F. It rejects the way of sensuality (5).

The wise man controls his sexual drives and expresses them in marriage. "Let your fountain be blessed, and rejoice in the wife of your youth. . . . Let her affection fill you at all times with delight, be infatuated always with her love" (vv. 18, 19). But beware, "for the lips of a loose woman drip honey, her speech is smoother than oil; but in the end she is bitter as wormwood" (vv. 3, 4). Take heed "lest afterwards you groan in anguish and in shame, when syphilis consumes your body, and you say, 'Oh, if only I had listened! If only I had not demanded my own way!' " (vv. 11, 12, Living Bible).

G. It reactivates the slothful (6:1-19).

Wisdom gives life to the lazy. "Go to the ant, O sluggard; consider her ways and be wise . . . . How long will you lie there, O sluggard? When will you arise from your sleep? A little sleep, a little slumber, a little folding of the hands to rest, and poverty will come upon you like a vagabond" (vv. 6, 9-11).

H. It represses the desires of lust (6:20-35).

The wise man will be preserved from the evil woman. He is exhorted: "Do not desire her beauty in your heart, and do not let her capture you with her eyelashes . . . . Can a man carry fire in his bosom and his clothes not be burned?" (vv. 25, 27). Those who play with the fire of lust will surely be burned.

I. It resists the evil woman (7).

This chapter contains one of the most vivid, forceful, and yet tasteful descriptions of temptation and harlotry in all literature. The foolish and lustful man is described as going after the evil woman "as an ox goes to the slaughter, . . . as a bird rushes into a snare" (vv. 22, 23). The wise man flees lust; he does not fall into it.

J. IT REJOICES IN GOD WHO BEGAT IT (8).

"Wisdom is better than jewels. . ." (v. 11). By it kings reign (v. 15) and all who diligently seek it find it (v. 17). It was by Wisdom (cf. John 1:2) that God created the world (vv. 22-30). Wisdom rejoiced in the presence of God from the very beginning. "I was beside him," cried Wisdom, "like a master workman, and I was daily his delight, rejoicing before him always. . ." (v. 30).

K. IT REPROVES THE RIGHTEOUS WHO USE IT (9).

Wisdom builds her house on the foundation of the fear of God (vv. 1, 10). "Reprove a wise man, and he will love you" but "do not reprove a scoffer, or he will hate you" (v. 8).

II. Word of the wise
— wisdom is practical; follow it (10-22a).

These chapters contain an assortment of Solomon's wise sayings. They cover a variety of subjects. Some of the important topics are indicated in the following outline and summaries. *Wisdom* entails these characteristics:

A. IT IS RICHES FROM GOD (10).

Over and over again the proverbs describe wisdom as a ruby, jewel, or treasure from God. "Treasures gained by wickedness do not profit. . ." (v. 2). But "the blessing of the Lord makes rich, and he adds no sorrow with it" (v. 22).

B. IT IS RIGHTEOUSNESS OF LIFE (11).

God hates cheaters and He will destroy the crooked (vv. 1, 3). But "the righteousness of the upright delivers them . . ." (v. 6). Indeed, "the fruit of the righteous is a tree of life; And he that is wise winneth souls" (v. 30, ASV).

C. IT IS RIGHTEOUS IN ITS LANGUAGE (12).

The wise man controls his tongue (cf. James 3). "An evil man is ensnared by the transgression of his lips . . ." but "truthful lips endure for ever . . ." (vv. 13, 19). "Lying lips are an abomination to the Lord, but those who act faithfully are his delight" (v. 22).

D. IT HAS REGARD FOR REPROOF (13).

"He who heeds reproof is honored" (v. 18). And "he who spares the rod hates his son, but he who loves him is diligent to discipline him"

(v. 24). As Hebrews puts it, "My son, do not regard lightly the discipline of the Lord . . ." (12:5).

E.   IT IS THE ROAD OF REWARD (14).

"He who walks in uprightness fears the Lord, but he who is devious in his ways despises him" (v. 2). God's path is not man's way. "There is a way which seems right to a man, but its end is the way of death" (v. 12). The path of righteousness, on the other hand, leads to life.

F.   IT EXHIBITS REGULATION OF THE TONGUE (15).

"A soft answer turns away wrath, but a harsh word stirs up anger" (v. 1). Our saying, "it is not so much what is said but how it is said," is based on this truth. "The mind of the righteous ponders how to answer, but the mouth of the wicked pours out evil things" (v. 28).

G.   IT RESTS IN THE PURPOSES OF GOD (16).

The wise man realizes that "the plans of the mind belong to man, but the answer of the tongue is from the Lord" (v. 1). For "the Lord has made everything for its purpose . . ." (v. 4). "A man's mind plans his way, but the Lord directs his steps" (v. 9).

H.   IT REFRAINS FROM STRIFE (17).

"Better is a dry morsel with quiet than a house full of feasting with strife" (v. 1). For "he who loves transgression loves strife" (v. 19). And by contrast, "a cheerful heart is a good medicine . . ." (v. 22).

I.   IT FINDS REFUGE IN GOD (18).

"A rich man's wealth is his strong city . . ." but "the name of the Lord is a strong tower; the righteous man runs into it and is safe" (vv. 11, 10). For the Lord is "a friend who sticks closer than a brother" (v. 24).

J.   IT RESPONDS TO POVERTY BY GIVING (if rich) (19).

Since it is so often true that "wealth brings many new friends, but a poor man is deserted by his friends" (v. 4), the rich are exhorted: "He who is kind to the poor lends to the Lord, and he will repay him for his deed" (v. 17).

K.   IT RESPONDS TO POVERTY BY WORKING (if poor) (20-21).

Drunkenness and sloth are two great breeders of poverty (20:1, 4). "Love not sleep, lest you come to poverty; open your eyes and you will have plenty of bread" (v. 13). "I fight poverty, I work" may be a modern slogan, but it is an ancient truth. Paul admonished the Thessalonians that those who refuse to work should be refused food (II Thess. 3:10).

"The plans of the diligent lead surely to abundance, but everyone who is hasty comes only to want" (21:5). This is the basis for the

English proverb, "haste makes waste." The lack of generosity and the love of pleasure are two more causes of poverty (21:13, 17).

L.   IT PROVIDES A REWARD TO THE POOR (22:1-16).
Wisdom rewards men, giving that which money cannot buy — a good name, humility, a faithful family. "A good name is to be chosen rather than great riches, and favor is better than silver or gold" (v. 1). And "the reward for humility and fear of the Lord is riches and honor and life" (v. 4).

III.   Words for the wise
— wisdom is admonitional; hear it (22b-24).

In this section wisdom speaks as a preacher with the admonition and exhortation to heed its call. Since it is valuable and practical for life, one should hearken to its voice.

A.   WISDOM IS PLEASANT (22b).
"Incline your ear, and hear the words of the wise. . .for it will be pleasant if you keep them within you . . ." (v. 17). As with the other virtues or positive characteristics of life mentioned by Paul, the believer should be admonished to "think about these things" (Phil. 4:8).

B.   WISDOM IS WORTHWHILE (23).
A wise son makes a father's heart glad (v. 15). And for the wise "surely there is a future, and your hope will not be cut off" (v. 18). The life of wisdom is worthwhile living.

C.   WISDOM IS PROSPEROUS (24).
The righteous man falls seven times but rises up again (v. 16). And "by knowledge the rooms are filled with all precious and pleasant riches" (v. 4). God blesses the wise.

IV.   Words from the wise
— wisdom is ethical; do it (25-31).

In this last section we hear from both Solomon and two other wise, but unknown oracles. Their words are definitely moral in tone.

A.   WORDS FROM SOLOMON (25-29).
1. *The king* (25) — A king's glory is to search out a matter and a king's downfall is evil men (vv. 2, 5). The heart of a king is unsearchable (v. 3) and he is persuaded with patience, not forwardness (vv. 6, 15).
2. *The fool* (26-27) — "Honor is not fitting for a fool" (26:1). And as a dog returns to his vomit, so is "a fool that repeats his folly"

(26:11). Fools boast of tomorrow when they do not know what a day may bring forth (27:1).

3. *The wicked* (28) — "The wicked flee when no one pursues, but the righteous are bold as a lion" (v. 1). "He who conceals his transgressions will not prosper, but he who confesses and forsakes them will obtain mercy" (v. 13). "Even his [the wicked man's] prayer is an abomination" (v. 9).

4. *The stubborn* (29) — "He who is often reproved, yet stiffens his neck will suddenly be broken beyond healing" (v. 1). Further, "the rod and reproof give wisdom, but a child left to himself brings shame to his mother" (v. 15).

B.   WORDS FROM AGUR AND LEMUEL (30-31).

1. *Truth and things* (30)—"Every word of God proves true" (v. 5). "Remove far from me falsehood and lying," the wise man requests of God (v. 8). There follows a number of "things" wonderful, unbearable, wise, and stately that impressed the sage (vv. 15f.).

2. *Wine and women* (31) — The words of Lemuel treat two very important aspects of life: (a) Strong drink (including drugs) is to be used as medicine but never as beverage (vv. 4-6); (b) "A good wife who can find? She is far more precious than jewels. The heart of her husband trusts in her..." (vv. 10, 11). There follows the most beautiful description of a good and virtuous wife to be found anywhere in the Bible. The wise man seeks this kind of life's companion, for he knows that beauty is only skin deep, and that the hidden virtues are invaluable.

STUDY QUESTIONS

1. What arguments can be given in favor of the Solomonic authorship of most of the Proverbs?
2. What is a proverb in the Old Testament sense?
3. Wisdom is probably the central concern of Proverbs. What is meant by wisdom, and on what is it based?

29

The Aspiration for Satisfaction in Christ
ECCLESIASTES

The title of this book means "the preacher" or "assembler." In Greek too it means "the assembler"; the Greek word for "assembly" or "church" *(ekklēsia)* is related to it. The theme of Ecclesiastes is a search for satisfaction; in the end it is found nowhere "under the sun" except in the words which come from the "one Shepherd" (12:11).

Who Wrote the Book of Ecclesiastes?

Despite the fact that the book claims to be written by "the Preacher, the son of David, king in Jerusalem" (1:1) who had surpassing wisdom (1:16), many scholars have held that the author was a later literary impersonator, not Solomon himself. They note that many of the literary forms found in Ecclesiastes are from a post-exilic period, that Solomon's day was one of prosperity not adversity, that the author said he *was* king (whereas Solomon remained king until death), that many kings (not just Saul and David) are said to have reigned in Jerusalem (1:16), that the author often speaks in the third person, as a citizen and not as the king (3:16), and that in the Hebrew Bible the book is not listed with the other books of Solomon. However, none of these arguments is decisive. The literary forms belong to a genre of their own and not to the post-exilic period; Solomon was not unaware of poverty and adversity; the text should be rendered "I the Preacher *have been* king. . ." or "I became king"; there were many kings or wise men in Jerusalem before Solomon; the author is speaking as *philosopher* and not as king; and the Hebrew Bible was not classified by authors, but by subject matter.

On the other hand there is substantial evidence to support the contention that Solomon wrote Ecclesiastes. (1) There is the direct claim of the book itself (1:1). (2) A literary impersonator in this context would be a moral deceiver. (3) Only Solomon fits the description as the wisest man who had ever taught in Jerusalem (1:16; cf. I Kings 4:29, 30). (4) And the description of riches, numerous wives, and great public works eminently fits Solomon (2:4-11). (5) There is also a marked similarity with both the overall theme ("the fear of the Lord is the beginning of wisdom") and specific teachings of the Book of Proverbs (cf. Eccles. 10:8, 9, 12, 13, 18; 12:9). (6) Further, the same person is writing throughout the book (cf. 1:1; 7:27; 12:8). The shift at times to the third person is a literary technique. (7) The intimate knowledge of evil women best fits Solomon (cf. I Kings 11:1f.). (8) The discovery of four fragments of Ecclesiastes among the Qumran scrolls refutes the critical theory that Ecclesiastes is a late post-exilic book. (9) Finally, Jewish teaching from the earliest times very explicitly attributes the book to Solomon (Megilla 7a and Shabbath 30), although there is indication that Hezekiah's men may have edited and published the text (Baba Bathra 15a) as they did some of Solomon's proverbs (Prov. 25:1).

WHEN WAS ECCLESIASTES WRITTEN?

According to Jewish tradition, Solomon wrote the Song in his early years, expressing a young man's love. He wrote the Proverbs in his mature years, manifesting a middle-aged man's wisdom. He reportedly wrote Ecclesiastes in his declining years, revealing an old man's sorrow (cf. 12:1). Perhaps Ecclesiastes is the record of Solomon's regret for and repentance from his grave moral lapses recorded in I Kings 11. The Book of Ecclesiastes, then, would have been written just before Solomon's death and the subsequent division of his kingdom that occurred in 931 B.C.

TO WHOM WAS ECCLESIASTES WRITTEN?

The book itself indicates that it was written to wise men or teachers in Jerusalem as well as to the people of the kingdom. The phrase "my son" (12:12) is often used of a disciple (cf. Elijah to Elisha and Paul to Timothy). The book also refers to the "sayings of the wise" (12:11) who would be teachers and declares that Solomon "taught the people knowledge" (12:9). Ecclesiastes, then, forms part of the wisdom literature of the Old Testament which is intended as a depository of wisdom and a guide for the people.

WHERE WERE THEY LOCATED?

The book clearly indicates that the audience of Ecclesiastes was in Jerusalem. It was from here, the seat of his kingdom, that Solomon's wisdom spread to the ends of the earth (I Kings 10).

WHY WAS ECCLESIASTES WRITTEN?

The purpose of Ecclesiastes is threefold:

The historical purpose.

The Book of Ecclesiastes provides a textbook on the true philosophy of life, on the answer to the question about life's *summum bonum.*

The doctrinal purpose.

(1) The fundamental teaching of the book is twofold: negatively, no true happiness is found in what this world has to offer and, positively, true satisfaction is found only in God. (2) In its basic teaching, namely, that the fear of God is the beginning of wisdom (cf. 12:13), Ecclesiastes is in accord with the rest of the wisdom literature of the Old Testament. (3) Included within its basic teachings are many other doctrines such as God's sovereignty (3), human depravity (7:29), divine sagacity (wisdom), and death's finality (3:17, 20).

The Christological purpose.

The person of Christ stands out in two significant ways in Ecclesiastes (1). He is the greatest good, the ultimate satisfaction for which the believer aspires (cf. John 4:13, 14). (2) Christ is the "one Shepherd" or teacher from whom the wisdom of this book comes (12:11; cf. John 10:1 and Col. 2:3). In brief, Christ is both the Water of Life that quenches our thirst for happiness and the Wisdom of God that satisfies our desire for knowledge.

WHAT IS ECCLESIASTES ABOUT?

Ecclesiastes is the most philosophical book in the Bible. There are three basic ways in which it has been interpreted. (1) Some have understood it as *purely naturalistic,* as though the book teaches a fatalistic (7:13), pessimistic (4:2), materialistic (3:19-21), hedonistic (2:24), agnostic (1:13) view of life. On this basis they have rejected the book as uninspired and therefore eliminated it from the canon of Scripture. (2) Others have understood Ecclesiastes to be *partially theistic* (i.e., God-centered). In this view everything from 1:3 to 12:12 is a record of what a natural man "under the sun" and apart from God thinks about life. Hence, only the conclusion of the book is what the author (and God) is teaching as true. The pessimism and agnosticism of the middle of the book are simply the record of the untrue beliefs of a natural man apart from God. (3) The third view holds that the book is *entirely theistic.* This view holds that in its proper context the book does not teach pessimism and agnosticism. That is, everything in the book is true. However, one must always keep in mind the overall purpose of the author as well as the fact that God's revelation is progressive and hence later revelation teaches more than what was available to Solomon and to natural wisdom. This third view fits best with the total content of Ecclesiastes as the following summary will indicate.

I. The problem stated
There appears to be no satisfaction in the world (1:1-11).

As the sage looked at the world everything appeared to run in cycles or circles. One generation goes and another comes; the sun rises and the sun sets; the wind blows round and round. Nothing is finally satisfying. The rivers run into the sea but the sea never gets full. "All things are full of weariness. . . ; the eye is not satisfied with seeing, nor the ear filled with hearing. . . .and there is nothing new under the sun [for satisfaction] (vv. 8, 9). All is vanity and a striving after the wind.

II. The problem studied
Satisfaction is sought in the world (1:12—12:8).

With this apparent futility firmly fixed in his mind, the wise Solomon sought to find ultimate pleasure and satisfaction in the world. He first sought it experientially (1:12 — 2:26) and then philosophically (3—12).

A. SATISFACTION SOUGHT EXPERIENTIALLY (1:12—2:26).

Perhaps no one has ever had more resources mentally, politically, and economically with which to research the question of pleasure than had Solomon. First, he tried *wisdom*. "I have applied my mind to know wisdom," he said. However, "I perceived that this also is but a striving after wind. For in much wisdom is much vexation, and he who increases knowledge increases sorrow" (1:17, 18). Turning from wisdom, Solomon tried *wit* as a source of satisfaction but concluded "of laughter, 'It is mad,' and of pleasure, 'What use is it?'" (2:2). Then he said, "I searched with my mind how to cheer my body with *wine*. . .and how to lay hold on folly, till I might see what was good for the sons of men to do under heaven during the few days of their life" (2:3). This too ended only in frustration, not in satisfaction. For as Solomon noted elsewhere, "Wine is a mocker, strong drink is raging: and whosoever is deceived thereby is not wise" (Prov. 20:1, KJV). From wine he turned to more constructive activities. "I made great *works;* I built houses and planted vineyards for myself." But the pleasure was sustained only in the process of building. The completed projects brought only incomplete satisfaction. From these pleasureless projects he turned to the prospect of great possessions. Of *wealth* Solomon said, "I had also great possessions of herds and flocks. . . . I also gathered for myself silver and gold and the treasure of kings and provinces" (2:7, 8). But treasures did not bring true joy, for he observed later, "He who loves money will not be satisfied with money; nor he who loves wealth, with gain: this also is vanity" (5:10). Both music and *women* were high on Solomon's pleasure list. "I got singers, both men and women, and many concubines, man's delight" (2:8). But neither song nor sex brought satisfaction to him. Neither a thousand wives and concubines (I Kings 11:3) nor a thousand and five choruses and poems (I Kings 4:32) brought abiding happiness to his heart. Likewise *worldly recognition* proved futile. "So I became great," he wrote, "and surpassed all who were before me in Jerusalem" (2:9). At the ends of the earth the half had not been told of his glory, but nevertheless at the bottom of his heart, the great Solomon was lonely and empty: "All is vanity." From fleeting fame he turned to the finest feelings and *worldly pleasures*. "Whatever my eyes desired I did not keep from them; I kept my heart from no pleasure . . ." (2:10). But in all of this pursuit of pleasure he saw that "all was vanity and a striving after wind, and there was nothing to be gained under the sun" (2:11). The whole experiment yielded a negative result. Experience with unlimited resources proved that there is nothing in this world that brings permanent pleasure or abiding satisfaction.

B.   SATISFACTION SOUGHT PHILOSOPHICALLY (3:1—12:8).

The second part of Solomon's search for the *summum bonum* (the greatest good) was conducted philosophically, in accordance with the highest wisdom his great mind could muster. Again, however, he discovered that ultimate satisfaction cannot be found in earthly things. Self-planned happiness fails, for God has determined a time and place for everything, including man's final judgment (3). Further, neither the oppressed nor oppressor is happy, for there is no one to deliver the former from his tears or the latter from his tyranny (4:1-3). Likewise, neither rivalry nor sloth brings happiness, for the life of rivalry is consumed by envy of others and the life of sloth is consumed by laziness (4:4-6). Neither is there satisfaction found in being either a rich miser or a popular king. The former is never satisfied with what he can get from others and the latter is never willing to take advice from others (4:7-16). Also, there is no joy in either a heart filled with empty religion or a house full of riches, for the former is repaid by divine judgment and the latter by sleeplessness and death. The power to enjoy riches is not within man; it is God-given (5:8—6:12). In addition, happiness is found in neither wisdom nor folly, neither righteousness nor wickedness. The latter is self-destructive and the former is unattainable by man in this life. What we do have of wisdom is destroyed by evil and death (7). Neither the obedient nor the rebellious are fully happy, for the submissive only do what pleases men and the rebellious do not do what pleases God (8). Likewise, neither the good man nor the evil man finds happiness, for the former places his hope for good reward beyond the grave (in God's hands) and the latter finds his evil rewarded by the grave (9a). Furthermore, neither wisdom nor folly is a guarantee of happiness, for the works of the wise are destroyed by fools while fools destroy their own works (9b-11a). The conclusion is this: rejoice in your youth, remove vanity from your life (11b), remember your Creator, and recognize that judgment is coming (12a).

III. The problem solved
Satisfaction is found beyond this world (12:9-14).

Solomon constantly saw the vanity and futility of the search for happiness in this world. There is no satisfaction "under the sun." Satisfaction is found only *beyond* the sun. It comes from the chief Shepherd (12:11), who teaches a true wisdom which begins with the fear of God. The Christian knows that Christ is the good Shepherd who alone brings abundant life (John 10:9, 10). That is, the aspiration for satisfaction can be fulfilled only in Christ. The reason for this is implied throughout the book: God has set eternity in man's heart and nothing in the temporal world can satisfy him (cf. 3:11). An infinite capacity for happiness will never be satisfied by mere finite things. The quest for ultimate happiness cannot be fulfilled in the less than ultimate life on this earth. As St. Augustine put it, the heart is restless until it finds its rest in God. Or, as Solomon stated it, "My son, beware of anything beyond these. . . . The end of the matter; all has been heard. Fear God, and keep his commandments; for this is the whole duty of man" (12:12, 13).

STUDY QUESTIONS

1. What indications do we have from Ecclesiastes itself that Solomon is its author?
2. Why is it that satisfaction can never be found in this world?
3. In the light of what this book teaches, which of the three interpretations best fits the book?
4. Where in the book would you find the basis for New Testament teachings such as those found in Galatians 6:7, I Timothy 6:10, and Hebrews 9:27?
5. What is the basic or root meaning of the word *philosophy* (see a dictionary) and in what sense does Ecclesiastes fit that definition?

30

The Aspiration for Union with Christ

SONG OF SOLOMON

In Hebrew the title of this book is "the song of songs." Both the Greek *asma* and the Latin *canticum* (from which we derive the word "Canticles") translate the Hebrew title literally. The theme of Canticles is the love of Solomon for his Shulamite bride. What we believe to be the purpose and original audience of the book depends largely on the interpretation we adopt.

WHO WROTE THE SONG OF SONGS?

There is good evidence to support the claim that Solomon is the author of this love ode. Let us briefly summarize that evidence.

(1) There is the direct claim of the first verse: this book is "the Song of Songs, which is Solomon's (1:1). This is not a dedication to Solomon but an attribution of the song to him as its author in the same way that a "psalm of David" is one composed by David, not one written for David.

(2) The vocabulary and style are very similar to the vocabulary and style of Ecclesiastes which is Solomonic in origin, as we have already seen (ch. 29).

(3) The natural history found in the Song corresponds to Solomon's encyclopedic knowledge in this area. Some twenty-one plants and fifteen animals are identified in the Song (cf. I Kings 4:33).

(4) The evidence of royal luxury and abundance of costly imports is eminently characteristic of Solomon's time (cf. 1:12, 13; 3:6, 9).

(5) The geographic references clearly favor a date during Solomon's reign. The absence of any reference to the later northern capital of Samaria (established after 885 B.C.) supports this view.

(6) All cities, both north and south, are spoken of as part of one undivided kingdom (cf. 6:4). This depicts a period during Solomon's reign.

(7) The allusion to horses and riches is characteristic of Solomon's time, for the king was very wealthy (cf. I Kings 4:26; 10:4-7).

(8) I Kings 4:32 informs us that Solomon wrote one thousand and five songs. This one is called his "Song of Songs," that is, it is his chief work.

WHEN WAS THE SONG WRITTEN?

Since Solomon died in 931 B.C., the Song was composed prior to this date. The bride of Solomon is a Shulamite (6:13), though Shulamites are not found in the list of his chief wives (I Kings 11:1). Possibly the wives mentioned in Kings were those acquired for political reasons or those who turned Solomon to idolatry. Since his marriage to Pharaoh's daughter is mentioned early (I Kings 3:1) and since there is an allusion to "Pharaoh's chariots" in the Song (1:9) and to "sixty queens and eighty concubines, and maidens without number" (6:8), it may be that the love affair with the Shulamite came later. It is possible that amidst all the marriages which represented political alliances (cf. I Kings 3:1 and 11:3), this young maiden taught Solomon the true beauty of monogamous love. In view of the number of his other wives and yet the vigor of Solomon's romance, it seems probable that the story occurred near the middle of his reign, that is, around 950 B.C.

TO WHOM WAS THE BOOK WRITTEN?

Here it may be helpful to distinguish between the Shulamite maiden from the province of Issachar (southwest of the Sea of Galilee) to whom the song was *written* (6:13) and the Jewish believers for whom the book was *published*. In the wake of Solomon's polygamy it may be that this book was put forth for an immoral society that had lost the sanctity of sexuality and the purity of marriage. Such was the sad state of both Israel and Judah after Solomon.

WHERE WERE THEY LOCATED?

The geographical citations within the Canticle refer to the whole land of Israel from north to south as a united kingdom. However, if the book was published by Hezekiah after Solomon's death, as was part of Proverbs (cf. 25:1), then of course the destination would be the southern kingdom of Judah centered in and around its capital, Jerusalem.

WHY WAS THE SONG OF SONGS WRITTEN?

Following our customary threefold breakdown, we may state the purpose of the Song of Songs as follows:

The historical purpose.

First and foremost, the Song aims to teach the sanctity and beauty of marriage as God intended it. Secondly, in Jewish usage the Song served a national role in that it was read at the feast of the Passover.

The doctrinal purpose.

The central teaching of the book concerns the nature of the union of lover and beloved. Hence, both compassion and union, love and oneness, are at the core of the doctrinal statement of the Song. Following from this, of course, are both a rebuke to polygamy and a reaffirmation of monogamous love as God's ideal for mankind.

The Christological purpose.

Solomon's love for his bride is a most beautiful illustration of Christ's love for His church (Eph. 5:25f.). Further, the bride's growth in love depicts the believer's maturation in the love of Christ, a growing realization of His acceptance of us in love. Truly, no book of the Bible is more holy and more sacred, yet few are more often scorned and rejected. Nevertheless, the aspiration for union with Christ in love is nowhere more fully and descriptively illustrated in all of Scripture.

WHAT IS THE SONG ABOUT?

The Canticle is difficult to outline. However, the basic divisions appear to be as follows:

I. The virgin and the vineyard (1:1—2:7).

Despite the fact that the beloved was scorched from hours of work in the vineyard under the blazing sun (1:6), she was the "fairest among women" and "the lily of the valleys" to her lover (1:8; 2:1). She was a Cinderella who became the king's lover.

II. The damsel and the dream (2:8—3:5).

She would dream of her lover coming "like a gazelle" and "leaping upon the mountains" (2:8, 9; cf. 3:1). He would say, "Arise, my love, my fair one, and come away" (2:13). And she responded confidently, "My beloved is mine and I am his..." (2:16).

III. The queen and the quest (3:6—5:1).

Finally one day her lover appeared. And with a "column of smoke" the horses of Solomon sped the couple to Jerusalem, where they were greeted by the "daughter of Jerusalem" (3:6-11). Here the romance grew. And there follows a poetical description by her beloved of the bride's elegant beauty (4). And the lovers rejoice in the sweetness of love as the wedding guests dine in the garden (5:1).

IV. Recollection and romance (5:2—6:9).

The bride reminisces about the budding romance and paints a glowing description of her lover, "My beloved is all radiant and ruddy, distinguished among ten thousand" (5:10). And even though her beloved be absent, her love has further matured to the point that she now emphasizes his love for her: "I am my beloved's and my beloved is mine" (6:3). Despite the fact that there are "sixty queens and eighty concubines, and maidens without number," he replies, "my dove, my perfect one, is only one" (6:9). The recognition by the man who had a thousand wives and concubines that he had only one true love may be the greatest rebuke against polygamy in all literature.

V. Romance and reality (6:10—8:4).

Again the lover extols the beauty of his bride. "O queenly maiden . . . . How fair and pleasant you are, O loved one, delectable maiden!" (7:1, 6). Her response depicts an even higher stage of their love. "I am my beloved's, and his desire is for me" (7:10). At first, she had said, "My beloved is mine" (2:16). Later she grew to recognize what is even better, "I am my beloved's" (6:3). Finally her love had blossomed into the full realization that "His desire is for me" (7:10). The maiden's understanding had grown from "I possess him" to "he possesses me" to "he not only possesses me but he desires me." This is the highest degree of mature love.

VI. The homestead and the honeymoon (8:5-14).

The romance is completed with a honeymoon trip. The hometown folk look on with amazement as the virgin of the vineyard returns arm in arm with the king. As the family reminisces in wonder (v. 5), the bride triumphantly recounts the power of love: "Love is strong as death. . . . Many waters cannot quench love, neither can floods drown it" (vv. 6, 7). She proudly proclaims herself the finest and purest fruit from Solomon's vineyard (v. 11). She is the chaste virgin who conquered the heart of Solomon and taught the polygamous king the beauty and sanctity of true, monogamous love.

How to interpret the Song of Solomon.

Despite the fact that the general outline of the story is clear and that the specifics manifest a most intimate love affair, there is no unanimity of opinion among scholars on how to interpret this canticle. There are three major views.

The literal interpretation. Those who take the ode literally fall into two groups. First there are those who take it as a purely secular story with no spiritual significance. They reject the Song's canonicity. Others see it as a literal story with deep spiritual significance concerning the holiness and wholesomeness of monogamous marriage.

The allegorical interpretation. It has been common among believing Jews and Christians to take this song symbolically, as an allegory of God's love for His people or of Jehovah's love for Israel (cf. Hosea).

The typical interpretation. Christians have often viewed the bride and groom as a prefiguration or type of Christ and His love for the church (cf. Eph. 5:28-32).

There may be an element of truth in all these views, but it seems best to ground our interpretation on the literal, actual love between Solomon and his Shulamite bride. It is always dangerous to spiritualize the meaning of what is apparently historical. The dictim is this: "If the literal, historical sense makes good sense, then seek no other sense lest it result in nonsense." And here the historical sense makes good sense. Love and marriage is of God (Gen. 2:23, 24). God created sex (Gen. 1:27) and gave it to men and women to enjoy (Prov. 5:17-19) within the bounds of monogamous marriage (I Cor. 7:1). Clearly it should not be forbidden (I Tim. 4:1f.). Indeed, God "richly furnishes us with everything to enjoy" (I Tim. 6:17). The Song of Solomon is a beautiful example of how God's riches are literally fulfilled within the true love of a biblical marriage. And it is within this ideal relationship that we may see an element of truth in the other interpretations. Truly a marriage of this kind is a dramatic *illustration* of Jehovah's love for Israel and a beautiful *picture* of Christ's love for His bride the church. But it seems unjustified to think of the story of Solomon and the Shulamite as purely allegorical on the one hand or as a type on the other. Technically, a type is a *picture* that *predicted* and was *fulfilled* in Christ (see ch. 7). Actually the Song lacks the last two of these three characteristics. It is not predictive and could not therefore be fulfilled in Christ, although its truth is certainly exemplified in Christ.

STUDY QUESTIONS

1. What is the evidence that Solomon wrote this book?
2. What type of marriage is taught in Canticles? What is ironic about this fact?
3. What are three basic ways to interpret Canticles, and which one seems best?

PART FIVE
The Books of Prophecy:

The Expectation of Christ

31

Introduction to the Books of Prophecy

The Law laid the *foundation* for Christ by the *election* (Gen.), *redemption* (Exod.), *sanctification* (Lev.), *direction* (Num.) and *instruction* (Deut.) of the nation through which the Messiah was to come.

In the books of History *preparation* was made for Christ by giving Israel the Holy Land for their possession (Josh.). Despite the *oppression* of foreign powers (Judg.) due to Israel's sin, there remained devotion within the nation (Ruth). God gave *stabilization* to the nation under king Saul (I Sam.), *expansion* under king David (II Sam.), and *glorification* of the nation during Solomon's reign (I Kings 1-10). With Solomon's death came the *division* of the nation (I Kings 11-22) into Israel in the north and Judah in the south. Both suffered *deterioration* and final *deportation* by foreign powers (II Kings). Likewise, the Temple suffered *deprivation* (I Chron.) and finally *destruction* (II Chron.) at the hands of the Babylonians. But God was faithful in the *reconstruction* of the Temple (Ezra), the *restoration* of the nation (Neh.), and the *protection* of His people (Esther). The holy nation returned to the Holy Land and preparation was made for Christ.

Meanwhile, in the Poetical Books there was *aspiration* for Christ. Whereas the Law laid down the *moral* basis for the people of God and the books of History provided the *national* framework, the books of Poetry revealed their *spiritual* aspirations. The implicit longing for what Christ alone would provide was fivefold. In Job the aspiration is for *mediation* by God and in Psalms for *communion* with Him. Solomon's aspiration for *wisdom* in Proverbs, for *union* in love in the Song of Songs, and for ultimate *satisfaction* in Ecclesiastes completes the spiritual longings of Israel for what was to be provided through Jesus Christ.

The Books of Prophecy look forward to Christ in *expectation*. The earlier prophets (Hosea, Joel, Amos) expect a *national restoration* by the Messiah. Isaiah and Micah predict *international salvation* through the coming of Christ. But Obadiah, Jonah, Nahum, Habakkuk and Zephaniah warn of God's *retribution on the nations*. Lamentations grieves over God's *retribution on His people* but Jeremiah looks for a *covenantal reaffirmation* in Christ. Ezekiel expects the nation's *religious restoration* and Daniel predicts its *political restoration*. After the Babylonian captivity Haggai and Zechariah exhort the people in their *religious reconstruction* and Malachi in their *social and moral reconstruction,* as they await the coming of the "sun of righteousness [that] shall rise, with healing in its wings" (Mal. 4:2).

THE MEANING OF PROPHECY.

As we approach the Books of Prophecy a few words of introduction will be helpful. The word *prophet* comes from the word meaning "to announce." A prophet was God's mouthpiece or the human instrument through which God declared His message to men.

The broad meaning of the word *prophecy* is to forth-tell; the narrow meaning is to fore-tell. The latter is more popular today but the former is by far the more common usage in the Bible. In forth-telling God's message to his day the prophet would often foretell what God was going to do in the future. These supernatural predictions form one of the strongest evidences that the Bible is the Word of God. Forth-telling involved *insight* into the will of God; fore-telling entailed *foresight* into the plan of God. The first was *exhortive,* challenging evil men to higher moral conduct; the latter was *predictive,* encouraging the righteous.

There are many descriptions of a prophet in the Bible. He is called a *man of God* (I Kings 12:22) since he was chosen by God, a *servant of the Lord* (I Kings 14:18) because of his faithfulness to the Lord, a *messenger of the Lord* (Isa. 42:19) as he was sent by God, a *seer* (I Sam. 9:9) because of his insight from God, a *watchman* (Ezek. 3:17) because of his alertness for God. But the most common description is the word *prophet* itself because he was a speaker for God.

TESTING A PROPHET.

There were true prophets and false ones. The Bible gives several ways to test for false prophets: (1) Do they ever predict things that do *not* come to pass? If so they are false prophets (Deut. 18:21, 22). (2) Do they turn people away from the true God to other gods? If so they are not God's prophets (Deut. 13:1-3). (3) Do they use instruments of divination (crystal balls, tea leaves, etc.)? No true prophet of God would use occult methods for contacting God (Deut. 18:10, 11). (4) Is Jesus

Christ the center of their predictions? If not, then they are not of God, for "the testimony of Jesus is the spirit of prophecy" (Rev. 19:10). It is noteworthy that all modern fortunetellers, astrologers, and so-called prophets are rendered "false prophets" on these grounds. The fact that some of a prophet's predictions come to pass does not mean he is a true prophet. Occasional fulfillments do *not* constitute irrefutable proof that he is a true prophet (Deut. 13:1, 2). Guesses, intuition, the power of suggestion, mind-reading, or contact with demons can easily account for occasional fulfillments of prediction apart from God. In this respect this test for a true prophet is not positive but negative: if some things *do* come to pass it is inconclusive, but if some *do not* come to pass then it proves the predictor is a false prophet. All of the prophecies of the Bible have come true as predicted; no alleged modern prophet can claim the same.

A prophet of God is one who speaks the Word of God and whose message is confirmed by a work of God (i.e., by a miracle). When Moses' prophetic office was challenged by Korah, God vindicated Moses by a miracle in which the earth swallowed Korah and his evil followers (Num. 16). Likewise Elijah was confirmed as a true prophet of God on Mt. Carmel when the fire of God consumed his sacrifice in the presence of the false prophets of Baal (I Kings 18). The New Testament declares that this is God's pattern: God bears witness to His spokesmen "by signs and wonders and various miracles and by gifts of the Holy Spirit distributed according to his own will" (Heb. 2:4). Christians are urged by God to beware of false prophets (Matt. 24:4, 23, 24), not to believe every spirit but to test them (I John 4:1), not to give heed to deceitful spirits and the doctrines of demons (I Tim. 4:1), and even to ignore any angel from heaven who preaches a gospel other than that of Christ (Gal. 1:8).

THE HISTORY OF PROPHECY.

The prophets did not begin with Elijah or even with Samuel. The first prophecy was about the coming Messiah, and was given by *God* to Adam and Eve (Gen. 3:15). *Enoch,* the descendant of Adam, also prophesied about Christ's coming (Jude 14). *Noah* made predictions about his three sons (Gen. 9:25-27). *Abraham* is called a "prophet" (Gen. 20:7) and both Jacob (Gen. 37:6, 7) and Joseph uttered prophecies (Gen. 49:10). *Moses* was considered a prophet (Deut. 18:15). There were other prophets between Moses and Samuel (Judg. 6:8) but it was *Samuel* who started a school of the prophets (I Sam. 19:20). Perhaps the most famous pair of prophets in the Old Testament is *Elijah* (I Kings) and his disciple and successor *Elisha* (II Kings). All these prophets are sometimes called the pre- or non-writing prophets. This is somewhat of a misnomer because there are those among them, like

Moses and Samuel, who did write parts of the Bible. What is meant by pre-writing prophets is that these prophets came before the prophets whose seventeen books comprise the last section of our Old Testament, which is commonly known as the Prophets (Isa.-Mal.), that is, they lived before 850 B.C.

The New Testament too continues the line of prophets from *John the Baptist* (Matt. 11:9) through *Jesus* (cf. Deut. 18:15) and the *"apostles and prophets"* (Eph. 2:20) who were the foundation of the early church to the last of the prophets, *John the Apostle* (Rev. 22:6, 9), who completed the canon of Scripture (cf. John 14:26 and 16:13 with Rev. 22:18, 19). But our concern here is with the writing prophets of the last section of the Old Testament.

Following is a chart which gives in chronological order the important features of each of the seventeen prophetical books. Note the meaning of the prophets' names, the kings during whose reigns they prophesied, and the theme of their books. Note that the first eleven books were written before the seventy-year Babylonian captivity (Obad.-Jer.), that the next three (Lam., Ezek., and Dan.) were written during the captivity, and that the last three (Hag., Zech., and Mal.) were post-exilic. The dominant theme of the pre-exilic prophets was *admonition* or warning of God's coming judgment. The keynote of the exilic prophets was *anticipation* of God's coming deliverance. And the central thrust of the post-exilic prophets was *exhortation* to rebuild for God in preparation for and expectation of the coming of Christ.

The basic message of prophecy is messianic, centering in Jesus Christ. However, since Israel was the channel through which the Messiah was to come, much of the prophets' message is directed generally to the life of the messianic nation rather than specifically to the messianic individual who would come to deliver them.

THE SOURCE OF THE PROPHETIC MESSAGE.

Hebrews tells us that "in many and various ways God spoke of old to our fathers by the prophets" (1:1). Sometimes God spoke through *dreams* (Gen. 37) and other times in *visions* (Dan. 7). On occasion God spoke in an *audible voice* (I Sam. 3), but probably more often He spoke by an *inner voice* (Hos. 1; Joel 1, etc.). Sometimes God spoke through a previously *written word* (Dan. 9) or by an *angel* (Gen. 19) and at other times through *nature* (Ps. 19) or a *miracle* (Judg. 6:37). But in whatever way God spoke, His servants received the message and faithfully delivered it to His people.

THE METHOD OF DELIVERING THE PROPHETIC MESSAGE.

The earliest and most common means of delivering God's message was *oral;* the prophets literally spoke for God. David confessed, "The

CHART OF PROPHETIC BOOKS

BOOK	MEANING	DATE	SCRIPTURE	KINGS*	THEME
1. OBADIAH	"Worshiper of Jehovah"	840-830	II Kings 8-12	Jehoram, Ahaziah, Athaliah, Joash (S)	Retribution
2. JOEL	"Jehovah is God"	830-820	II Kings 12	Joash (S)	Visitation
3. JONAH	"Dove"	780-760	II Kings 14	Jeroboam II (N)	Commission
4. AMOS	"Burden bearer"	755-750	II Kings 14	Jeroboam II (N)	Threatened
5. HOSEA	"Salvation"	760-710	II Kings 14-17	Jeroboam II, Zechariah, Shallum, Menahem, Pekahiah, Pekah, Hoshea (N)	Estrangement
6. ISAIAH	"Jehovah is salvation"	740-690	II Kings 15-21	Jotham, Ahaz, Hezekiah, Manasseh (S)	Salvation
7. MICAH	"Who is like Jehovah"	735-700	II Kings 15-20	Jotham, Ahaz, Hezekiah (S)	Arraignment
8. NAHUM	"Compassionate" (Counselor, Comforter)	650-620	II Kings 21-23	Manasseh, Amon, Josiah (S)	Doom
9. ZEPHANIAH	"Hidden by Jehovah" (Protected)	630-620	II Kings 22-23	Josiah (S)	Vindication
10. HABAKKUK	"Embraced"	620-605	II Kings 22-24	Josiah, Jehoahaz, Jehoiakim (S)	Justice
11. JEREMIAH	"Established by Jehovah"	625-585	II Kings 22-25	Josiah, Jehoahaz, Jehoiakim, Jehoiachin, Zedekiah (S), Nebuchadnezzar	Warning
12. LAMEN.	"Grieving"	585-580	II Kings 25	Nebuchadnezzar	Disconsolate
13. EZEKIEL	"Strength of God"	593-570	II Kings 24-25	Zedekiah (S)	Glory
14. DANIEL	"God is my Judge"	606-530	II Kings 23-25; Ezra 1-4	Jehoiakim (S), Nebuchadnezzar, Belshazzar, Darius, Cyrus	Dominion
15. HAGGAI	"Festal"	520	Ezra 5-6	Zerubbabel, Darius I (Persian)	Consider
16. ZECHARIAH	"Remembered by Jehovah"	520-480	Ezra 5-6	Zerubbabel, Darius I, Xerxes	Consummation
17. MALACHI	"My Messenger"	430-420	Nehemiah 13	Artaxerxes, Darius II	Apostasy

PRE-EXILIC (1-11)
EXILIC (12-14)
POST-EXILIC (15-17)

*N = Northern Kingdom
 S = Southern Kingdom

Spirit of the Lord speaks by me, his word is upon *my tongue*" (II Sam. 23:2). As was indicated earlier, the root meaning of the word *prophet* is to announce or speak for God. This the prophets did faithfully, consistently speaking to the ears of God's people.

Sometimes, however, the prophets would give a *visual* message. They would pictorially present the word of God for the eyes of God's people. Hosea dramatically illustrated God's unfailing love by a *marriage* to an unfaithful wife (Hos. 1). The prophet Ahijah illustrated the division of the kingdom of Solomon by *tearing a garment* into twelve pieces (I Kings 11). At God's command Ezekiel built a brick *model* of Jerusalem being besieged by the enemy (Ezek. 4). In addition, every miracle seen by God's people was a visual presentation of God's word; there is always a message in the miracle, a sermon in the sign.

Of course, much of what the prophets *said* and *showed* they also *wrote,* and this at God's command. Habakkuk was told by God, "*Write* the vision; make it plain upon tablets..." (2:2). Jeremiah, likewise, was commanded, "*Write* in a book all the words that I have spoken to you" (30:2). It is in this way that future generations — including you and me — are able to have the words that God spoke through His prophets. Indeed, it is the *written words* given by the Holy Spirit (I Cor. 2:13) and recorded in Holy Scripture (II Tim. 3:16) that are inspired of God.

THE SUBJECT OF THE PROPHETIC MESSAGE.

Christ is the central subject of the prophetic Word. He said, "It is written of me in the roll of the book" (Heb. 10:7) and "everything written about me in the Law of Moses and the prophets and the psalms must be fulfilled" (Luke 24:44). Peter declared, "To Him all the prophets bear witness..." (Acts 10:43). Not always did the prophets themselves fully understand what they wrote about Christ's coming for they searched their own writings to discover "what person or time was indicated by the Spirit of Christ within them when predicting the suffering of Christ and the subsequent glory" (I Peter 1:11). During our survey of the prophetic books we will have opportunity to see what it was that they did predict about the coming Messiah and the messianic age.

The message of the prophets was far broader than statements about a coming messianic *individual* (Christ); there was also much about the messianic *instrument* (Israel). Statements about the individual were *predictive* and related to Christ and the future; statements about the instrument were largely *exhortative* and spoke about Israel and her present. The first were *messianic* and the latter *moral* in nature, although often the two are inseparably connected. Messianic predictions about the future kingdom seem to blossom right out of moral exhortation about the present conditions. Israel is the tree and Christ is her righteous Branch (cf. Zech. 3:8).

THE SIGNIFICANCE OF THE PROPHETIC MESSAGE.

The overall significance of the prophetic message was to show God at work in human history, to reveal that history is His-story. The prophets' predictions about a coming messianic and golden age provided a Goal or End of history. That is, the prophets wanted to show that history is going somewhere, that it is heading for an Omega point. Hence, the Jewish prophets are rightly credited by modern historians with providing the western world with a linear view of history as opposed to the cyclical view of history espoused by eastern and Greek thought.

We may relate the significance of the prophets' message to the past, to the present, and to the future. (1) The *past* events were used as lessons for the present. Moral history does repeat itself; falling away from God repeatedly leads to disaster and destruction. The lessons of the past serve as exhortations to the present (cf. I Cor. 10:11). (2) In the *present* the prophets served two primary roles: they were *reformers* in a day of apostasy, and *reminders* in a day of prosperity. (3) The *future* was the goal of the present. History in the view of the present was a moral process leading to the messianic age in which the moral principles laid down by God in the past and neglected by His people in the present would be brought to full social fulfillment in the future. This same truth is vividly set forth in the teaching of Jesus about the kingdom of God.

STUDY QUESTIONS

1. What does each prophet's name tell you about that prophet?
2. What is a prophet and how can one tell a true one from a false one? Is Jeane Dixon a true or false prophet according to these standards?
3. What are the two basic meanings of the word *prophecy* and how do these meanings relate to the broad and narrow subject matter of prophecy?
4. What three major chronological divisions do the seventeen prophets fall into and what characterizes each period?
5. What was the full and final way God spoke through the prophets? Why was this way final?

32

The Expectation of National Restoration by Christ

HOSEA, JOEL, AMOS

As the chart of the prophets (see ch. 31) indicates, Joel, Amos, and Hosea were among the earliest prophets of Israel. Their central common concern was *national restoration* in expectation of Christ. We will treat them in chronological order in order to fit their message into the context of their day.

JOEL

WHO WROTE JOEL?

Joel, the son of Pethuel, a prophet of Judah, is the author of this book. This fact is supported by an explicit claim (1:1), and is so corroborated by the content that even many critics of the Book of Joel accept Joel as the author.

WHEN WAS JOEL WRITTEN?

The book is early pre-exilic, dating from about 830 B.C. (cf. II Kings 12) during the reign of young king Joash. This is substantiated by several facts: (1) the array of Israel's enemies mentioned in Joel fits this period (note the absence of the Assyrians and Babylonians who came later); (2) many similarities can be seen between Joel (3:18) and Amos (9:13), which dates from this period; (3) the lack of reference to a king (but to ruling elders and priests instead) suggests the book was written during the reign of a youthful king like Joash (cf. II Kings 11:4). The arguments against this date are inconclusive. For example, the reference to the Greeks (3:6) is not to the major world power of the fourth century, but to a remote country involved in slave-trading.

TO WHOM WAS JOEL WRITTEN?

The internal evidence indicates that Joel's message was directed to Jerusalem and Judah in the south where the Temple and priests were located (cf. 1:9, 13, 14; 2:15), although his prophecy does speak of the Assyrian invasion which ultimately captured northern Israel in 722 B.C. (ch. 2).

WHERE WERE THEY LOCATED?

It will be remembered that when Solomon's united kingdom was split in two, Jeroboam, his captain, took over the northern ten tribes, Samaria was established as the capital, and centers of idolatry were set up at Dan and Bethel. The southern tribe of Judah (and Benjamin) kept Jerusalem as its capital and Solomon's Temple as the center of the worship of the Lord. It is to Jerusalem and Judah in the *south* that Joel addresses his message.

WHY WAS JOEL WRITTEN?

The historical purpose.

Joel was given as a warning of God's impending judgment on Judah.

The doctrinal purpose.

Two teachings are central: the day of the Lord (judgment) and the coming of the Spirit of the Lord (blessing).

The Christological purpose.

Christ is presented as the one who gives the Holy Spirit (2:28), who judges the nations (3:2, 12), and who is the Refuge and Stronghold for His people (3:16).

WHAT IS JOEL ABOUT?

The prophets often had two words: good news and bad news. First, for the bad news: judgment for man's evil is coming from God. Next, for the good news: God holds out a promise of future blessing to the faithful. Joel is no exception to this common prophetic pattern.

I. Desolation from the Lord (1:1–2:17).

A. THE HISTORICAL ASPECT (1:1-20).

It is not uncommon for a prophet to have both a near view (the immediate historical situation) and a far view (future application) in his message. The opening verses of Joel seem to indicate that a literal plague had swept the land (vv. 1-4). Thus an exhortation for God's people to humble themselves before Him (vv. 5-18) is followed by the prophet's supplication to God because of the plague (vv. 19, 20).

B. THE PROPHETICAL ASPECT (2:1-17).

From the immediate past the prophet turned to the immediate future. "Blow the trumpet in Zion . . . for the day of the Lord is coming, it is near" (v. 1). This indicates a day of judgment. The literal locusts of the past are now used as pictures of the invading northern army of the future. And in view of this the people are called to a solemn fast. The *destruction* is described (vv. 1-11) and then their *contrition* is commanded (vv. 12-17).

II. Deliverance of the Lord (2:18—3:21).

All is well that ends well. The prophet announces the good news: God will send deliverance from destruction to His people both in the present and in the future.

A.   THE PROMISE OF PRESENT BLESSING (2:18-27).

Following the plague God will send a plentiful harvest. The northern enemy will be removed and *restoration* will come from God to His land. "And my people shall never again be put to shame."

B.   THE PROMISE OF FUTURE BLESSING (2:28—3:21).

The pivotal phrase "and it shall come to pass *afterwards*" introduces this section. It indicates a shift from the near view to the far view. Indeed, it is a prediction of Pentecost when God poured out His spirit upon His people in *revival* (cf. Acts 2:1f., 17f.). First, Joel speaks of the *restoration* of Judah (2:30—3:3), then of the *condemnation* of their enemies (3:4-8); this is followed by a *proclamation* to the nations to prepare for the final battle (Armageddon) (3:9-15). All of this will be climaxed by the salvation of the Lord as "the Lord roars from Zion, and utters his voice from Jerusalem" (3:16-21).

AMOS

WHO WROTE AMOS?

The book was written by Amos, a herdsman (7:14) from Tekoa (near Bethlehem). This is substantiated by the claim of the book (1:1), the pastoral (shepherd's) language (cf. 7:10 f.), and the historical contents. Although Amos never went to the school of prophets (7:14), nevertheless he was called of God to prophesy to Israel (7:15).

WHEN WAS AMOS WRITTEN?

Amos' ministry can be dated around 755 B.C. (II Kings 14) during the later part of the reign of Jeroboam II of Israel (1:1). This was a time of great military success and materialism for the northern tribes, a fact that became a target of the prophet's scorching attack.

TO WHOM WAS AMOS WRITTEN?

Amos directed his message to the wicked but prospering northern ten tribes (cf. 3:1, 12; 7:10, 14, 15), although he himself was from Judah

Young shepherds in the fields outside Tekoa. Photo by Charles W. Turner

in the south (1:1). Hence, his warnings had obvious implications for his own countrymen as well (cf. 2:4, 5).

WHERE WERE THEY LOCATED?

Israel was located in the northern half of Palestine. Bethel, a center of their idol worship, was singled out by Amos for God's judgment (4:4f., 7:13).

WHY WAS AMOS WRITTEN?

The historical purpose.

The purpose of Amos was to call the prosperous and materialistic northern tribes under Jeroboam II to repentance of their sins.

The doctrinal purpose.

The book teaches God's hatred of evil, His jealousy for His own good, and the sanctity of His law. On the last point there are numerous references in Amos to the law of Moses (cf. 2:7 with Deut. 23:17, 2:8 with Exod. 22:26; 2:12 with Num. 6:1-21).

The Christological purpose.

The book presents Christ as the Rebuilder of David's Tabernacle (9:11, ASV) and the Husbandman of His people (9:13).

WHAT IS AMOS ABOUT?

The Book of Amos is divided into three sections. There are eight oracles, three sermons, and six visions of judgment and restoration.

I. The declarations of sin and judgment (1-2)
— eight oracles.

Beginning with the nations surrounding Israel, Amos swings in a kind of counterclockwise circle proclaiming God's judgment on *Syria* for their cruelty (1:3-5), on *Philistia* for slavery (1:6-8), on *Phoenicia* for breaking a treaty (1:9-10), on *Edom* for its revengeful spirit (1:11, 12), on *Ammon* for violence (1:13-15), on *Moab* for injustice (2:1-3), and on *Judah* for perverting the law (2:4-6). Amos then zeros in on Israel for her part in perverting the law (2:6-16).

II. The exhortations about sin and judgment (3-6)
— three sermons.

Each sermon begins with "Hear this word. . . ." The first message states the *reason* for God's judgment—sin (3); the second gives the *result* of God's judgment—destruction (4); and the third sermon calls for *repentance* in view of the sin and God's impending judgment (5-6). Amos speaks about the nature of true repentance (5a) and pronounces woes on false repentance (5b-6).

III. The visions of judgment and restoration (7-9)
— six visions.

In this final section the prophet presents six lively pictures—five of God's judgment and one of promised restoration. Each begins with "the Lord God showed me" or "I saw." The vision of the *locusts* (7:1-3) depicts the all-consuming nature of God's wrath. The vision of the *fire* indicates the scorching drought that would follow the plague (7:4-6). The *plumb line* reveals that God had already measured Israel by the rule of His justice and marked them for their due (7:7-9). After a short historical interlude in which Amos courageously announces his call and commission (7:10-17), the prophet manifests the immediacy of Israel's doom in the *basket of summer fruit,* which indicated that the end of their fruitful years had come (8:1-14). The last judgment is the *smiting of the Temple,* indicating the worldwide dispersion of Israel (9:1-10). But in the end there will be a *restoration:* "I will restore the fortunes of my people Israel," says the Lord. "I will plant them upon their land, and they shall never again be plucked up" (9:11-15).

HOSEA

WHO WROTE HOSEA?

Hosea, the son of Beeri, was apparently a citizen of northern Israel (cf. 7:5). This is the claim of the book (1:1) and the critics generally agree.

WHEN WAS HOSEA WRITTEN?

Some of the book appears to have been written before the death of Jeroboam II (753 B.C.), since the first chapter regards the end of Jehu's dynasty as yet future. Hosea 5 seems to have been intended for king Menahem (d. 742 B.C.) and Hosea 7 may have been written during Hoshea's dealings with Egypt (d. 722 B.C.). So the final product was no doubt completed by around 720 B.C. His ministry extended from at least 760 to 710 B.C. (II Kings 14:17).

TO WHOM IS HOSEA ADDRESSED?

Hosea is clearly directed to the northern ten tribes of Israel (1:1; 5:1). They are often referred to as "Ephraim" (cf. 5:3, 5, 11, 13; 12:1; 13:1).

WHERE WERE THEY LOCATED?

Israel, of course, was the northern division of the tribes who split on Solomon's death. Their capital city was Samaria (10:5).

WHY WAS HOSEA WRITTEN?

The historical purpose.

Hosea is a dramatic illustration of God's love for unfaithful Israel.

The doctrinal purpose.

The futility of formalism, the depravity of man, and the unending charity of God are three strong emphases of the Book of Hosea.

The Christological purpose.

The Messiah is presented as the Son of God (11:1), the only Savior of His people (13:4), the one who will ransom us from the dead (13:14; cf. I Cor. 15:55), but primarily as our compassionate lover (11:4) and the healer of the backslider (6:1).

WHAT IS THE BOOK OF HOSEA ABOUT?

The name *Hosea* means "salvation," and his message to Israel was one of saving love. God commanded him to remain faithful to his adulterous wife. This represented God's unfailing love despite Israel's spiritual harlotry with other gods (cf. Exod. 20:3).

I. A faithful husband and unfaithful wife
— personal affection (1-3).

These first chapters relate an amazing story of faithful love. Hosea was commanded to marry a wife (Gomer) who proved to be unfaithful to him. The *children* born to them were *signs* of God's dealings with Israel. "Jezreel," the name of the first son, meant "God will scatter" His people. "Lo-Ruhamah," the daughter, meant "not pitied" by God because of their sin. And, "Lo-Ammi," the second son, meant "not my people," indicating God's desire to disown them because of their sin (1). The *wife* proved *sinful*. She was a harlot and yet Hosea was to be faithful to her in his love (2). The *husband* Hosea was representative of *salvation*. He had to buy his wife back from the slavery in which adultery had involved her, yet loved her in spite of her sin (3).

II. A faithful Lord and an unfaithful Israel
— national reflection (4-14).

A. THE TRANSGRESSION OF ISRAEL (4-8).

Their sins were multiple. *Idolatry* (4) and *iniquity* (5) in the face of God's *fidelity* and *charity* (6) were followed by their *depravity* (7) and *apostasy* (8). "Come, let us return to the Lord; for he has torn, that he may heal us," Hosea pleaded (6:1). "What shall I do with you, O Ephraim?" God inquired (6:4). "For I desire steadfast love and not sacrifice, the knowledge of God, rather than burnt offerings" (6:6). Their religion was empty formalism. It had a "form of godliness, but denied the power thereof" (cf. II Tim. 3:5, ASV). Religious ceremony was a cover-up for their rebellious lives. They were without faith toward God; nevertheless, God remained faithful to them for He cannot deny Himself (cf. II Tim. 2:13).

B. THE VISITATION OF ISRAEL (9-10).

In the Old Testament a divine visitation signals judgment. The judgment, of course, was because of *Israel's disobedience* (9). And the form of the visitation was manifested in *Israel's dispersion* (10): God would scatter them. "Its people shall mourn for . . . its glory which has departed from it. Yea, the thing itself shall be carried to Assyria, as tribute to the great king" (10:5, 6).

C. THE RESTORATION OF ISRAEL (11-14).

Like Joel and Amos, Hosea stressed God's final restoration of His people. God loves His people with a love that will not let them go. He said, "I led them with cords of compassion, with the bands of love . . ." (11:4). With tender pity God cries, "How can I give you up, O Ephraim! How can I hand you over, O Israel!" (11:8). God's *compassion* is emi-

nently manifest (11) but Israel's *provocation* was likewise great (12).
Consequently, God's *condemnation* will come on the wicked (13). None-
theless, his *invitation* to salvation is extended, "Return, O Israel, to the
Lord your God . . ." (14).

STUDY QUESTIONS

1. What features do all three of these books have in common?
2. What do the names of these prophets mean, and what significance
   does this have for their times and message?
3. What are the particular conditions to which each prophet addresses
   his message?
4. Was all of Joel's prophecy completely fulfilled on the day of Pentecost (cf. 2:28-32)? If not, when will the rest be fulfilled?
5. How would you reconcile the fact that believers are commanded
   not to marry unbelievers with the fact that Hosea was commanded
   to marry an adulterous woman (cf. 1:2 with II Cor. 6:14)?

33

The Expectation of International Salvation Through Christ

ISAIAH, MICAH

The word *Isaiah* means "Jehovah is salvation" and *Micah* means "who is like Jehovah." These contemporaries provided respectively a major and minor voice demonstrating that God is salvation, not only for His chosen people, but for all the nations of the world. God promised Abram that through him He would bless all the nations of the world (Gen. 12:3); Isaiah and Micah prophesy the coming fulfillment of this promise.

ISAIAH

In many respects Isaiah is a miniature Bible. It has sixty-six chapters; the Bible has sixty-six books. The first thirty-nine chapters correspond to the thirty-nine books of the Old Testament, speaking largely about Israel before the coming Messiah. The last twenty-seven chapters parallel the New Testament, speaking largely about the Messiah and His messianic kingdom. Isaiah is one of the Old Testament books most often quoted in the New Testament. When one reads Isaiah it sometimes seems as though he is reading from the pages of the Gospels (cf. Isa. 9, 11, 40, 53).

WHO WROTE ISAIAH?

The author of this book claims to be Isaiah, son of Amos. He was a great poet, orator, and statesman. Isaiah was highly educated, knowledgeable in international affairs, and on familiar terms with the royal court. He was no doubt the greatest of the writing prophets both in the extent and comprehensiveness of his message and in his ability to communicate.

Critics have disputed whether Isaiah is a unified whole or whether there is a second (called Deutero-Isaiah, chs. 40-66) or even a third section (called Trito-Isaiah, chs. 56-66). The evidence is firmly in favor of *one Isaiah:*

(1) The book as a whole claims to be the work of one Isaiah. The introductory claim that Isaiah is the author (1:1) stands for the whole book, as is seen by its repetition in succeeding chapters (7:3; 20:2; 38:4; 39:5). The unified character and contents of the rest of the book also fit this claim.

(2) All of Jewish tradition attributes the whole book to one Isaiah. This tradition extends from the time of the intertestamental Book of Ecclesiasticus (48:17-25) (c. 150 B.C.) to the Talmud and into modern times.

(3) The same literary style, thoughts, phrases, and even figures of speech run throughout the whole book. The special formula, "thus saith the Lord," is found throughout the whole book; and the phrase for God, "the Holy One of Israel," which is rarely found in the rest of the Old Testament, occurs a dozen times or more in each of the two major sections of Isaiah. Biblical scholars have noted some forty or fifty other phrases common to both sections of Isaiah (see Archer, *A Survey of Old Testament Introduction,* pp. 333f.).

(4) The details of the entire book are Palestinian and not Assyrian. The latter half of the book would have to be Assyrian in its details if the critics be correct about a second Isaiah writing chapters 40-66. But even in 45:22 (which is from the second section), Jerusalem is the center from which God speaks to the whole earth.

(5) The failure of the critics to come up with another historical person who had the literary abilities reflected in Isaiah or with any textual evidence of separate Isaiahs indicates the insufficiency of their view. The earliest manuscripts of Isaiah discovered among the Dead Sea Scrolls support the fact that Isaiah is one complete and whole book. Further, it is highly unlikely that an unknown "second Isaiah" could have produced a literary masterpiece which rivals and corresponds with the first part of Isaiah.

(6) At the heart of the critics' objection is their aversion to the fact that Isaiah contains supernatural predictive prophecy. For example, parts of Isaiah name Cyrus (who became king of Persia) more than one hundred fifty years before he lived (44:28; 45:1). But no one who believes in a God who created this world should have any problem believing that He can reveal the future in advance. In fact, even if we were to adopt the most radical dating of the Old Testament prophets (say, the third or second century B.C.), we would still have dozens of predictions about Christ given hundreds of years in advance and literally

fulfilled. They include where He would be born (Mic. 5:2), that He would be born of a virgin (Isa. 7:14), when He would be born (Dan. 9), and even how He would die (Ps. 22). The God who can do all this has no problem in knowing and naming a king one hundred fifty years before his time.

(7) The conclusive evidence that there was only one Isaiah who wrote the whole book is that our Lord and the writers of the inspired New Testament attributed *both sections* of the book to one and the same *Isaiah*. John the Baptist cited Isaiah 40 in Matthew 3:3. Jesus quoted Isaiah 61 in Luke 4:18f. John 12:38 refers to Isaiah 53, while verse 40 quotes Isaiah 6. Paul also cited Isaiah 53 in Romans 10:16.

WHEN WAS ISAIAH WRITTEN?

The time of Isaiah's ministry extends from around 740 to about 690 B.C. It covers the reigns of Jotham, Ahaz, Hezekiah, and Manasseh, all kings of Judah. The historical background for this period is found in II Kings 15-21.

TO WHOM WAS ISAIAH WRITTEN?

Isaiah as a prophet ministered primarily to the southern kingdom of Judah. His message was generally directed toward Judah's sinful people (1:4) and particularly to its evil leaders (1:23).

WHERE WERE THEY LOCATED?

Judah, of course, was located in southern Palestine. Its capital was Jerusalem where throughout the book Isaiah centered his activity (1:1; 2:1; 52:2; 62:1).

WHY WAS ISAIAH WRITTEN?

The historical purpose.

Isaiah was sent of God to warn Judah of the sins that lead to Israel's downfall and to warn of the evil that would lead to their own. His message to them was twofold: God will bring condemnation on Israel and Judah through the nations but He will also one day provide salvation through Israel and Judah to the nations.

The doctrinal purpose.

This book comprehends all the great truths of the Old Testament regarding salvation from man's sin (1) through Christ's redemptive work (53) as well as the final glorious restoration of this earth (65).

The Christological purpose.

Isaiah presents perhaps the most complete and comprehensive descriptions of Christ found in the Old Testament. For example, Christ is referred to as the "Lord . . . high and lifted up" (6); the son of a virgin (7:14); the "Wonderful Counselor, Mighty God, Everlasting Father, Prince of Peace" (9:6); a Branch from Jesse and Anointed of the

Lord (11:1, 2); the "Comfort" of His people (40); the "Redeemer" and "Holy One of Israel" and their Creator and King (43); the Deliverer of the captives (61) and more.

WHAT IS ISAIAH ABOUT?

The message of Isaiah is one of salvation both for Israel in particular and for all nations in general. The book has been called "The Gospel According to Isaiah." The book may be divided into three sections: the prophetic (1-35), the historic (36-39), and the messianic (40-66).

I. Prophetic condemnations (1-35).

A. CONDEMNATIONS CONCERNING JUDAH AND ISRAEL (1-12).

This first section deals primarily with God's judgments through the hands of the Assyrians on the sins of His people. There is the judgment concerning Judah and Israel in which God *charges* His people with sin (1-5) and *calls* His prophet (6) to *warn* Judah of the coming judgment (7:12).

B. CONDEMNATION ON THE SURROUNDING NATIONS (13-23).

Turning the attention of his prophetic "oracles," Isaiah moves from one country to another, predicting the judgment of God on Babylon (13-14a), on Philistia (14b), on Moab (15-16), on Damascus (17-18), on Egypt (19-20), on Babylon, Dumah, and Arabia (21), and finally on Jerusalem (22) and Tyre (23). God is a holy God and He will not tolerate sin; He will visit the nations in wrath for their wickedness.

C. CONDEMNATIONS CONCERNING ALL NATIONS (24-35).

God's holy anger will not be restricted to Israel and her neighbors: the whole world will feel its stinging effects. (1) This coming wrath is given as *warning of the "Day of the Lord"* (24-27), which is a time of desolation (24a) to be followed by a time of restoration (24b-27). (2) Then Isaiah pronounces five *woes on the people of the Lord* (28-33): one on the drunkards and scoffers (28), one on the deceivers of God (29), one on the rebellious who place confidence in man not God (30), one on those who make alliance with the enemy (31-32), and one on treacherous destroyers (33). Finally, the prophet speaks of the *judgment and salvation of the Lord* (34-35). "Draw near, O nations, to hear.... For the Lord is enraged against all the nations" (34). But to the faithful He says, "Be strong, fear not! Behold, your God. . . . He will come and save you" (35).

II. Historic confiscation (36-39).

This section deals with the confiscation of Israel and Judah by the Assyrians and the Babylonians.

A. LOOKING BACK TO THE ASSYRIAN INVASION (36-37).

Isaiah reminds the Judean king Hezekiah of what the Assyrians did to the northern kingdom of Israel in 722 B.C. and warns him of Assyria's threat to Judah. But Hezekiah's *trouble* with the Assyrians (36) becomes his *triumph* in the Lord (37) when he turns to God and God delivers him from the Assyrians, thus sparing Jerusalem.

B. LOOKING FORWARD TO THE BABYLONIAN INVASION (38-39).

God heard Hezekiah's cry during the *sickness* which nearly caused his death and added fifteen years to his life (38). But because Hezekiah showed all his treasures to the messengers of the king of Babylon, God condemned him for his *sin* and predicted that the king of Babylon would one day carry his treasure and his sons to Babylon (39).

III. Messianic consolation (40-66).

The first sections of Isaiah contain many messianic prophecies (cf. chs. 7, 9, 11, 14, 26). But this final section of Isaiah is more explicitly messianic. In it the emphasis shifts from condemnation to consolation.

A. THE DELIVERANCE FROM GOD (40-48).

The stress in these chapters is on the consolation to be found in God's deliverance of His people. "Comfort, comfort my people, says your God" (40:1). The deliverance is *proclaimed* (40-42), *promised* (43-45), and *prophesied* (46-48). "Behold my servant, whom I uphold, my chosen, in whom my soul delights; I have put my Spirit upon him, he will bring forth justice to the nations" (42:1). He will be sent to "open the eyes that are blind, to bring out the prisoners from the dungeon, from the prison those who sit in darkness" (42:7, 8). This section abounds with messianic descriptions: "your Redeemer, the Holy One of Israel" (43:14); "the Creator of Israel, your King" (43:15); "God of Israel, the Savior" (45:15). Messiah will bring deliverance to Israel.

B. THE DELIVERER FROM GOD (49-57).

In this section special emphasis is placed on this One through whom the deliverance will come, the Messiah. He it is who *called* Isaiah (49-50) and who has *compassion* on His people (51-53), for "surely he has borne our griefs and carried our sorrows. . . . But he was wounded for our transgressions, he was bruised for our iniquities" (53:4, 5). His death will bring *comfort* to His people (54-55) and to the Gentiles as well (56). "Sing, O barren one, who did not bear; break forth into singing and cry aloud, you who have not been in travail" (54:1). "Ho, every one who thirsts, come to the waters; and he who has no money, come, buy and eat!" (55:1). A final note of *condemnation* on the wicked is sounded (57).

C.   THE DELIVERED OF GOD (58-66).

This last section centers on those who will be delivered of God, that is, on those people who trust in Him. God's *condition* for their deliverance is that "they seek me daily, and delight to know my ways . . ." (58-59). For "behold the Lord's hand is not shortened, that it cannot save, or his ear dull, that it cannot hear"; it is only "your iniquities [that] have made a separation between you and your God . . ." (59:1, 2). The *completeness* of their deliverance is spelled out in the glorious era of peace and prosperity (60-65a) in which Israel will be returned to the land of Palestine (60), the Savior will come (61), Zion will be restored (62), Israel will be converted (63-64), and the Gentile nations who call on God will be saved (65a). The *consummation* of the deliverance will come about when God creates a new heaven and earth (65b) and true worship of God will be restored (66). "For as the new heaven and the new earth which I will make shall remain before me, says the Lord; so shall your descendants and your name remain. From new moon to new moon, and from sabbath to sabbath, all flesh shall come to worship before me, says the Lord" (66:22, 23). Thus will God deliver the faithful of both Israel and the nations; His *international salvation* will endure forever.

MICAH

Micah was a contemporary of Isaiah and his book is a miniature of Isaiah's. He too spoke of God's international salvation through Christ. Only brief treatment is needed of the truth repeated in Micah.

WHO WROTE MICAH?

The author is Micah, the Morasthite (from Moresheth near Gath), the prophet of Judah, and contemporary of Hosea and the great prophet Isaiah. The evidence that Micah wrote this book is found in its claim (1:1), the character and unity of the whole book (cf. 1:2; 3:1; 6:1), its similarity in content to Isaiah (cf. 4:1-3 and Isa. 2:2-4), the confirmation of early Jewish teaching, and general agreement of the critics.

WHEN WAS MICAH WRITTEN?

Micah was an early pre-exilic prophet during the reigns of Jotham, Ahaz, and Hezekiah, kings of Judah (see II Kings 15-20). This time period extends from about 735 to 700 B.C.

TO WHOM DID MICAH WRITE?

Micah was *about* both Israel (Samaria) and Judah (Jerusalem) but it seems to be primarily directed *to* Judah, since only southern kings are mentioned in the address (cf. 1:1).

WHERE WERE THEY LOCATED?

Micah refers to cities of northern Israel (e.g., Samaria) and of southern Judah (e.g., Jerusalem, Bethlehem), but the home of the prophet (near Gath) and the direction of his message indicate that he lived in the southern kingdom.

WHY WAS MICAH WRITTEN?

The historical purpose.

Micah shows God's hatred of His people's passionless ritual and sin (cf. 6:7) and His offer of pardon to them.

The doctrinal purpose.

Several important teachings are stressed including God's hatred of empty formal religion (6:7), His concern for social justice (6:8), His pardoning grace (7:18), and His faithfulness to His covenants (7:20).

The Christological purpose.

This book presents Christ as the God of Jacob (4:2), the Judge of the nations (4:3), and the Ruler in Israel who will be born in the city of Bethlehem (5:2; cf. Matt. 2:1-6).

WHAT IS MICAH ABOUT?

"Micah" means "who is like Jehovah" (as Michael means "who is like God"). In spirit and content his message was like Isaiah's—a message of salvation to the nations. As is common for a prophetic book, Micah has two basic divisions: denunciation and consolation.

I. The denunciation of the Lord (judgment) (1-3).

The denunciation of God is pronounced on *Samaria* for its idolatry (1:1-7), on *Judah* for its idolatry and wickedness (1:8—2:13), and on the *princes and prophets* for their injustice and deception (3).

II. The consolation of the Lord (glory) (4-7).

But one day God will rescue His people. Micah gives a *prophecy* (4-5) that includes both the salvation of Gentiles (cf. 4:1-3) and an unusual prediction about the birth of Christ (5:2). God's *pleading* with Israel to do good (6) is succinctly stated: "What does the Lord require of you but to do justice, and to love kindness, and to walk humbly with your God?" (v. 8). Finally, Micah reminds them of God's *pardoning* grace for their sins (7): "Who is a God like thee, pardoning iniquity and passing over transgression for the remnant of his inheritance?" (v. 18). The book closes with the consolation that this God will "show faithfulness to Jacob and steadfast love to Abraham, as he hast sworn to our fathers from the days of old" (v. 20).

STUDY QUESTIONS

1. What evidence is there that only one author wrote the entire Book of Isaiah?
2. Study Isaiah 53. How much of the life and death of Christ, as recorded in the Gospels, can you identify in this chapter?
3. In what respects is Isaiah a miniature Bible?
4. How much of the picture of the future can you put together from Isaiah?
5. Study the descriptions of Christ in Isaiah. What do they tell us about Him?
6. About what is Micah's social concern?

34

The Expectation of Retribution on the Surrounding Nations

OBADIAH, JONAH, NAHUM

A characteristic of this group of pre-exilic prophets is that they all predicted God's retribution or judgment on the nations. *Obadiah* may be the earliest of all seventeen prophets (ninth century). He announced God's judgment on proud Petra in the clefts of Edom's rocks. *Jonah* originally proclaimed impending judgment on the people of Nineveh (eighth century), but because they repented God spared them for one hundred and fifty years. *Nahum* was also written about Nineveh, but it was directed to the southern kingdom. Later both *Zephaniah* and *Habakkuk* (seventh century) declared doom for Judah and the surrounding nations just before the Babylonian captivity (see ch. 35). A brief statement on each book will be given in the order in which they were written.

OBADIAH

The name *Obadiah* means "Worshiper [or servant] of Jehovah." He wrote the shortest book in the Old Testament. It is a prophecy about Petra in Edom.

WHO WROTE OBADIAH?

The author is Obadiah, an otherwise unknown prophet of Judah (1:1), cited by Jeremiah 49:7-22 (cf. Obad. 1-9). The claim of the book, its basic unity, its citation by Jeremiah, and early Jewish teaching support authorship by Obadiah.

WHEN WAS OBADIAH WRITTEN?

The time is uncertain. Some biblical scholars say Obadiah was written very early, that is, during *Jehoshaphat's time* (ninth century). Others say it was written very late, perhaps during the *Babylonian cap-*

tivity (sixth century), and still others take a middle course, placing it during the reign of *Ahaz* (eighth century). If verses 11 and 20 refer to the Babylonian captivity, then the late date is called for; but the quotation by Jeremiah (49:7-22) would seem to eliminate this possibility since the passage from Obadiah is included with citations of earlier prophets (e.g., Isaiah and Amos). Likewise, the view that Obadiah was written in the eighth century is faced with the serious problem that the historical record of the attack of the Edomites and Philistines at that time (II Chron. 28:17) makes no mention of the capture and desolation of Jerusalem depicted in Obadiah 11. It therefore seems best to adopt, as many scholars do, the ninth century as the date and to identify the capture and temporary destruction of Jerusalem with that inflicted by Edom in the days of Jehoram (II Kings 8:20). Thus Obadiah should be dated 840-830 B.C.

To whom was Obadiah written?

If Obadiah did indeed write around 840-830 B.C., the book was addressed to the people of Judah just after Jehoram and during the reigns of the wicked queen Athaliah, the evil king Ahaziah, and the young Joash. It was a prophecy *about* Edom's doom but it was a comfort *to* Judah, which had just suffered bitter defeat at the evil hands of Edom.

Where were they located?

Petra was located in Edom, due south of the Dead Sea. But the Book of Obadiah was written to Judah centered in Jerusalem (cf. vv. 11, 21).

Why was Obadiah written?

The historical purpose.

The purpose of Obadiah is to pronounce doom on Edom (Petra) and to predict the restoration of the land to Judah.

The doctrinal purpose.

This tiny book declares the justice of God, His faithfulness in restoring the land given to Abraham, and the perils of anti-Semitism. It teaches that pride comes before a fall (cf. I Cor. 10:12).

The Christological purpose.

The book pictures the Messiah as both Savior and possessor of the kingdom (21).

What is Obadiah about?

I. The doom of Edom pronounced (1-16).

Obadiah speaks of the *certainty* of Edom's overthrow (1-9), the *cause of* their overthrow, namely, violence and pride (10-14), and the *character* of their overthrow, that is, they would receive the same treatment they had given Judah (15, 16).

II. The deliverance of Judah (17-21).

Whereas the doom of Edom will be dark and terrible, the deliverance of Judah will be bright and beautiful. Obadiah speaks of the *triumph* of Judah over her enemies (17, 18), the *treasures* of Judah in their possession of the land (19, 20), and the *triumph* of Judah as the Lord possesses the kingdom (21).

JONAH

The word *Jonah* means "dove." This prophet is one of the most interesting in the Bible. He preached repentance, but actually hoped for the doom of Israel's brutal enemies at Nineveh, capital of Assyria.

WHO WROTE JONAH?

Jonah, the son of Amittai, a prophet from Galilee in the northern kingdom of Israel, is the author. This is confirmed by the claim of the book (1:1), the historical character of the book which names real places and persons, corroboration from another historical source (II Kings 14:25), and the testimony of Jesus in the New Testament (Matt. 12:40).

WHEN WAS JONAH WRITTEN?

Jonah's ministry is dated around 780 to 760 B.C., during the reign of Jeroboam II of Israel. Thus Jonah is an early pre-exilic prophet to the northern kingdom (II Kings 14).

TO WHOM WAS JONAH WRITTEN?

Jonah wrote to his proud and patriotic fellow-countrymen who were already under taxation by the notoriously evil Assyrian empire.

WHERE WERE THEY LOCATED?

Nineveh was the capital of the great Assyrian empire sprawling to the north and east of Israel. Jonah wrote about Nineveh but the book is directed to the northern tribes of Israel.

WHY WAS JONAH WRITTEN?

The historical purpose.

Jonah provides a strong rebuke to the proud patriotism of the Jews that blinded them, keeping them from seeing God's love for the Gentiles.

The doctrinal purpose.

Jonah teaches the universality of God's salvation, the need for obedience to God, the secret of true revival by repentance from sin, and the truth that "salvation is of the Lord" (2:9, KJV).

The Christological purpose.

The New Testament mentions Jonah as a type of Christ's resurrection (Matt. 12:40). Through Jonah, Christ is pictured as a prophet to the nations, while in Jonah's life He is shown as the Savior and Lord (2:9).

WHAT IS JONAH ABOUT?

The message of Jonah is captured by a study of the outline headings for the four chapters.

I. The disobedient prophet
Running away from the Lord (1).

Jonah was called by God to proclaim Nineveh's doom unless the city repented, but Jonah disobeyed and took a ship west to Tarshish (Spain). God prepared a great fish to swallow Jonah in which the prophet spent three restless days and nights.

II. The disciplined prophet
Running back to the Lord (2).

Recognizing the hand of God upon him, Jonah cried out to the Lord from the fish's belly. God delivered him, causing the great fish to vomit Jonah out on dry land.

III. The dynamic prophet
Running with the Lord (3).

Having learned the lesson of obedience to God, the prophet was recommissioned to go to Nineveh and cry out against their wickedness. The repentance of Jonah was exceeded by the repentance of Nineveh. And God, seeing their contrition, repented of the judgment He would have executed on Nineveh and spared the city.

IV. The disappointed prophet
Running ahead of the Lord (4).

The proud and patriotic Israelite prophet was disappointed that the evil enemies of Israel were not destroyed. But God tenderly taught the pouting prophet that He is gracious and forgiving, even to the Gentiles if they repent. God's major concern, as He told Abraham (Gen. 12:3), is to bless the world, not to judge it.

NAHUM

The name *Nahum* means "consolation," but his message was anything but that for the Ninevites. What Jonah had hoped for, namely,

God's judgment on the wicked Assyrians, was predicted by the pen of Nahum over one hundred fifty years later.

WHO WROTE NAHUM?

This book was written by Nahum, who was probably a prophet of Judah (cf. 1:15). The identification of his city, translated "Elkosh" in the Revised Standard Version, is in dispute. (1) Jerome held that it was Elkesi in Galilee; (2) others say it was Capernaum, which means "city of Nahum" (Kephar-Nāhūm); (3) some say it refers to Alqush near Mosul in Assyria; (4) but it was probably Elecesei, a city in Judah between Jerusalem and Gaza, since the internal evidence indicates Nahum was a native of Judah. The explicit claim (1:1), internal unity, and confirmation by historical evidence indicate that Nahum was the author.

WHEN WAS THE BOOK WRITTEN?

Nahum refers to the fall of Thebes in Egypt (661 B.C.) as a past event. Further, he predicted the fall of Nineveh, which took place in 612 B.C. Nahum probably wrote between 650 and 620 B.C., when Nineveh fell victim to a flood and the besieging armies of Medes and Chaldeans. This would place Nahum during the reigns of Manasseh, Amon, and Josiah, kings of Judah (II Kings 21).

TO WHOM WAS NAHUM WRITTEN?

Nahum was written to the kingdom of Judah though it concerned the fall of Nineveh. It was no doubt an encouragement to the Jews to hear that the Lord would vindicate His holiness on the inhumane brutality of the ruthless empire of Assyria.

WHERE WERE THEY LOCATED?

Nineveh was to the north of the former land of Israel, which had fallen to the Assyrians almost one hundred years earlier. Judah lay restless to the south in mortal fear of the God-defying Assyrian empire.

WHY WAS NAHUM WRITTEN?

The historical purpose.

Nahum comforted the faithful in Judah by describing the justice of God in the condemnation of Nineveh.

The doctrinal purpose.

This book manifests both the justice of God in dealing with evil and the goodness of God in the eyes of the righteous. It dramatizes the truths, "The wicked shall depart to Sheol [Hell], all the nations that forget God" (Ps. 9:17), and "Vengeance is mine, I will repay, says the Lord" (Rom. 12:19).

The Christological purpose.

Nahum sees Christ as the jealous God (1:2) and the Avenger of His adversaries.

WHAT IS NAHUM ABOUT?

The theme of Nahum is retribution; God vindicated His holiness on this pagan nation. The revival of Jonah was a century and a half past, and "Nineveh's cup of iniquity" was now full.

I. The judgment on Nineveh declared (1).

Judgment is made necessary by the nature of a holy God. First, the *character* of God is described by the prophet in powerful, poetic terms (vv. 1-7). "The mountains quake before him, the hills melt.... Who can stand before his indignation?" (vv. 5, 6). Next, the *condemnation* of Nineveh is declared (vv. 8-15). "But with an overflowing flood he will make a full end of his adversaries" (v. 8).

II. The judgment on Nineveh described (2).

One can almost hear the invading army as Nahum writes of the *siege of the city* (vv. 1-8): "Man the ramparts; watch the road.... The chariots rage in the streets...they gleam like torches, they dart like lightning.... Nineveh is like a pool whose waters run away" (vv. 4, 8). Following the siege, the *sack of the city* is described (vv. 9-13): "Plunder the silver, plunder the gold.... Desolate! Desolation and ruin!" (vv. 9, 10).

III. The judgment on Nineveh defended (3).

Finally, the prophet justifies God's judgment on Nineveh. Her *sin and wickedness demanded God's judgment* (vv. 1-7): "Woe to the bloody city, all full of lies and booty—no end to the plunder!" (v. 1). And her *strength and wealth cannot detour God's judgment* (vv. 8-19): "All your fortresses are like fig trees with first-ripe figs.... Your princes are like grasshoppers.... Your shepherds are asleep, O king of Assyria" (vv. 12, 17, 18). God is holy and He will punish the wicked.

STUDY QUESTIONS

1. What evil deeds of the Edomites called for the judgment of God described in Obadiah?
2. Why was Jonah disappointed when the Ninevites were converted?
3. How long did Nineveh's revival under Jonah delay God's judgment and why did Nahum call that judgment down?

35

Retribution on Judah and the Nations

ZEPHANIAH, HABAKKUK

Obadiah, Jonah, and Nahum predicted God's retribution on the nations surrounding Judah. Zephaniah and Habakkuk later predicted God's judgment on both Judah and the Gentile nations.

ZEPHANIAH

The name *Zephaniah* means "hidden by Jehovah." The theme of the book is the vindication of God. Despite appearances to the contrary, God is in firm control of the world and will prove this by His chastisement of Judah and destruction of idolatrous Gentile nations.

WHO WROTE ZEPHANIAH?

The book claims to be written by Zephaniah, the son of Cushi, the great-grandson of Hezekiah (1:1). This could be Hezekiah the king. If so, Zephaniah is the only prophet of royal blood. The character and content of the book fit its claim to be the work of Zephaniah.

WHEN WAS ZEPHANIAH WRITTEN?

This is a late pre-exilic book written during the reign of Josiah (cf. 1:1) prior to the revival of 621 B.C. (II Kings 22-23). If Zephaniah 2 is making reference to the Scythian invasion of about 630 B.C., then the prophet wrote between 630 and 621 B.C. He was a contemporary of Jeremiah and Habakkuk.

TO WHOM WAS ZEPHANIAH WRITTEN?

The prophet addresses his message to the people of Judah whose moral and religious interest had been dulled by the influence of the evil reigns of Manasseh and Amon (cf. 3:1-7).

WHERE WERE THEY LOCATED?

The prophet apparently lived in Jerusalem, since he referred to it as "this place" (1:4). His message was definitely to the inhabitants of Judah and Jerusalem.

WHY WAS ZEPHANIAH WRITTEN?

The historical purpose.

This book served to warn Judah of the impending doom on both Judah and the nations for their sins, and to call on them for repentance.

The doctrinal purpose.

Zephaniah teaches that God desires to demonstrate His holiness and hence will be just in executing judgment on the world. In this regard, the prophet Zephaniah stresses "the day of the Lord" (ch. 1). Nonetheless, God will be faithful to all in every nation who call upon Him (cf. Rom. 10:13). Further, God will keep His promise and restore the fortunes of Israel, regathering them as a nation (3:20).

The Christological purpose.

The Savior is presented as the righteous Lord within Israel (3:5), the witness against the nations (3:8), and "the King of Israel, the Lord" (3:15).

WHAT IS ZEPHANIAH ABOUT?

Zephaniah divides into three sections: retribution, repentance, and redemption.

I. The execution of retribution
God's jealousy is kindled against Judah (1).

Zephaniah tells *who* will bring the judgment—God (v. 1); *what* He will do—"I will utterly sweep away everything from the face of the earth" (vv. 2, 3); *why* He will do it—because of idolatry (vv. 4-6); *on whom* it will fall—the officials, princes, and inhabitants of Judah (vv. 7-13); and *how great* the judgment will be—"The great day of the Lord is near. . . . A day of wrath is that day, a day of distress and anguish. . . . In the fire of his jealous wrath, all the earth shall be consumed" (vv. 14-18).

II. The exhortation to repentance
God's jealousy is kindled against the Gentiles (2-3a).

Before the judgment falls there is time for repentance. Zephaniah gives God's *call to Judah:* "Seek the Lord, all you humble of the land" (2:1-3). But God's *condemnation on the Gentiles* is coming (2:4-15): "The Lord will be terrible against them; yea, he will famish all the gods of the earth, and to him shall they bow down . . . ." Nor will God overlook the *corruption of Jerusalem* (3:1-7): "Woe to her that is rebellious and defiled, the oppressing city! She listens to no voice, she accepts no correction."

III. The expectation of redemption
God's jealousy quenched for Judah (3b).

The final heat of God's wrath will accomplish the *cleansing of the nations* (vv. 8-10): "For my decision is to gather nations, to assemble kingdoms, to pour out upon them my indignation, all the heat of my anger." Yet "at that time I will change the speech of the peoples to a pure speech, that all of them may call on the name of the Lord and serve him with one accord." Then will follow the *restoration of Israel* (vv. 11-13): "For I will leave in the midst of you a people humble and lowly. They shall seek refuge in the name of the Lord, those who are left in Israel." This restoration of the remnant will result in the *jubilation of Israel* (vv. 14-20): "Sing aloud, O daughter of Zion; shout, O Israel! Rejoice and exalt with all your heart, O daughter of Jerusalem!"

HABAKKUK

The name *Habakkuk* is of uncertain origin; it may mean "to embrace." But the message of Habakkuk is clear: God is holy, and He cannot look with approval on sin.

WHO WROTE HABAKKUK?

Habakkuk was a Judean prophet with a levitical (priestly) background (cf. 3:19). The whole book claims to come from Habakkuk (1:1; 3:1), but critics challenge the third chapter because it is a psalm not a prophecy and because it mentions musical terms which these critics claim came later in Israel's history. But these arguments are fallacious because levitical music existed long before Habakkuk's time; David originated much of the levitical music (I Chron. 25 and Amos 6:5). Further, it is only natural for someone within the levitical tradition (like Habakkuk) to be interested in music and psalms (cf. "Shigionoth" in Hab. 3:1 with the title of Ps. 7).

WHEN WAS HABAKKUK WRITTEN?

Since the book demonstrates awareness of the notoriety of the conquering Babylonians (1:6-10), Habakkuk's ministry appears to be during the reign of Jehoiakim of Judah. This would be just after the fall of Nineveh to the Babylonians (612 B.C.), or perhaps even after the exploitation of the poor upon the death of Josiah (609 B.C.), as

1:2-4 may indicate. It seems that Babylon had not yet invaded Judah (605 B.C.), although invasion appears imminent (1:6; 2:1). Habakkuk's prophecy, then, was probably written shortly before 605 B.C. and no earlier than late in Josiah's day (620 B.C.). Habakkuk was a contemporary of Jeremiah and lived during the reigns of Josiah, Jehoahaz, and Jehoiakim (II Kings 22-24).

To whom was Habakkuk written?

Habakkuk directs his message of condemnation at the greedy nobles and the shameless religious leaders who were oppressing the common people of Judah (1). God's promises were conveyed to the faithful who were apparently dismayed that God had not intervened to vindicate justice (2).

Why was Habakkuk written?

As with the other books, a threefold purpose may be seen:

The historical purpose.

To comfort the faithful in Judah with the justice of God's coming judgment on the evil Chaldeans was Habakkuk's historical purpose.

The doctrinal purpose.

To teach the holiness and justice of God and the necessity of faith for the righteous, to show that God is just and that the just live by faith in Him: these were the doctrinal purposes.

The Christological purpose.

Christ is pictured as the Holy One (1:12), the one who justifies the righteous by faith (2:4), and the one who will some day fill the earth "with the knowledge of the glory of the Lord, as the waters cover the sea" (2:14).

What is Habakkuk about?

Although often neglected, Habakkuk's prophecy is one of the most influential in the Bible. Habakkuk 2:4 is quoted three times in the New Testament (Rom. 1:17; Gal. 3:11; Heb. 10:38), more than almost any other verse. It served as the basis for the Protestant Reformation and, through Luther's Commentary on Galatians, the conversion of John Wesley. Habakkuk is a book of faith.

I. Faith tested (1).

The prophet *requested* that God answer his cry about violence and corruption in the land (vv. 1-4). God *replied* that He would bring in the Chaldeans to chastise Judah (vv. 5-11). But the prophet *remonstrated* that God was holy and he could not understand how God could use a nation more evil than Judah as His instrument of judgment.

II. Faith taught (2).

"I will take my stand to watch . . . and look forth to see what he [God] will say to me," wrote Habakkuk (2:1). So the *waiting prophet* (v. 1) was met by a *willing Lord* (vv. 2-5) who told him that while "the righteous live by faith," "he whose soul is not upright in him shall fail." Therefore Habakkuk lamented the sins of his *woeful nation* (vv. 6-20), particularly the sins of those who rob the poor and spread violence throughout the land.

III. Faith triumphant (3).

Habakkuk's faith was both tested and taught; his faith then gave triumphant expression first to the *person of God* who taught him (vv. 1-5): "His glory covered the heavens, and the earth was full of his praise"; then to the *power of God* (vv. 6-12): "Thou didst bestride the earth in fury, thou didst trample the nations in anger"; and finally to the *purpose of God* (vv. 13-19): "Thou wentest forth for the salvation of thy people."

STUDY QUESTIONS

1. What impact did Zephaniah's message have on the evil people of Judah (cf. II Kings 22:1, 2)?
2. What is God jealous about (Zeph. 1:18; 3:8) ? Is it right for God to be jealous?
3. What does the phrase "the day of the Lord" signify in Zephaniah? Compare Joel 2:1f.
4. What does Habakkuk teach us about the character of God?
5. Study the New Testament quotations of Habakkuk 2:4. If the verse is divided into three parts (The just—shall live—by faith), in which New Testament book(s) is each part of the verse stressed?

36

The Expectation of Covenantal Reaffirmation in Christ

JEREMIAH, LAMENTATIONS

Both of these books were written by Jeremiah, the weeping prophet. Lamentations looks backward in agony over God's retribution on Israel, and Jeremiah looks forward to God's reaffirmation of the covenant with Israel after the seventy-year captivity. Jeremiah's prophecies were given both before and after the fall of Jerusalem (605 B.C.). Hence, he is both a pre-exilic and early exilic prophet.

WHO WROTE JEREMIAH?

This book was written by Jeremiah, the son of Hilkiah the priest. The supporting evidence for Jeremiah's authorship is more than sufficient.

(1) The title of the book claims that the prophecies are those of Jeremiah (1:1).

(2) The character and contents of the book fit the tumultuous era in which Jeremiah lived—just before and during the Babylonian exile.

(3) Daniel, a contemporary of Jeremiah, possessed and cited from the prophecies of this book, verifying that Jeremiah wrote them (Dan. 9:2; cf. Jer. 25).

(4) Later sources such as Ecclesiasticus 49:6, 7 and Josephus, *Antiquities,* X.5.1, attribute the book to Jeremiah.

(5) In the field of archaeology the Lachish letters (dating from 588 B.C.) offer both linguistic and historical support for the authorship of Jeremiah.

(6) The New Testament quotes this book as the work of Jeremiah several times (cf. Matt. 2:17; 21:13; Heb. 8:8-12).

There were probably several editions of Jeremiah. The first edition was burned by king Jehoiakim in anger (Jer. 36:2, 23). Jeremiah rewrote it and added more words to it at God's command (Jer. 36:32).

This may account for the fact that the Septuagint (LXX) version of Jeremiah is about an eighth shorter than the Hebrew (Masoretic) text. The final version was no doubt put together by Baruch, Jeremiah's secretary, after Jeremiah's death (cf. 36:1-4). He incorporated the additional prophecies of Jeremiah and published the longer work which is the basis for the Hebrew and English texts.

Jeremiah was one of the more colorful Old Testament characters. A word about his life is in order. (1) He was from a priestly background (1:1). (2) He was predestined to the prophetic office before he was born (1:5, 6). (3) He began his preaching ministry under Josiah (II Chron. 35:25). (4) His times were perilous (16:1-4). (5) He spent a good deal of time in prison for his unfavorable prophecies (37:15). (6) He shared in the sufferings of the remnant left in the land after the Babylonian captivity and was finally exiled to Egypt (43:1-7).

WHEN WAS JEREMIAH WRITTEN?

Jeremiah began his ministry at about twenty years of age in the thirteenth year of the reign of Josiah (1:2). He continued to prophesy after the destruction of Jerusalem in 585 B.C. (cf. Lamentations). The times of his various prophecies are indicated below in the outline of the book. Jeremiah's ministry covered the reigns of Josiah, Jehoahaz, Jehoiakim, Jehoiachin, and Zedekiah (II Kings 22-25). He was a contemporary of Nahum, Zephaniah, Habakkuk, Daniel, and Ezekiel.

TO WHOM WAS JEREMIAH WRITTEN?

Jeremiah's early prophecies were directed to the people of Judah in the declining days before the Babylonian captivity (1-39). The remaining chapters were directed to the discouraged and dismayed peoples scattered around the land of Palestine as a result of the Babylonian captivity and the destruction of Jerusalem.

WHERE WERE THEY LOCATED?

The audience of the first section of Jeremiah was the nation of Judah—the invasion of the Babylonians was still in the future (1-39). The last part of Jeremiah is directed to the guerrilla remnant who stayed in the land after Judah fell (40-43), to those who fled to Egypt to avoid being taken captive (44), and to the captive remnant in Babylon (45-52). Jeremiah's readers, then, were scattered in three major areas: Palestine, Egypt, and Babylon.

WHY WAS JEREMIAH WRITTEN?

The historical purpose.

Jeremiah's prophecies served as God's final warning of the impending judgment of the Babylonian captivity.

The doctrinal purpose.

The book lays great stress on morality and on the supremacy of the one God (as opposed to idolatry). It teaches that "righteousness exalts a nation, but sin is a reproach to any people" (Prov. 14:34).

The Christological purpose.

There are many presentations of Christ: He is the fountain of living waters (2:13; cf. John 4:14), the balm of Gilead (8:22), the good Shepherd (23:4), a righteous Branch (23:5), and the Lord our righteousness (23:6). Overall He is the weeping Prophet to His people (cf. Matt. 23:37, 38).

WHAT IS JEREMIAH ABOUT?

The name *Jeremiah* probably means "established by the Lord." This name is certainly characteristic of the man. Jeremiah was an anchor in turbulent waters. His prophecies were unpopular with the political and religious establishment but an encouragement to the remnant. The prophecies here are slightly rearranged into chronological order for a better understanding of the history of his times.

I. Prophecies before the fall of Jerusalem (1-39).

These early prophecies fall into three categories: those reflecting the *mourning* of Jeremiah about his people's condition, those giving a prophetic *warning* about the coming captivity, and those looking beyond the captivity to the bright prophetic *morning* awaiting God's people.

A. PROPHECIES DURING JOSIAH'S REIGN (1-12).

These first chapters provide us with the *prophet's call* from his mother's womb (1), the *prophet's concern* for his people's idolatry, injustice, and iniquity (2-6), the *prophet's compassion* for his people's lives (7-10): "Thus says the Lord of hosts, the God of Israel, Amend your ways and your doings . . ." (7:3). "Why then has this people turned away in perpetual backsliding?" asked the Lord (8:5). "O that my head were waters, and my eyes a fountain of tears, that I might weep day and night for the slain of the daughter of my people!" cried the prophet (9:1). Further, the *people's complacence* toward God's commands dismayed Jeremiah (11-12): "They have turned back to the iniquity of their forefathers, who refused to hear my words; they have gone after other gods to serve them" (11:10). Jeremiah recognized, "Righteous art thou, O Lord, when I complain to thee." Nonetheless, he

pleaded with God: "Why does the way of the wicked prosper?" (12:1).
God was quick to answer Jeremiah in no uncertain terms with the
judgment on Judah at the hands of Nebuchadnezzar.

B. PROPHECIES DURING JEHOIAKIM'S REIGN (13-20; 25-26; 35-36).

1. *The prophet's experiences* (13-20). God spoke through dramatic
illustrations using a rotten loincloth (13a) and a jar filled with wine
(13b) to show how the inhabitants of the land would be filled with
drunkenness. Jeremiah spoke of coming drought: "Let my eyes run
down with tears night and day, and let them not cease..." (14). But
the people rejected Jeremiah's compassionate warning of persecution,
making him feel like a "man of strife and contention to the whole
land" (15). God forbade Jeremiah to marry and father children because
of the tumultuous days ahead (16). Jeremiah said, "The sin of Judah
is written with a pen of iron; with a point of diamond it is engraved
on the tablet of their heart..." (17a). Standing in the Benjamin Gate
at God's command, the prophet charged them: "Keep the sabbath day
holy. . . . But if you do not listen to me, to keep the sabbath day holy,
and not to bear a burden. . . , then I will kindle a fire in its gates, and it
shall devour the palaces of Jerusalem and shall not be quenched" (17b).
Down at the potter's house God taught Jeremiah that "like the clay in
the potter's hand, so are you in my hand, O house of Israel" (18). Finally,
Jeremiah was told to buy and break a potter's earthen flask to illustrate
how God would shatter Judah and Jerusalem (19). At this the out-
raged people beat Jeremiah and put him in public stocks (20).

2. *The prophet's exhortations* (25-26). It was during this period in
the reign of Jehoiakim that Jeremiah uttered his famous prophecy
about the captivity: "This whole land shall become a ruin and a waste,
and these nations shall serve the king of Babylon seventy years" (25:11).
Of course, through the mouth of Jeremiah, God gave Israel one last
chance to repent. But "all the people laid hold of him, saying, You
shall die!" (26:8). Thus they sealed their own doom by bitter rejection
of God's patient pleading through the prophet.

3. *The prophet's exigencies* (35-36). Jeremiah rebuked Judah
because they were not as faithful as were the Rechabites to their
Father's command not to drink wine nor to build houses to dwell in.
"Therefore, thus says the Lord, the God of hosts, the God of Israel: Behold, I am bringing on Judah and all the inhabitants of Jerusalem all the
evil that I have pronounced against them" (35). Hence, God commanded Jeremiah to "take a scroll and write on it all the words that I
have spoken to you against Israel and Judah and all nations . . . ." It
was read to king Jehoiakim, column by column, and his response was
prompt: he "cut them off with a penknife and threw them into the fire in

the brazier." But God commanded Jeremiah to rewrite the scroll and to add many similar words (36).

C. Prophecies during Zedekiah's reign (21-24; 27-34; 37-39).

The Babylonians invaded Judah in 605 B.C., taking Jehoiakim captive just as Jeremiah had predicted. Zedekiah, the last of Judah's kings, was little more than a puppet of Babylon's Nebuchadnezzar. During these dark days in Judah's history, Jeremiah uttered several more prophecies.

1. *Prophecies about Judah's political future* (21-24; 27-29). These prophecies were both unpleasant and hopeful. On the unpleasant side were the predictions about Zedekiah's downfall and Jerusalem's destruction (21), and the curse upon Jeconiah's heirs (22). Likewise, all ungodly prophets and priests who held out false hope to Judah came under the woeful condemnation of God (23). Nevertheless, there remained a ray of hope for the exiled remnant in Babylon. The Lord promised, "I will set my eyes upon them for good, and I will bring them back to this land. I will build them up, and not tear them down; I will plant them, and not uproot them" (24). But the false prophets who said there would be no captivity were severely condemned by Jeremiah (27-28). The only consolation that was offered was that a faithful remnant would return after seventy years (29).

2. *Prophecies about Judah's spiritual future* (30-33). The immediate political future was very bleak indeed, but the spiritual future beyond that was bright. "For behold, the days are coming, says the Lord, when I will restore the fortunes of my people, Israel and Judah . . ." (30). And "at that time, says the Lord, I will be the God of all the families of Israel, and they shall be my people." For "behold, the days are coming says the Lord, when *I will make a new covenant* with the house of Israel and the house of Judah . . . . I will put my law within them, and I will write it upon their hearts; and I will be their God, and they shall be my people" (31). And despite the imminent destruction of Jerusalem, Jeremiah sealed his faith in the future by buying property for his relatives (32). The day was coming in which God would "cause a righteous Branch to spring forth for David; and he shall execute justice and righteousness in the land. In those days Judah will be saved and Jerusalem will dwell securely. And this is the name by which it will be called: 'The Lord is our righteousness'" (33).

3. *Prophecies about Judah's immediate future* (34; 37-39). Jeremiah predicted that the Babylonians would capture Jerusalem but would not kill Zedekiah the king (34). Jeremiah was thrown in prison as a traitor for his prophecies (37), and eventually he was cast into a cistern to die. But the king came to his rescue and delivered him (38).

When the Babylonians broke through the walls of Jerusalem, they captured king Zedekiah as he attempted to flee and destroyed Jerusalem as Jeremiah had forecast (39).

II. Prophecies after the fall of Jerusalem (40-52).

These last prophecies fall into three categories denoting the geographical location of the people involved: the guerrilla remnant remaining in Palestine after Babylon's conquest, those who fled to Egypt (as Jeremiah did), and those taken captive into Babylon (586 B.C.), just as Daniel and the three Hebrew children had been earlier (605 B.C.).

A. PROPHECIES TO THE REMNANT IN PALESTINE (40-43).

Jeremiah was given the choice to stay in Judah with Gedaliah the puppet governor that Nebuchadnezzar set up over the land (40). But Ishmael, a royal descendant, killed Gedaliah and many Jews as well (41). Johanan and all the other remaining military leaders were exhorted by Jeremiah to remain faithful to the Lord and stay in the land rather than go down into Egypt (42). But they disbelieved Jeremiah's prophecy and, capturing him and all the people, fled to Egypt. Thereupon Jeremiah predicted that Nebuchadnezzar would either capture or slay them (43).

B. PROPHECIES TO THE REMNANT IN EGYPT (44).

Down in Egypt the remnant burned incense to the queen of heaven. Jeremiah gave them the word of the Lord: "I will punish those who dwell in the land of Egypt, as I have punished Jerusalem, with the sword, with famine, and with pestilence, so that none of the remnant of Judah who have come to live in the land of Egypt shall escape or survive or return to the land of Judah . . . except some fugitives."

C. PROPHECIES TO THE REMNANT IN BABYLON (45-52).

The final section of prophecies is directed to the Babylonian captives. Jeremiah forecast the fall of Jehoiakim and Judah (45) followed by the invasion of Egypt by Nebuchadnezzar (46). Surrounding nations too were to come under God's judgment: the Philistines would be overrun (47), Moab would be laid waste (48), the Ammonites would be dispossessed (49a), and Edom's pride destroyed (49b). Both Damascus and Kedar would be smitten by Nebuchadnezzar, and Elam would be chosen (49c). This judgment on Israel's wicked enemies was intended to encourage the remnant with a realization of the justice of God. Even mighty Babylon would one day finally fall to a nation from the north and Judah would be stirred to repentance (50-51). To Jeremiah's predictions is added an eyewitness account of the fall of Jerusalem in the eleventh year of Zedekiah's reign (586 B.C.) (52).

LAMENTATIONS

The title of this book in Hebrew is taken from the word *how!* The title in the Greek Septuagint (LXX) means "Tears of Jeremiah." The book is a lamentation over the destruction of Jerusalem and the Temple of the Lord. It is really the first of three exilic books; Ezekiel and Daniel are the others. Lamentations concentrates on the past, whereas the other two exilic books look forward. It is treated here because of its immediate connection with Jeremiah.

WHO WROTE LAMENTATIONS?

The author seems unquestionably the same as the author of the Book of Jeremiah. The evidence is substantial: (1) Lamentations is attributed to Jeremiah in the Greek Old Testament (LXX) and in the Arabic Targums of Jonathan. (2) II Chronicles 35:25 informs us that Jeremiah was a writer of lamentations, albeit it is probably not referring to this book. (3) The author was an eyewitness of the destruction of Jerusalem (1:13-15; 2:6, 9; 4:10). (4) There are striking similarities in style and phraseology with the Book of Jeremiah (cf. 1:15 with Jer. 8:21; 1:16 with Jer. 9:1; 2:22 with Jer. 6:25). (5) Both books anticipate similar judgment on the nations which rejoice in Jerusalem's fall (4:21; cf. Jer. 46:25). (6) The same sensitive soul and sympathetic sorrow for the nation of Judah are reflected in both books.

WHEN WAS LAMENTATIONS WRITTEN?

There seems to be little doubt that the whole book was composed immediately following the fall of Jerusalem (586 B.C.). As one reads the book one can almost feel the tears yet in the eyes of the Jews as they watch their city smolder. The acrostic form—each verse beginning with a different letter of the Hebrew alphabet—insures the unity and completeness of the book.

TO WHOM WAS LAMENTATIONS WRITTEN?

Here again there is little question that the audience is the exiled Jewish nation whose land had been captured by the Babylonians and whose Temple had just been burned.

WHERE WERE THEY LOCATED?

Since those Jews who fled to Egypt were killed or later exiled to Babylon with the rest, the destination of Lamentations was ultimately, if not immediately, the Jews of the Babylonian captivity.

WHY WAS LAMENTATIONS WRITTEN?

The historical purpose.

Lamentations served as an expression of sorrow at the destruction of Jerusalem and as a reminder of God's faithfulness to His word and to His people.

The doctrinal purpose.

Lamentations is an unusual but compatible mixture of the wrath and mercy of God. It stresses His faithfulness to His promise to punish evil and yet His steadfast love and compassion for His people (3:22, 23).

The Christological purpose.

There are many prophetic pictures of Christ. Christ is the afflicted of the Lord (1:12), despised of His enemies (2:15, 16), the laughingstock of all peoples (3:14), and the smitten and insulted one (3:19). But behind the movement of the whole book, Christ is the man of sorrows who is acquainted with grief (cf. Isa. 53:3).

WHAT IS LAMENTATIONS ABOUT?

Written in the rhythm of a funeral dirge, this book laments, in the form of five metaphors, the downfall of Zion, the city of God.

I. The pain of Zion's fall (1)
—a mourning widow.

The author gives a *pathetic description* of the fallen city: "How like a widow has she become, she that was great among the nations!" (vv. 1-11). The *national desperation* is described forcefully in these words: "Is it nothing to you, all you who pass by? Look and see if there is any sorrow like my sorrow which was brought upon me . . ." (vv. 12-22).

II. The plight of Zion's fall (2)
— a weeping daughter.

What God did to Zion is depicted: "The Lord in his anger has set the daughter of Zion under a cloud!" (vv. 1-10); and *why God did it* is summed up succinctly: "The Lord has done what he purposed, has carried out his threat; as he ordained long ago . . ." (vv. 11-22). All who pass by wonder, "Is this the city which was called the perfection of beauty, the joy of all the earth?" (v. 15).

III. The purpose of Zion's fall (3)
— an afflicted man.

Here Jerusalem is depicted as a "man who has seen affliction under the rod of his [God's] wrath" (v. 1). The prophet took *comfort in Jerusalem's calamity* (vv. 1-39) because "the steadfast love of the Lord never ceases, his mercies never come to an end; they are new every morning; great is thy faithfulness" (vv. 22, 23). Assured that "the Lord will not cast off forever," he asked, "why should a living man complain, a man, about the punishment of his sins?" (vv. 31, 39). Thus he received *confidence through confession* (vv. 40-66). "Let us test and examine our ways, and return to the Lord. . . . We have transgressed and rebelled, and thou hast not forgiven." Therefore, "my eyes will flow without ceasing, without respite, until the Lord from heaven looks down and sees" (vv. 40, 42, 49, 50).

IV. Pondering Zion's fall (4)
— tarnished gold.

"How the gold has grown dim, how the pure gold is changed," cried Jeremiah! Their *present punishment* (vv. 1-15) is described as "greater than the punishment of Sodom. . ." for "the hands of compassionate women have boiled their own children; they became their food in the destruction of the daughter of my people" (vv. 6, 10). The *future prospect* (vv. 16-22) seems very dim: "The Lord himself has scattered them, he will regard them no more"; yet "the punishment of your iniquity, O daughter of Zion, is accomplished, he will keep you in exile no longer" (vv. 16, 22).

V. Plea on behalf of Zion's fall (5)
— a fatherless child.

In this last chapter Zion is pictured as an orphaned child. Zion's *cause is presented* (vv. 1-18): "Remember, O Lord, what has befallen us; behold, and see our disgrace! . . . Women are ravished in Zion, virgins in the towns of Judah. Princes are hung up by their hands; no respect is shown to the elders" (vv. 1, 11, 12). The *cause is pleaded* (vv. 19-22): "But thou, O Lord, dost reign for ever. . . . Why dost thou forget us for ever, why dost thou so long forsake us? Restore us to thyself, O Lord, that we may be restored!"

STUDY QUESTIONS

1. What was it about the character of the man Jeremiah which particularly suited him for the very unpleasant task to which God called him?
2. Compare the old covenant God made with Israel and the new covenant applied to the church. What are the similarities and what are the differences (Jer. 31:31; cf. Heb. 8:8—10:25)?
3. What evidence do we have that Jeremiah also wrote the Book of Lamentations?
4. What does Lamentations teach about the character of God?

37

The Expectation of the Nation's Religious Restoration by Christ

EZEKIEL

Of the two forward-looking books of the captivity, Daniel looks forward to the *political* restoration of Israel while Ezekiel previews their *religious* restoration. The former is concerned about world kingdoms and the kingdom of God; the latter is interested in the restoration of the Temple and religious system. Respectively, their perspectives are from the prophetic and priestly points of view.

WHO WROTE EZEKIEL?

Ezekiel, a member of the priestly family of Buzi and contemporary of Jeremiah and Daniel, is the author of this book. The evidence for this is quite substantial.

(1) There is the clear claim of the book (1:1), all of which is given autobiographically (phrases like, "I looked," and "the word of the Lord came to me" occur throughout).

(2) There is a unity of apocalyptic (visions) style through the entire book.

(3) The whole book is written from the priestly point of view that one would expect given Ezekiel's priestly background (note sacrifices, the Temple, etc.).

(4) Both early Jewish teachers and many Bible critics agree that Ezekiel was the author.

(5) The bases upon which some critics reject Ezekiel's authorship are insubstantial. For example, they say that Ezekiel purports to give eyewitness accounts of events which occurred in Jerusalem years after he was exiled (chs. 8, 11, 12). But these critics overlook the fact that the "I saw" is a description of his visions from God rather than his direct observation—the whole style of the book is apocalyptic (cf. 8:3). Critics

also mistakenly suppose that the same prophet could not pronounce both doom and future blessing on his people. But this criticism ignores the dual role to which virtually every prophet, including Isaiah, Micah, Amos, and Hosea, was called.

In brief, there is no plausible reason why Ezekiel could not have written this book and there are good reasons to believe that he did.

When was Ezekiel written?

Ezekiel ministered between about 593 and 570 B.C. He was taken into exile in 597 B.C. by Nebuchadnezzar with the second group of captives. There were three major invasions of Judah by Nebuchadnezzar:

(1) In 605 B.C. during Jehoiakim's reign—Daniel was taken to Babylon (cf. Dan. 1).

(2) In 597 B.C. during Jehoiachin's reign—Ezekiel was taken to Babylon (Ezek. 1).

(3) In 586 B.C. during Zedekiah's reign—Jeremiah was left in the land while Zedekiah was taken to Babylon (Jer. 39).

Now Ezekiel was called to his prophetic ministry in 593 B.C. (the fifth year of the captivity of king Jehoiachin) when he was about thirty years of age (1:1). The Book of Ezekiel was written between 593 and 570 B.C. (cf. 29:17).

To whom was Ezekiel written?

Ezekiel addressed his book to the exiles in Babylon who were discouraged and deluded with false hopes of an early return to their homeland (cf. 12:25).

Where were they located?

Ezekiel was taken captive to a community near Nippur called Tell-Abib on the river Chebar (about fifty miles south of Babylon on the Euphrates River) (1:1). Here he received his visions and ministered to the Jews in Babylonian exile.

Why was Ezekiel written?

The historical purpose.

As a prophet of the exile Ezekiel's intentions were to comfort and encourage God's people by revealing God's plans for their full and final restoration and to counteract any false hope of an early return to their homeland.

The doctrinal purpose.

The central doctrinal teaching of Ezekiel concerns the glory of God (cf. 1:28; 10:4). Connected with God's glory is the need for judgment on sin in the vindication of His righteousness (cf. 11:12). And finally the book stresses God's faithfulness to His promises (cf. "for my name's sake," 20:44).

The Christological purpose.

Ezekiel anticipates Christ as the glory of God (10:18, 19), the Renewer of the covenant (16:60), the Shepherd of the flock (34:23), the Cleanser of the Temple (36:24f.), the Regenerator of Israel (36:25, 26); and throughout the book He is presented as the Restorer of Israel.

WHAT IS EZEKIEL ABOUT?

Ezekiel is the prophet of the glory of God (1:28). The name *Ezekiel* means "strengthened of God" and Ezekiel exhibited this quality as he spoke to the captives concerning God's mighty hand in judgment on the nations and in the religious restoration of Israel.

Ezekiel begins with a vision of the glory of God, explaining that Judah no longer experiences it because of their sin (1-24). He then speaks of God's visitation in judgment on the nations surrounding Judah in preparation for the return of God's glory (25-32). The book concludes with a description of the return of God's glory and the restoration of Israel (33-48).

I. God's denunciation of Judah (1-24)
— the departure of God's glory.

A. THE ORDINATION OF THE PROPHET (1-3).

Ezekiel's call to the prophetic ministry came through a staggering *vision* of the glory of God (1). Summarizing the vision he said, "Such was the appearance of the likeness of the glory of the Lord. And when I saw it, I fell upon my face, and I heard the voice of one speaking" (v. 28). The *voice* commissioned Ezekiel: "Son of man, I send you to the people of Israel, to a nation of rebels, who have rebelled against me" (2). The *venture* of Ezekiel was difficult. God warned that the people would not listen to him, but if Ezekiel did not warn them of their sins, then, said God, "That wicked man shall die in his iniquity; but his blood I will require at your hand" (3). Then Ezekiel saw the glory of God arise from its place and he said, "I went in bitterness in the heat of my spirit, the hand of the Lord being strong upon me" (vv. 12, 14).

B. THE PROCLAMATION OF THE PROPHET (4-24).

When Ezekiel began his ministry (593 B.C.) Jerusalem had not yet fallen (586 B.C.). His first commission was to declare the imminence of her doom.

1. *The nearness of God's judgment* (4-7). Ezekiel was commanded to make a brick replica of Jerusalem and dramatize how it would be besieged. Then God told him to lie on his side for over a year, symbolizing the times of judgment on Israel and Judah (4). Ezekiel next cut off his hair and beard and burned a third of it, struck a third with the

sword about the city, and scattered a third to the wind, thus symbolizing the three ways the people of Jerusalem would be judged by Babylon's invasion (5). This judgment was to fall not only on Jerusalem but also on the idolatrous high places in the mountains of Israel. And when it happens, "They shall know that I am the Lord; I have not said in vain that I would do this evil to them" (6). Their sin is complete: "An end! The end has come upon the four corners of the land.... Your doom has come, injustice has blossomed, pride has budded" (7).

2. *The need of Jerusalem's judgment* (8-11). Ezekiel was given visions in which he saw the abominable idolatry and violence of Jerusalem (8). He saw God's executioners (angels of judgment) draw near the city and unleash their swords on everyone except the remnant who grieved over the abominations of the city (9). Then the prophet saw again a vision of the glory of the Lord in the holy of holies (10), after which the Lord departed from Israel, for "the glory of the Lord went up from the midst of the city, and stood upon the mountain which is on the east side of the city" (11). The judgment on the wicked notwithstanding, God promised Israel, "I will gather you from the peoples, and assemble you out of the countries where you have been scattered.... And I will give them one heart, and put a new spirit within them" (vv. 17-19). Judgment was needed; the glory had departed, but it would one day return to them through the same eastern gate through which it had departed in the person of their king.

3. *The nature of God's judgment* (12-24). God's judgment is sure. As predicted, king Zedekiah will be taken captive to Babylon for "the days are at hand, and the fulfillment of every vision" has come (12). God will judge the false prophets whose delusive visions and lying divinations misled the people to say "peace, when there is no peace" (13). So certain is God's judgment on Israel that "if Noah, Daniel, and Job were in it, as I live, says the Lord God, they would deliver neither son nor daughter; they would deliver but their own lives by their righteousness" (14). Just as the wood vine of the forest is "given to the fire for fuel, so will I give up the inhabitants of Jerusalem," says the Lord (15). Jerusalem is forcefully described as an abominable harlot: "You [have] trusted your beauty, and played the harlot because of your renown, and lavished your harlotries on any passer-by." Israel has broken her vows to God (16). Yet, says the Lord, "I will remember my covenant with you in the days of your youth, and I will establish with you an everlasting covenant.... and you shall know that I am the Lord (vv. 60, 62). God has judged the king of Judah for treason. Yet He will plant again His people in their land and they will bear fruit (17). What brings God's judgment down is Israel's failure to be righteous (cf. 18:5-8). But no one shall suffer for another's sins; "the soul that sins shall die. The son

shall not suffer for the iniquity of the father, nor the father suffer for the iniquity of the son" (18). God tenderly calls them to repentance: "Why will you die, O house of Israel? For I have no pleasure in the death of anyone, says the Lord God; so turn, and live" (vv. 31, 32). But they do not turn and Ezekiel is commanded to take up a lamentation for them (19).

Ezekiel recounts for Israel their long history of rebellion against God—their blasphemy, idolatry, and profanity—which brings down the judgment of God (20). "Son of man, set your face toward Jerusalem and preach against the sanctuaries...; and all flesh shall know that I the Lord have drawn my sword out of its sheath" (21). Again the prophet lists their many sins: murder, contempt for parents, extortion, exploitation of widows, profanity, slander, moral lewdness, sodomy, sexual impurity, adultery, bribery, robbery and oppression. "Therefore I have poured out my indignation upon them; I have consumed them with the fire of my wrath" (22). Again Israel's sin is described as the lewdest form of harlotry, to which God responds, "Your lewdness shall be requited upon you, and you shall bear the penalty for your sinful idolatry; and you shall know that I am the Lord" (23). The last prophecy of judgment on Jerusalem came the very day of the Babylonian destruction of Jerusalem (586 B.C.; cf. 24:1), the very day Ezekiel's wife died (24:18). By this the people knew that He was the Lord: His glory would not be tarnished nor His judgment delayed (24).

II. God's visitation on the nations (25-32)
— preparation for glory.

Like Obadiah, Nahum, Zephaniah, and Habakkuk before him, Ezekiel called down the judgment of God on Israel's enemies. They too had transgressed God's law and they deserved His wrath. Beginning in the east with Ammon and proceeding clockwise to the north at Tyre and Sidon (25-28), the prophet strikes a fatal blow at the heart of each nation's sin. He reserves the last and largest description of judgment for Egypt (29-32). (1) The *Ammonites* stood condemned for rejoicing in the desolation of the Temple (25:1-7). (2) *Moab* would be judged for declaring that Judah was not God's special people (25:8-11). (3) *Edom* would be cursed of God because of their revenge on Judah (25:12-14). (4) The *Philistines* too acted with revenge and even malice to destroy God's people (25:15-17). (5) *Tyre* would be cast into the sea because she wished to be replenished at Israel's expense (26:1–28:19). (6) *Sidon* too would be punished because she did not acknowledge that God is Lord (28:20-26). (7) *Egypt* would receive God's condemnation because they selfishly refused support to Israel beleaguered by her enemies (29).

Egypt would be destroyed by the Babylonians (30). Pharaoh would be cut down like a proud cedar (31) and captured like a dragon in the sea (32).

III. God's restoration of Israel (33-48)
— the return of God's glory.

Judgment on evil is God's preparation for blessing. There are two movements in the full restoration of Israel's place of blessing: the bestowal of a new life upon them by God (33-39) and the establishment of a new order within them (40-48).

A. NEW LIFE WILL BE BESTOWED ON ISRAEL (33-39).

God desires life, not death, for His people. But in order to provide this resurrection of Israel (35-37), God would give exhortations to His people (33-34) and would make a final visitation in judgment on their enemies (38-39).

1. *Exhortations to God's people* (33-34). Israel must repent and confess their sins before God can revisit them with life. "And you, son of man, say to the house of Israel, Thus have you said: 'Our transgressions and our sins are upon us, and we waste away because of them; how then can we live?' " (33). Then "Son of man, prophesy against the shepherds of Israel.... Should not shepherds feed the sheep?" In fact, the Lord said, "I will bring back the strayed, and I will bind up the crippled.... And I, the Lord, will be their God, and my servant David will be prince among them" (34).

2. *Resurrection of God's people* (35-37). A final exhortation is given to Edom (Mt. Seir) because of their perpetual enmity against Israel. God's people will never be fully restored until the enmity of their enemies ceases (35). Of the mountains of Israel God prophesied: "I will multiply men upon you, the whole house of Israel, all of it.... For I will take you from the nations, and gather you from all the countries, and bring you into your own land. I will sprinkle clean water upon you, and you shall be clean from all your uncleanness, and from all your idols I will cleanse you. A new heart I will give you, and a new spirit I will put within you" (36). Israel like a valley of dry bones scattered among the nations will be revived and restored to her land: "Prophesy to these bones, and say to them, O dry bones, hear the word of the Lord.... Behold, I will open your graves, and raise you from your graves, O my people; and I will bring you home into the land of Israel" (37).

3. *Visitation on Israel's enemies* (38-39). Ezekiel turns his attention to Israel's last enemies, the confederacy of kingdoms against her in the end time. The prince of Meshech (Moscow) and Tubal (Tobolsh) in Russia, along with Persia, Cush (Egypt), Put (Libya), and Gomer (Ger-

many) will invade Israel after she dwells safely in the land again (38). But God will miraculously defend His people, sending fire on their enemies in their homelands and slaying their armies on the mountains of Israel (39). God has returned His people permanently and He will defend them through His visitations of judgment on their enemies.

B.   A NEW ORDER WIL BE ESTABLISHED IN ISRAEL (40-48).

This final section of Ezekiel looks beyond Israel's last foes to their future kingdom. It is a description of their Temple-centered messianic age, a portrayal of the full and final religious restoration.

1. *The messianic Temple* (40-43). The first four chapters in this final section give a detailed description of the messianic Temple. This Temple is built after the same pattern and with the same basic dimensions as Solomon's Temple, and features the reinstitution of the sacrificial blood offerings.

2. *The messianic worship* (44-46). An elaborate system of levitical worship is described, following the pattern laid down by Moses. It will include laws of defilement (44), of the priesthood and offerings (45), and of feasts (46). It represents a full and complete religious restoration for Israel.

3. *The messianic land and river* (47-48). Out of the restored Temple will flow a river from Jerusalem (47a). The city of Jerusalem within the land will measure over five miles in circumference (18,000 cubits). "And the name of the city thenceforth shall be, The Lord is there." And the land will be apportioned again for the twelve tribes in the following way (47b-48):

HOW TO INTERPRET EZEKIEL 40-48.

There are two basic ways to interpret this passage. It can be interpreted spiritually as a symbolic representation in Old Testament Jewish terms of the New Testament Christian church. Or, it may be interpreted literally as a restoration of the Old Testament sacrificial system in a restored earthly kingdom of Israel.

The spiritual interpretation.

The following reasons are given for interpreting this passage symbolically as fulfilled in the New Testament church but not involving a literal future Temple nor the reinstitution of blood sacrifices:

1. The New Testament teaches that Christ fulfilled and did away with the Old Testament system of priestly sacrificial offering (Heb. 8:8-10).

2. The Book of Revelation describes the Heavenly City of the future as having no Temple or sacrifices, only Christ the Lamb (21:22f.).

A section of the Ishtar Gate of ancient Babylon which is now displayed in the Berlin Museum. Photo by Charles Pfeiffer

3. Ezekiel pictures the Gentiles as excluded from Israel's Temple; this is contrary to the New Testament teaching that Jew and Gentile are one in Christ (Gal. 3:28; Eph. 2:12-22).

4. The New Testament speaks of the church as a spiritual Israel and indicates that Old Testament predictions are fulfilled spiritually or symbolically in the Christian church (Gal. 6:16; Heb. 8:8-10).

The literal interpretation.

According to this interpretation there will be a literal restoration of the Temple and sacrificial system for Israel during the thousand-year messianic reign of Christ (Rev. 20). This interpretation seems better for the following reasons:

(1) Ezekiel presents highly detailed descriptions, numerous measurements, and historical scenes that do not fit with a symbolical interpretation.

(2) The general rule of hermeneutics (interpretation) is this: "when the literal sense makes good sense, seek no other sense lest it result in nonsense." The literal sense makes good sense here. If this passage is spiritualized, then on similar grounds one could spiritualize away most of the Old Testament prophecies including the obviously literal ones about Christ's first and second comings.

(3) The Bible makes a clear distinction between the Christian *church* (which began after Christ; cf. Matt. 16:18; Acts 1:6; I Cor. 12:13) and the nation of *Israel* (I Cor. 10:32; Rom. 9:11). Promises unique to Abraham and his descendants, such as the promise of the Holy Land (Gen. 12:1-3), are not fulfilled in the Christian church.

(4) The picture in Revelation 21 (no Temple or sacrifices) is not that of the thousand-year messianic reign (Rev. 20) but of the eternal state to follow. Ezekiel's prediction (40-48) is to be literally fulfilled during the thousand years; later in the New Heaven and Earth there will be no Temple or sacrifices.

(5) The sacrifices of the messianic kingdom have no atoning significance; they are merely memorial in nature, looking back to the accomplished work of Christ on the cross. This is similar to what the elements of the Lord's Supper do for a Christian.

(6) If the thousand-year reign described in Revelation is a literal restoration of the Kingdom to Israel and if the Christian church as Christ's bride reigns with Him, there is no reason to doubt that the picture in Ezekiel applies distinctively to Israel and not to Gentiles. However, even in the Old Testament, believing Gentiles were envisioned as being brought into a united society of God's people under the Lord (Isa. 11:10-16). Ezekiel's picture should not be pressed in such detail as to exclude what other Old Testament prophets foresaw.

STUDY QUESTIONS

1. In what social issues was Ezekiel interested (cf. 18:5-9; 22:6-16)?
2. What is the glory of God (study 1:28; 3:12, 23; 8:4; 9:3; 10:4, 18, 19; 11:22, 23; 31:18; 39:21; 43:2, 4, 5; 44:4)?
3. No direct quotations of Ezekiel are found in the New Testament. Do you think the New Testament writers knew and accepted Ezekiel (compare Ezek. 1:10 and Rev. 4:7; Ezek. 11:19 and John 3:3; Ezek. 18:20 and Rom. 6:23; Ezek. 33:8 and Acts 20:26)?

38

The Expectation of the Nation's Political Restoration by Christ

DANIEL

Of the three books written during the captivity, Lamentations looked back in regret at Israel's destruction and Ezekiel and Daniel looked forward to Israel's restoration. Ezekiel anticipated the restoration of their Temple, and Daniel expected the restoration of their nationhood. Ezekiel speaks from the priestly point of view and Daniel from the prophetic and political standpoint.

WHO WROTE THE BOOK OF DANIEL?

Despite the fact that critics argue that all of Daniel (or at least chs. 7-12) was written in the Maccabean period (i.e., c. 165 B.C.), the evidence definitely favors a date around 530 B.C.

(1) The whole book claims to come from the same Daniel who was taken captive by Nebuchadnezzar in 605 B.C. (1:1) and who lived at least until the third year of Cyrus (536 B.C.; cf. 7:1; 8:1; 9:1; 10:1, 2; 11:1; 12:5).

(2) Our Lord Jesus Christ referred to the last section of the book (9:27; 11:31; 12:11) as the work of Daniel the prophet (Matt. 24:15). This is the very section the critics most often dispute. The Christian chooses Christ over the critics.

(3) The Book of Ezekiel, which is recognized even by critics as a work of the sixth century, refers three times to Daniel as a famous believer (Ezek. 14:14, 20; 28:3).

(4) The teaching of the Jewish Talmud attributes this book to the Daniel of the sixth century B.C.

(5) A careful comparison of the linguistic style and vocabulary of Daniel with books from the Maccabean period (second century B.C.) reveals that Daniel is not from that period but from an earlier one.

(6) The basic objection behind critical attempts to give a late date to Daniel is the alleged impossibility of anyone knowing several centuries in advance the details of the great successive world governments. But this antisupernatural bias is not a sound basis for scholarship, nor is there any problem for one who believes in the existence of the Creator of this world. The real problem of the critics is Genesis 1:1, not supernatural prophecy. It is also worth noting that Jesus considered Daniel a *prophet* of future events and not merely a historian of events that had already happened (Matt. 24:15).

(7) Several objections raised by the critics can and should be briefly answered. (a) These critics ask why, if Daniel was strictly a prophet, the Hebrew Bible lists his book in the Writings rather than in the Prophets. The biblical answer rests in the fact that his call was not primarily prophetical but political. Further, the contents of Daniel are mixed, most of the book being clearly historical. Also, unlike the other prophets Daniel is not a direct mouthpiece of God to a specific audience of Jews. Finally, the basic classification of Old Testament books was twofold (Law and Prophets, see ch. 1) and not threefold (Law, Prophets, and Writings) and in that basic twofold division Daniel was listed with the Prophets. (b) These critics also object that there are historical errors in Daniel. But none of these allegations has been proven to be true, many have been shown to be false, and there are plausible explanations for the rest (see Archer, *A Survey of Old Testament Introduction*, chs. 28, 29). As it turns out, the errors reside not in the Bible but in its critics. (c) Some critics claim that many of Daniel's theological views on subjects like angels, the Messiah, resurrection, and the judgment, are so highly developed that the book must have been written at some late date. But all of these doctrines are taught in other books of the Old Testament; Job refers to the resurrection (19:25, 26); Zechariah stresses angels (2:3; 5:9); and both Malachi and Zechariah refer to the Messiah (Mal. 3:1; 4:2; cf. Zech. 3:1; 6:12, etc.).

WHEN WAS DANIEL WRITTEN?

Daniel, a contemporary of Jeremiah and Ezekiel, was taken captive during the reign of Jehoiakim (605 B.C.). His book records events and visions dating from 605 B.C. (1:1) to 536 B.C. (10:1). Hence, Daniel must have completed his book by around 530 B.C. Since Daniel was in his teens in 605 B.C. he undoubtedly lived the full fourscore years allotted by God.

TO WHOM WAS DANIEL WRITTEN?

No specific audience of Jewish people is indicated in Daniel. The immediate audiences of his interpretations of dreams and visions were the Gentile kings under whom he worked (cf. 2:36; 4:19). Most of the book, however, appears to be Daniel's memoirs of God's revelations to him during the internment of the Babylonian captivity. These revelations, inasmuch as they showed that God would restore again the kingdom to Israel, were preserved for the encouragement of the exiles (cf. 2:44; 12:1f.).

WHERE WERE THEY LOCATED?

Daniel himself was located in the Babylonian capital. He played a highly important political role under several kings, including Nebuchadnezzar (1:1), Belshazzar (5:1), Darius the Mede (probably Gurbaru) (5:31), and Cyrus the Persian (10:1).

WHY WAS DANIEL WRITTEN?

The historical purpose.

Daniel's prophecies served to comfort the exiled people of Israel with news that their nation would be restored. But in addition they were meant as an encouragement to the Jews to withstand the command to worship the emperor (cf. ch. 3) and to remain true to the Lord God of Israel no matter how difficult the circumstances (cf. ch. 6).

The doctrinal purpose.

There is a twofold stress in the teaching of this book: it condemns the existing (beastly) powers of this world and at the same time communicates the plan of God to set up His kingdom in this world. In so doing Daniel emphatically teaches that history has a goal, that it is His-story, and that God is sovereign over the affairs of this world (cf. ch. 4).

The Christological purpose.

The chief portrait of Christ in Daniel is the coming Messiah (the anointed one, 9:26). But Christ is also portrayed as the great stone who will crush the kingdoms of this world (2:34, 45), the son of man (7:13), and the Ancient of Days (7:22). The vision of 10:2-9 is probably a Christophany (appearance of Christ).

WHAT IS DANIEL ABOUT?

The name *Daniel* means "God is [my] judge." It is not an inappropriate name for one who lived out the entire time of God's judgment on His people in the seventy-year Babylonian captivity. The book is divided basically into two sections: the historical (1-6) and the prophetical (7:12). The first section centers largely around the dreams of Nebuchadnezzar while the second part revolves around the visions of Daniel himself.

I. The historical narration (1-6).

The first half of Daniel has a definite historical setting; the last six chapters are prophetical.

THE TIMES OF THE GENTILES
Luke 21:24

	MONARCHY	ARISTOCRACY	AUTOCRACY	"DEMOCRACY"		
	UNITY (2:37)	DUALITY (7:5)	FOURFOLD (7:6)	IMPERIAL	TENFOLD	POPULAR
				(2:44, 45; 7:7, 24; Rev. 13:1)		

STONE (2:45)

MONSTER (Lion-Bear-Leopard) (7:7; Rev. 13:2)

LION (7:4)	BEAR (7:5)	LEOPARD (7:6)	ROME
		GREECE	

BABYLON

MEDO-PERSIA

[GOLD] · [SILVER] · [BRASS] · [IRON] · [IRON & CLAY]

| 1260 |
| 42 |
| 3½ |

TRIBULATION

483 YEARS (9:24)

70 YEARS CAPTIVITY

606 B.C. · 536 B.C. · 444 B.C.

KINGDOMS	GOD'S VIEW	WILD BEASTS
	MAN'S VIEW	METALLIC MAN
	CHRONOLOGY	

Copyright N.L. Geisler

A. THE SELECTION OF DANIEL (1).

Despite the fact that Nebuchadnezzar changed the country, language, education, diets, and names of Daniel and his friends, he could not change their hearts (v. 8). Daniel determined not to defile himself with the king's wine or meats (perhaps associated with idols) and therefore God both prospered and promoted Daniel in the kingdom. He was selected to be an administrator over the wise men of the kingdom (v. 20), for God had blessed him.

B. THE SECRETS OF GOD (2).

Not only had Nebuchadnezzar misunderstood his strange dream, but he forgot what it was about as well. No one but Daniel was able to recall it and interpret it for the king. The dream portrayed a great metallic man (see chart below) with a golden head, shoulders and arms of silver, thighs of brass, and legs of iron built on feet of mixed iron and clay. According to Daniel's interpretation this metallic man represented successively four great world kingdoms: Babylon, Medo-Persia, Greece, and Rome. The feet represented a ten-member confederacy of kings in the end time which would eventually be smitten by the great Rock (Christ), who would thereupon set up His endless kingdom (v. 44).

C. THE STEADFASTNESS OF GOD'S SERVANTS (3).

The kingdoms of this world are man-centered and idolatrous. In Nebuchadnezzar's dream he was only the head of gold; in real life his pride prompted him to make a whole image of gold which he commanded all to worship. But the three friends of Daniel refused and were cast into the fiery furnace as punishment. There they were saved by the Angel of the Lord (Christ), one "like the Son of God" (v. 25, AV). They would not bend or bow to idolatry and they did not burn; God delivered them.

D. THE SOVEREIGNTY OF GOD (4).

Nebuchadnezzar, the mighty potentate of the great and glorious ancient Babylonian empire, learned the hard way that there was a Sovereign over him. His vision of the huge tree (his empire) cut down by God was to teach him "that the Most High rules the kingdom of men, and gives it to whom he will, and sets over it the lowliest of men" (v. 17). God is sovereign in the affairs of men. Men may rule but God overrules. Ultimately, history is His-story.

E. THE SIN AND FALL OF BABYLON (5).

MENE, MENE, TEKEL, UPHARSIN. That is what the hand wrote on the wall: Your kingdom is numbered, weighed, and divided. That very night the kingdom of the Babylonians fell to Darius and the

Medes who, having diverted the waters of the Euphrates, swarmed through the river channel under the city wall. Belshazzar's impious feast ended in God's judgment, as Daniel had forecast from the writing on the wall.

F. THE SUPPLICATION AND DELIVERANCE (6).

Daniel was not only a man of firm convictions (1:8) but also a man of regular prayer. It was in this that his envious colleagues trapped him. Through the king's proclamation that forbade prayer to any god other than Darius himself, these jealous men were able to arrest Daniel and have him thrown to the lions. But God delivered Daniel from the den of lions and Daniel was further exalted in the kingdoms of Darius and Cyrus.

II. Prophetical revelations (7-12).

Through a series of visions God revealed to Daniel in political exile how the kingdoms of this world would crumble one after the other and would become the kingdom of our Lord and of His Christ (cf. Rev. 11:15).

A. THE SYMBOL'S SIGNIFICANCE (7).

Like the Book of Revelation, which is patterned after it, the Book of Daniel involves a series of symbols. Nebuchadnezzar had seen the kingdoms of this world symbolized by a shining metallic man (ch. 2); this is man's self-glorifying image of himself. God's perspective is quite different; He sees the kingdoms of this world as raging beasts (ch. 7). The head of gold is a mighty lion (Babylon); the arms of silver are really a ravenous bear (Medo-Persia); the thighs of brass are, from God's view, a vicious leopard (Greece); the legs of iron are pictured as a monster partaking of some of the qualities of all three of its predecessors (Rome). And the horn (power) that arose out of Rome, that is, the Antichrist, prevailed over the saints until the Ancient of Days (Christ) came and subdued him and his ten-horned confederacy (cf. the ten toes of 2:42).

B. SACRILEGE IN THE SANCTUARY (8).

In this vision Daniel foresaw the victory of Alexander the Great (the he-goat) over the Persians (the ram) and the subsequent division of Alexander's kingdom into four parts by his four generals—Cassander, Lysimachus, Seleucus, and Ptolemy (vv. 8, 9, 22). He foresaw also the rise of Antiochus Epiphanes and his sacrilege of the Temple when he stopped the Jewish sacrifices and offered up instead a sow (an unclean animal) (vv. 10-14). These amazing predictions, hundreds of years before the events occurred, are an evidence of the supernatural origin of the Bible and a constant source of embarrassment to and object of attack by the critics.

C. THE SEVENTY SEVENS (OF YEARS) (9).

One of the most amazing predictions in the Bible foretold the very time of Christ's coming. While meditating on the seventy-years captivity, as Jeremiah (ch. 25) had predicted it, Daniel was told by the angel Gabriel that seventy sevens (of years) would be decreed upon Jerusalem and the Jewish people before the messianic age would come. The first sixty-nine sevens (483 years) would run from the command of Artaxerxes to rebuild Jerusalem (445 B.C.) to the cutting off of the Messiah (the Crucifixion). Taking these to be lunar years (i.e., twelve 30-day months = 360 days) one comes up with about 476 solar years, which takes us to A.D. 31, the time of the Crucifixion of Christ. Some scholars believe this is the exact number of years, even days, to Christ. Others are content with a round-number approximation (70x7). Whatever the case, it is sufficiently close to be amazing, especially in view of the fact that the most skeptical critic admits that the prophecy was given at least 165 years before Christ! The last of the seventy periods of seven years speaks of the future tribulation, the time when the Antichrist will reign (cf. Rev. 11-13). It is divided into two parts of 3½ years (Daniel uses the word "times") —42 months or 1260 days. In the middle of this period, the Antichrist will stop the sacrifices in the Jewish Temple of the future and demand that all men worship him (cf. II Thess. 2 and Rev. 13).

D. STRENGTH FROM THE SAVIOR (10).

Daniel was frightened by the momentous reality of his vision from the Lord (vv. 1-9). His supplication for strength went unanswered for three weeks while the angel struggled with the demonic powers behind the great world kingdoms (cf. Matt. 4:8; Eph. 6:12). But eventually his prayer was answered and strength came to Daniel from the Lord (vv. 17, 18). The angel then promised to show him the truth of things to come.

E. THE SINISTER SAVIOR (11).

The truth shown by the angel included a detailed description of the exploits of Alexander the Great (vv. 2-4), of the wars between Ptolemy and Seleucus (vv. 5-20), of the persecution of Israel by Antiochus IV (Epiphanes) (vv. 21-39), and of the Antichrist of the end time (vv. 40-45) of whom Antiochus was a prototype or foreshadowing. It is this last sinister figure who will "at the time of the end" go forth "with great fury to exterminate and utterly destroy many. And he will pitch his palatial tents between the sea and the glorious holy mountain; yet he shall come to his end, with none to help him" (vv. 44, 45).

F. THE SALVATION OF THE SAINTS (12).

But "at that time shall arise Michael, the great prince who has charge of your [Jewish] people. And there shall be a time of trouble, such as never has been since there was a nation till that time [cf. Matt. 24 and Rev. 6].... And many of those who sleep in the dust of the earth shall awake, some to everlasting life, and some to shame and everlasting contempt" (vv. 1, 2). Of this revelation about the tribulation period before Christ returns to earth, Daniel was told to "seal the book, until the time of the end," for meanwhile "many shall run to and fro, and knowledge shall increase"—an amazing prediction of advances in communication and education in modern times! The wicked will not understand these things, but the saints will purify themselves and know that it will be 1260 days from the time the Antichrist takes away the Jewish sacrifices and sets up his own image for worship in the Temple to the end of the tribulation period. Then it will take another thirty days to restore order after the terrible judgments and deaths culminating in the battle of Armageddon (see Rev. 9:13-21 and 16:12-21). But "blessed is he who waits and comes to the thousand three hundred and thirty-five days," that is, he who waits forty-five more days—this may signify the official inauguration of the messianic age with the celebration of the feast of booths (tabernacles) (cf. Zech. 14:16-19). In any event, Christ will return as the great Rock that smites the kingdoms of this world and He will reign for ever and ever. Hallelujah!

STUDY QUESTIONS

1. In view of the detailed predictions of Daniel about Alexander and Antiochus, why is it so important to the Bible critic to try to date these prophecies around 165 B.C.? What evidence renders their attempts futile?
2. What does a study of the chart of the great metallic man reveal to you about the progressive tendency within the kingdoms of this world? Are they getting stronger or weaker? More unified or less? Do the metals get heavier or lighter?
3. What do Revelation 13 and II Thessalonians 2 add to our knowledge about the Antichrist?
4. How do we know Daniel's prophecies about the Antichrist were not fulfilled in Antiochus (11:40-45; Matt. 24:15; Rev. 13)?

39

The Spiritual and Moral Reconstruction of the Nation

HAGGAI, ZECHARIAH, MALACHI

There are only three post-exilic prophets: Haggai, Zechariah, and Malachi. All spoke to encourage the spiritual and moral reconstruction of the returned remnant. Haggai and Zechariah spoke primarily about their spiritual and religious needs centered around rebuilding the Temple; Malachi spoke of their moral and social needs centered around rebuilding the nation itself.

Haggai and Zechariah were contemporaries. Haggai challenged the people to build the Temple of the present (Zerubbabel's); Zechariah encouraged them to behold the Temple of the future (the Messiah's). Haggai was practical, with his feet on the ground, and thus he spoke mostly to the present; Zechariah was visionary, with his head in the clouds, and he therefore prophesied much about the future. The two combined to challenge the remnant returned from Babylon to restore the spiritual vitality of the nation.

HAGGAI

The name *Haggai* means "festal," perhaps indicating that he was born on some major feast day. His main challenge to the remnant was to rebuild the Temple now that they were back in Palestine after the seventy years of captivity.

Who wrote Haggai?

Haggai the prophet, a contemporary of Zechariah the prophet and Zerubbabel the governor, is the author of this book. This is supported by the claim of the book (1:12, 13; 2:1, 20), its obvious unity of message, style, and time, and an important historical reference in Ezra (6:14). Both Jewish tradition and virtually every critic concur.

WHEN WAS HAGGAI WRITTEN?

Haggai's post-exilic prophecies are the most precisely dated writings in the Old Testament. The first message was given on the first day of Elul (Aug.-Sept.), 520 B.C. The second message was delivered on the twenty-first of Tishri (Sept.-Oct.), 520 B.C. The last messages came on the twenty-fourth of Chisleu (Nov.-Dec.) of the same year.

TO WHOM DID HAGGAI WRITE?

The remnant returned in about 538 B.C. and began working to rebuild the Temple around 536 B.C. But discouragement and indifference set in and the site lay idle for some sixteen years before God stirred up the people through the prophetic ministries of Haggai and Zechariah (cf. Ezra 5-6).

WHERE WERE THEY LOCATED?

Cyrus had decreed that the Jews could return to Jerusalem (Ezra 1:1f.). Over fifty thousand availed themselves of this opportunity to return to the land (Ezra 1, 8). They settled in and around Jerusalem (Ezra 1:11; 7:7).

WHY WAS HAGGAI WRITTEN?

The historical purpose.

Haggai wrote to exhort the returned remnant to rebuild the Temple in Jerusalem.

The doctrinal purpose.

There are many lessons in Haggai: (1) God blesses His people when they put Him first (cf. Matt. 6:33); (2) when we are in God's service we should never "weary in well-doing" (cf. Gal. 6:9); (3) God's promise for tomorrow is our hope for today.

The Christological purpose.

Our Lord is represented as the Restorer of the Temple's glory (2:7-9), the Overthrower of the kingdoms of this world (2:22), and a signet ring for Israel (2:23).

WHAT IS HAGGAI ABOUT?

Haggai had four brief but potent words for the remnant: a word of reproof (1), a word of support (2a), a word of blessing (2b), and a word of promise (2c).

I. The word of reproof (1)
— about the Temple's construction (Elul 1, 520 B.C.)

Haggai forcefully reminded the people that the *Temple of the Lord was unfinished* (vv. 1-6), while they were settled snugly in their paneled homes. The *trouble of the people was explained* to be the result of this indifference to God's house (vv. 7-11): God had not blessed them domestically because they had forgotten Him spiritually. Due to the moving of God's Spirit in the hearts of the remnant, the *testimony of the prophet was heeded* (vv. 12-15) and they resumed building the Temple.

II. The word of support (2:1-9)
— about the Temple's consolation (Tishri 21, 520 B.C.)

But when the older generation, who had seen the great and glorious Temple of Solomon, saw the much less spacious and less splendorous Temple of Zerubbabel taking shape before their eyes, Haggai was faced with the *perplexity of the people* (1:3); this Temple seemed unworthy in their eyes. But Haggai provides a *promise from the Lord* (vv. 4, 5) that God is with them in their efforts, and adds a *prediction about the future Temple* (vv. 6-9) that the "splendor of this house shall be greater than the former."

III. The word of blessing (2:10-19)
— about the Temple's sanctity (Chisleu 24, 520 B.C.).

Haggai reminded the people that *perversity* (evil) *is contagious* (vv. 10-13) and that the *people were contaminated* with it (vv. 14-17). But when they began to put God first, then the *promise was certain* (vv. 18, 19): "From this day on I will bless you," said the Lord.

IV. The word of promise (2:20-23)
— about the Temple's strength (Chisleu 24, 520 B.C.)

One day in the future the *heavens will be shaken* (vv. 20, 21), the *heathen will be overthrown* (v. 22) and the *Holy One* (Messiah) *will be exalted* (vs. 23). Zerubbabel, the leader of the restored remnant, is singled out as a symbol of the Messiah to come. Thus the promise of future blessing provided strength to the Temple-centered hope of Israel's remnant.

ZECHARIAH

WHO WROTE ZECHARIAH?
Zechariah was the son of Berechiah, the grandson of Iddo, the priest who led the Levites (Neh. 12:4), and a contemporary of Haggai the prophet (Ezra 6:14).

WHEN WAS ZECHARIAH WRITTEN?
Many critics attempt to date Zechariah 9-14 in the third or second

century B.C. because of its supposedly different style and its references to Greece (9:13) and to the defeat of Tyre and Sidon by Alexander the Great (9:1-4) in 330 B.C. However, the evidence supports the date of 518 B.C. for chapters 1-8 (1:1) and a date just after 480 B.C. for chapters 9-14:

(1) The whole book claims to come from Zechariah (1:1).

(2) There are many striking similarities in style between the two sections. For example, phrases like, "Lord of hosts" (cf. 2:10 and 9:15), the eyes of the Lord (cf. 8:6 and 12:4), "word of the Lord" (cf. 1:7 and 9:1), and "saith the Lord" (1:17 and 12:1, KJV) are common to both sections. The differences between the two sections are easily accounted for by the forty-year time span between the dates of composition; both circumstances and style can change slightly over four decades.

(3) The message of the entire book is remarkably similar to that of Haggai, who wrote in the sixth century. Compare Ezra 6:14.

(4) The same evangelistic flavor is found throughout the whole book.

(5) The objections of the critics are insufficient: (a) Greece came to international prominence with the defeat of Xerxes at the battles of Salamis, Plataea and Mycale (480-479 B.C.). Zechariah was written just after that time. (b) The defeat of Tyre and Sidon by Alexander is a prophecy and is introduced as such in 9:1. (c) The style and spirit of the book is the same throughout, despite some reasonable minor differences due to the forty-year gap.

(6) The divergent dates suggested by critics and their general lack of agreement on this issue tend to indicate the inadequacy of their attempts to push Zechariah to a later date.

(7) The amazing prophecy of Alexander's victory at Tyre is the prime object of the critics' antisupernatural bias. They insist that this passage (9:1-4) could not have been written about one hundred fifty years before the event happened.

To whom was Zechariah written?

Like Haggai, the prophet Zechariah wrote to the remnant, returned from Babylon, who were discouraged with the small size of the Temple as compared to Solomon's (Ezra 3:12). The prophet asserted that "whoever has despised the day of small things shall rejoice . . ." (Zech. 4:10). In other words, he encouraged them by pointing out that this little beginning showed promise of greater things to come.

Where were they located?

The remnant, of course, had returned home from the Babylonian captivity. They were settled in and around Jerusalem.

WHY WAS ZECHARIAH WRITTEN?

The historical purpose.

Zechariah's intent was to encourage the returned remnant by showing that God was at work in the world restoring Israel to their spiritual inheritance in preparation for the coming of the Messiah.

The doctrinal purpose.

Several teachings stand out in Zechariah: (1) the centrality of the Temple in God's spiritual restoration of Israel; (2) the providence of God in bringing back His people to their land; (3) the preeminence of the Messiah in the future spiritual restoration of Israel.

The Christological purpose.

Zechariah presents Christ as the angel of the Lord (3:1), the Righteous Branch (3:8), the Crucified Savior (12:10) and the Coming King (9:9).

WHAT IS ZECHARIAH ABOUT?

The name *Zechariah* means the "Lord has remembered." Zechariah was also concerned with rebuilding the Temple, but his visions of the future go far beyond those of Haggai. He received eight visions about Zion's sanctuary, four messages about Zion's services, and two burdens about Zion's Savior.

I. Zion's sanctuary (1-6)
— eight visions.

Here are eight visions about Israel's future among the nations and their spiritual restoration by God. The first vision, the *angelic horsemen* (1:7-17), represents God's providential activity among the nations to return His people to Jerusalem so they can rebuild their Temple. The second vision, the *four horns and smiths* (1:18-21), symbolizes the four world powers under whose dominion Israel was to come. The vision of *the man and the measuring rod* (2) illustrates God surveying the land for the remnant to reinhabit. *Joshua the high priest* (3) is a vision of Christ in the Temple interceding for Israel so that Satan would not destroy her (cf. Rev. 12). The vision of the *lampstand and olive trees* (4) declares that the renewed light of Israel among the nations is dependent on the oil of the Holy Spirit (cf. v. 6). The vision of the *flying scroll* (5:1-4) indicates that the judgment of God's Word would fall upon the Jews because they broke His commandments. The *woman in the ephah* (bushel basket) (5:5-11) portrays the purging away of Israel's idolatry by her captivity in Babylon, the seat of idolatry. Finally, the *four chariots and horses* (6) are the providential agents of God who oversee the events of the nations to assure Israel's return to their land and reconstruction of the Temple.

II. Zion's services (7-8)
— four messages.

The heart of Israel is Jerusalem, and the heart of Jerusalem is the Temple of God. Zechariah's burden for the returned remnant was four-fold with regard to this spiritual center of the people. First, he spoke out against the *worldly ritual practiced in it* (7:1-7), that is, against pure formalism in serving God. He then reminded them of the *wide retribution* or judgment of God that came on Israel because they would not heed the former prophets—they were scattered by God among the nations (7:8-14). The third message concerned the *worldwide restoration* of Israel (8:1-19): "Thus says the Lord of hosts: Behold, I will save my people from the east country and from the west country; and I will bring them to dwell in the midst of Jerusalem." And there will be a *worldwide religion* (8:20-23): "Many peoples and strong nations shall come to seek the Lord of hosts in Jerusalem, and to entreat the favor of the Lord."

III. Zion's Savior (9-14)
— two burdens.

This last section is highly messianic. It contains two burdens: one about the rejection of the Messiah and one about the reign of the Messiah.

A. THE REJECTED SAVIOR (9-11)—THE FIRST COMING OF CHRIST.

One of the most frequently cited passages in the Bible is in this section—the prediction of the triumphal entry of Christ into Jerusalem on Palm Sunday, just before His crucifixion. "Rejoice greatly, O daughter of Zion! Shout aloud, O daughter of Jerusalem! Lo, your king comes to you; triumphant and victorious is he, humble and riding on an ass, on a colt the foal of an ass" (9:9 cf. Matt. 21:5; Mark 11:1-10; Luke 19:28-40; John 12:12-15). But He was rejected and "became the shepherd of the flock doomed to be slain for those who trafficked in the sheep" (11:7). Indeed He would be betrayed for "thirty shekels of silver" (11:13; cf. Matt. 26:15; 27:9).

B. THE REIGNING SAVIOR (12-14)—THE SECOND COMING OF CHRIST.

When Christ returns the Jews will "look on him whom they have pierced" (Zech. 12:10 cf. Rev. 1:7). And "on that day there shall be a fountain opened for the house of David and the inhabitants of Jerusalem to cleanse them from sin and uncleanness" (13:1). "Behold, a day of the Lord is coming.... For I will gather all the nations against Jerusalem to battle, and the city shall be taken.... Then the Lord will go forth and fight against those nations as when he fights on the day of battle. On that day his feet shall stand on the Mount of Olives which lies before Jerusalem on the east" (14:1-4; cf. Acts 1:10, 11). And "the Lord will become king over all the earth; on that day the Lord will be one and his name one. . . . Then every one that survives of all the nations that have come against Jerusalem shall go up year after year to worship the King, the Lord of hosts, and to keep the feast of booths" (14:9, 16). In short, after the battle of Armageddon (cf. Rev. 16:12-21), Christ will judge the nations (cf. Matt. 25:31f.) and He will set up His messianic kingdom and reign for a thousand years (Rev. 20:1-6).

MALACHI

Malachi prophesied some one hundred years after Haggai and Zechariah began to write. Malachi lived in a day of moral and social decline against which he spoke forcefully while placing hope in the expectation of the Messiah. The name *Malachi* means "my messenger," that is, Malachi was the messenger of the Lord.

WHO WROTE MALACHI?

An otherwise unknown prophet named Malachi was the author of this book, although one unsubstantiated Jewish tradition claims it was Nehemiah (interpreting the word *Malachi* as a designation of an unnamed messenger). That Malachi was the author is supported by the claim, unity, and contents of the book as well as by the bulk of Jewish teaching.

WHEN WAS MALACHI WRITTEN?

The evidence indicates that Malachi wrote between about 430 and 420 B.C., while Nehemiah was in Babylon:

(1) The date was definitely after the completion of the Temple in 516 B.C. (1:7, 10; 3:1).

(2) It was during the time of Persian rule (note the word *pehah* in 1:8 [Persian for "governor"]).

(3) It was not while Nehemiah was in the land, since the sins denounced are those which were corrected when Nehemiah was present (cf. Neh. 13).

(4) Hence, it was probably while Nehemiah was back in Babylon following 433 B.C. (Neh. 13:6, 7).

TO WHOM WAS MALACHI WRITTEN?

Malachi wrote to the remnant a few generations after the Temple had been rebuilt. They had lost the spiritual fervor of their forefathers and both priests and people had backslidden. It was a day of moral and social decline.

WHERE WERE THEY LOCATED?

Malachi's audience was in the land of Palestine and the message centered particularly around the worshipers at the Temple in Jerusalem.

WHY WAS MALACHI WRITTEN?

The historical purpose.

Malachi rebuked Israel's social and moral decay, thus warning the backslidden remnant.

The doctrinal purpose.

Malachi teaches that unless there is purity in God's people there will be purging by God's hand. It stresses that sincerity and purity are prerequisites for serving God.

The Christological purpose.

Christ is the messenger of the covenant (3:1), the refiner's fire (3:2), and the sun of righteousness (4:2).

WHAT IS MALACHI ABOUT?

The message of Malachi strikes home to several areas of the life of the backslidden remnant. He speaks of their religious decline, their social debasement, their moral defection, and their material dissipation.

I.   Religious decline (1:1—2:9).

Malachi begins with a *revelation of God's love to Israel* (1:1-5) and a *rebuke to the priests' sins* (1:6—2:9); they were despising His name and polluting His altar by using sickly sacrifices rather than using the best animals as God demanded.

II.   Social debasement (2:10-16).

Socially the tide was as low as it was spiritually. *Idolatry was present* (vv. 10-13) despite the lesson learned in Babylon. *Divorce was practiced* (vv. 14-16) even though it is written, "I hate divorce, says the Lord the God of Israel."

III.   Moral defection (2:17—3:6).

The justice of God was questioned by the people (2:17): "Where is the God of justice?" they cried. But *the judgment of God is coming*, replied the Lord (3:1-6). "Behold, I send my messenger to prepare the way before me, and the Lord whom you seek will suddenly come to his temple; . . . behold, he is coming, says the Lord of hosts. But who can endure the day of his coming, and who can stand when he appears?"

IV. Material dissipation (3:7-18).

Because they had not tithed as God commanded, they were *robbing from God* (vv. 7-12). Furthermore, the *resistance of the people* was stout and arrogant (vv. 13-15), but the *reply of the Lord was* clear: He would remember the righteous in the day of judgment, sparing them as a father spares his son (vv. 16-18).

V. Messianic declaration (4:1-5).

The *condemnation of the wicked* will be accomplished with the coming of the Messiah (v. 1): "For behold, the day comes, burning like an oven, when all the arrogant and all evildoers will be stubble." But this day will be a *consolation for the righteous* (v. 2), for therein "the sun of righteousness shall rise, with healing in its wings." The book ends with a *command to obey the law* (v. 4) and a prediction about the *coming of Elijah* in preparation for the Lord (cf. Matt. 3:1 and 11:14).

In conclusion, our study has brought us from the foundation laid for Christ in the Law, through the preparation made for Christ in the Books of History, and the aspiration for Christ in Poetry, to the expectation of Christ in Prophecy. The Old Testament began with creation (Gen. 1:1) and it ends here in Malachi (4:6) with a curse. Man's sin brought death and the curse of God. But salvation is coming. The anticipation in the Old Testament for deliverance will become a realiza tion in the New Testament. It is also interesting to observe that the New Testament begins "the book of . . . Jesus Christ" (Matt. 1:1) and ends with "the grace of the Lord Jesus . . ." (Rev. 22:21). Amen!

STUDY QUESTIONS

1. What common concern gripped all three post-exilic prophets?
2. What distinguished the messages and approaches of Haggai and Zechariah?
3. What circumstances occasioned the need for Haggai's rebukes to the remnant?
4. Why were the older members of the remnant crying (while the younger ones rejoiced) when Zechariah challenged them not to despise the day of little things (Zech. 4:10; cf. Ezra 3:12)?
5. What conditions of Malachi's day called forth his strong social and moral exhortations?